A must-read for anyone and family.

— Susan Garmon

Estell Sims Halliburton's strong love for God and family inspired her and encouraged her to move her family from Brooklyn, New York, back to the South during the early 1970s. This move with her husband and their daughters was quite unsettling for them as a result of racism in housing, education, and the job force. Estell's journey—told in this sequel—continues to speak volumes about her persistence, resilience, ability to embrace change, and the many ways in which she triumphs in the face of adversity. All who undertake a similar journey will certainly draw inspiration from the life, times, testimony, and legacy of Ms. Estell Halliburton.

— Dr. Natasha N. Johnson, faculty, Georgia State University

Estell Sims Halliburton masterfully captures the heart of this baby boomer with her latest memoir, *If Grits Could Talk*. Halliburton skillfully had me in the car with her and her husband as they made the road trip from New York to Atlanta. I am an Atlanta native, so with each sentence, Halliburton mentally took me to each location in Atlanta with her. I felt as if Halliburton transported me from my house and I was there on Peachtree Street back in the 1970s. Walking down Whitehall Street, I was there. Waiting for the Marta bus, I was there. Going to The Varsity, Burger King, Paschal's (on Hunter Street), Greenbriar, Rich's, or Kroger, OMG, I was there. This book actually took me back to a time when things were much simpler, and all I wanted were chocolate chip cookies from Rich's bakery before walking down the street to catch the 18 North Decatur bus headed to Kirkwood.

The way Halliburton chronicles her journey is so interesting. She paints a picture of very modest and humble beginnings that literally touched my heartstrings as I thought of the journey of my own mom and how she used to share similar stories with us, reflecting on growing up on a farm in the country in Georgia. Anyone growing up in Atlanta or in the South in the 1960s, '70s, or even the '80s will find *If Grits Could Talk* to be very relaxing, somewhat comical at times, and somewhat angering at times with references to racial prejudices, but without question, very enjoyable. This is a great read by an author who is very transparent about many of her life's transitions.

Let it help you reminisce about a different time and space in your own life. You've got to read it. You've got to share it. You've got to talk about it.
> ~ Sam Thurman, mentor and change champion

Returning from the North to the South in the 1970s, a Black woman born on a Mississippi plantation continues to face discrimination as she arrives with her husband and daughters in Atlanta from New York City. There, she rejoins her Southern family and begins to replant her roots. Filled with colorful sensory details, the agonies and gems of this segment of her journey will transport and transform the reader of this true story.
> ~ Gelia Dolcimascolo, writing assistant and former facilitator,
> The Writers' Circle, Georgia State University
> Perimeter College, Dunwoody

If Grits Could Talk

A Southern Girl's Return Home

ESTELL SIMS HALLIBURTON

© 2023 Estell Sims Halliburton

All Rights Reserved. No part of this publication may be reproduced, distributed, or transmitted in any form or by any means, including photocopying, recording, or other electronic or mechanical methods, without the prior written permission of the publisher, except in the case of brief quotations embodied in critical reviews and certain other noncommercial uses permitted by copyright law. For permission requests, contact Halliburton Publishing Co., LLC, PO Box 567191, Atlanta, Georgia 31156

ISBNs:
978-1-7374462-4-8 (paperback)
978-1-7374462-3-1 (hardcover)
978-1-7374462-5-5 (eBook)

Library of Congress Control Number: 2024903113

Halliburton Publishing Co., LLC
6065 Roswell Road #450
Atlanta, Georgia 30328

Edited by Candace Johnson, Change It Up Editing
Cover illustration and cover design by Jennifer Pradhan
Interior design by Jera Publishing

Unless otherwise noted, all photos © Estell Sims Halliburton

Disclaimer: The author has tried to re-create events, locales, and conversations from her memories of them. Some names and identifying details have been changed to protect the privacy of individuals.

"Don't ever stop. Keep going.
If you want a taste of freedom, keep going."
~ Harriet Tubman

"I have learned over the years that when one's mind is made up, this diminished fear; knowing what must be done does away with fear."
~ Rosa Parks

This book serves to keep our memories alive.

I am dedicating this book to my parents, Wardell Sims and Estell Sims.

My home on Matubba Street in Aberdeen, Mississippi, was as joyful as being wrapped in a warm blanket. I was a rather naughty child, which tested my parents' patience, but they never wavered in their love for me.

In addition to their struggles to hold our family together, Momma and Daddy endured daily indignities. I did not appreciate the sacrifices they made for our family when I was growing up.

My home was a refuge of kindness and love. I am grateful that my parents provided me with a nurturing home where I felt safe. I will always cherish their memories!

In the summer of 1964, I got off the Trailways bus in New York City at the Port Authority near Forty-Second Street. My cousin from Aberdeen picked me up at the station and introduced me to Joseph Halliburton that first day. He had broad shoulders, walnut-brown skin, and an accent that was different from that of any guy I'd met in Aberdeen. Joseph showed me so many possibilities, and I wanted to be a part of his life. Months later, I married this handsome soldier. Although our life together was often difficult, it was worthwhile. I will never forget his smiles at our daughters and grandchildren. I will always love you, Joseph.

Contents

Foreword xi
Preface xiii

Introduction. 1
1 From New York to Atlanta 3
2 Searching for a New Home 13
3 Our Place of Worship 17
4 Estell Finds Work 21
5 Trouble in Paradise 27
6 Welcome Home. 33
7 Reunited in Aberdeen 37
8 Our Place on Rex Avenue 47
9 Ben Hill School. 57
10 My Neighbors on Rex Avenue 61
11 A Big Change for the Halliburton Family 65
12 How Sweet It Is! 75
13 Bringing Home Our New Baby. 83
14 Bus Ride to Visit the Doctor 93
15 Fun Days at School 99
16 Daughters and Discipline 107
17 Soul Train 113
18 Joseph's Story 115

19	Missing Aberdeen	119
20	Visiting Parks	131
21	Returning to Work	137
22	Got the Job—Now What?	147
23	Lucinda, the Babysitter	153
24	A New Adventure Begins	159
25	Oh, Waitress!	165
26	Working Mom	173
27	Hold Your Head High and Keep Going	179
28	A Homemaker Once Again	187
29	Joseph's Security Job	195
30	All Is Not Well	203
31	A New Beginning for Joseph	213
32	Joseph Gets His Groove Back	217
33	Fun in the Yellow Station Wagon	223
34	An Afternoon of Quilting	229
35	The Inspection	235
36	Flying Bugs Are Eating Our Home	239
37	Family Meeting: Let's Tell Our Daughters About Our Home	245
38	Sharing Our Unhappy News	251
39	Silver Linings	255
40	Leaving Our House with the Burgundy Door	263

Acknowledgments	273
About the Author	275

Foreword

I knew my great-grandfather Wardell Sims to be a stoic man of few words who moved slowly and with purpose. In reading my grandmother's book, *Leaving Aberdeen*, I had the opportunity to know him more in depth. When my great-grandfather's friend was killed, when the owner of the land he sharecropped acted threateningly, he would always turn to his faith.

Today's racism often masquerades as an "elephant in the room"; the racism my ancestors experienced was more of a "bull in a china shop." My grandfather, Joseph R. Halliburton, was a revolutionary and a member of the Black Panther Party. He stood beside armed men, protecting china shops from bulls. Grit is characterized as remaining resilient when faced with adversities. My lineage has a lot of grit.

Grits are made from the grinding of whole kernels of corn between two slabs of stone. It is the friction that gives the grits their form, just as it is life's challenges that shape us. The manner in which my great-grandfather dealt with his trials caused him to be held in high regard within his community, leading him to become one of the first prominent African American employee at the Aberdeen City Hall.

In my grandmother's memoir, one can see how the challenges in Aberdeen inspired her to move to New York, where she attributes the expansion of her consciousness to seeing African Americans blossom in Harlem.

As I sit before my breakfast of grits and butter today, I am reminded of all the work that went into the formation of grits. I am reminded of the efforts that led to my own formation. I send gratitude to my ancestors before finishing what's on my plate.

~ Xavier Sparks

Preface

I wrote this book to continue sharing my parents' legacy. Estell and Wardell Sims are gone, and I miss them. When they were alive, they were just poor people living on the colored side of town in Aberdeen, Mississippi. My parents were good people who never owned a car, but they did own their home. Nevertheless, they shared whatever they had with their family and friends. Every night, we sat down in our tiny kitchen and ate the dinner my mother cooked, and we went to church on Sundays. My home provided a foundation of love, and I felt safe and loved as the youngest child; my daddy called me Sis[1]. After school, my mom had me doing my chores, like planting flowers and feeding the chickens in the hen house. But I learned the lesson of hard work and independence. I am forever grateful to my parents for providing a loving home.

    I left Aberdeen when I was nineteen years old because I felt trapped by the rules of segregation. I remember going to the doctor with my mother and seeing signs that read WHITE ONLY and COLORED ONLY. My mother and I went to the back door, and I wondered why we had to use separate doors. I kept quiet and said nothing because my mother looked scared and held my hand tightly. I never forgot feeling like my life did not matter.

---

[1] "Sis" was my childhood nickname, and my parents and siblings still called me that as an adult.

If Grits Could Talk

In December 2021, when I self-published my first book through my company, Halliburton Publishing, I was thrilled. It was a significant milestone for me. I felt a surge of momentum, and it was like a light bulb went off inside of me. I learned that I enjoy writing about my life. Honestly, it was a challenge to reveal my pain, hurt, and shortcomings. I used my imagination to create essential stories. In both books, I wrote to expose the truth and change the narrative about our lives.

For many years, I was underemployed; I did not fit in on the job. I was bored and couldn't wait until my shift ended. I just worked to pay the bills and keep a roof over my head. I was not doing work that made use of my education and my skills. I worked a lower-paying job, and I earned less than white people. So, when I began writing, I was doing something that helped me get out of a rut. In fact, I am the best version of the person I always wanted to be. I don't give up, and I continue to work on my dream and get it done.

I am inspired to write my stories. I want to share the Black experience to document our history and expose the truth about our heritage. I am sharing stories about the people I love and respect: hardworking families who just want to live in a good home and educate their children and people trying to find meaning in their lives, overcoming obstacles and hard times and finding a way to push through. Through my books, I want us to show empathy toward each other and for my readers recognize our similarities and difference. My story is an American story that needs to be told.

Introduction

After nine years in New York, I went home to the South. I never thought I would leave New York because I loved living in our brownstone in Brooklyn, but with a growing family, we began looking for a home we could afford. I wanted my family to live in a quiet neighborhood with trees and flowers. This move was different because I was returning with my husband, Joseph, and my two daughters, Fatima and Rabia. Later, my third daughter, Aisha, was born in Atlanta at Grady Hospital. I decided on Atlanta because Black Southerners were gaining political and economic power. Atlanta was a catalyst for change and the center of the Civil Rights movement with Dr. Martin Luther King, Jr. and Mayor Maynard Jackson, the first African American mayor in the South, who was a good businessman and improved race relations in the city. Besides, I saw Atlanta as a place where I could feel comfortable and learn more about our culture.

I was ready to come home to the South, but I had a bittersweet feeling of coming back to the land of my ancestors. Returning to the South was like returning to my childhood and seeing that not much had changed. Even the large Coca-Cola signs remained the same. But my perspective on life had changed, and I no longer felt that those limiting beliefs of my past could hold me back. When I got to Atlanta, I discovered that I had changed, and I had a new perspective on the South, too. I saw that it had charm but still had the attitude that skin color made a difference. I felt the mental stress of being a Black woman seeking financial security for my family. But I knew I was stronger, and I was confident that I was connecting to my roots and our lives would blossom.

1
From New York to Atlanta

I MOVED TO NEW YORK when I was nineteen years old, and now I was returning to the South. I knew I belonged near my parents, and in the South, but I was moving with some regret because the South was where I struggled to find my identity. Yet this was a homecoming because I was coming back to a land that had the sweat of my ancestors in the soil. This time, I was bringing a family: my husband of seven years, Joseph, and our daughters, Fatima and Rabia.

Joseph had the same strength that my dad exhibited in my birth family. For years, I did not tell anyone except my husband about my life in Aberdeen, Mississippi. I did not want to tell anyone that I used an outhouse for the bathroom and fed the hogs in the pen. After I married Joseph in Harlem in 1965, I began to tell my friends that my daddy had been a sharecropper, that I was born on a plantation and wore a sack on my back to pick cotton. I still had thoughts of my stomach growling in my one-room schoolhouse and walking in the woods with holes in my shoes. Yet I realized that my parents' faith in God kept them going, and nothing ever stopped them from sharing their love with me. I decided that moving back was something I had to do, and this time, I was settling into my own with my family.

New Beginnings

On a warm Friday morning in the spring of 1974, Joseph was speeding on Georgia's State Route 400 in heavy traffic. Joseph tapped me on the shoulder and shouted over the roaring engine, "Babe, wake up!" I opened my eyes to huge billboards flashing by on the highway: "Gun Show Down the Road," "Church on Sunday," "Peanut Country," and "The City Too Busy to Hate." I had never seen traffic like that, and all those crazy signs! I yawned, thinking about how people in the South called this "God's Country."

I could almost smell BBQ chicken on the grill and taste potato salad made with hot mustard, pickles, and boiled eggs. Coming home brought up good memories! We had left New York City about twelve hours earlier and only stopped to pick up sandwiches at an orange-roofed Howard Johnson's, and those signs made me hungry.

For a moment, it seemed as if I had just crossed the George Washington Bridge that spans the Hudson River, and it was scary to leave our brownstone on Halsey Street in Brooklyn and our puppy, Buddy. *And*, I thought, *I may not ever see my friends again, and our two girls are not here with me. They are in Aberdeen*. I decided that re-creating my identity in the South was, so far, a painful journey.

Joseph began looking at his map book. "I read somewhere that those fifteen streets are named Peachtree Street," he grumbled. "I thought that I had the streets figured out, Babe, but Peachtree Street is everywhere."

As we drove along the narrow lanes with trees hovering above the street, I held my daughters' framed picture and the small silver Statue of Liberty that my friend Jasmine gave me the day before I crossed the

From New York to Atlanta

George Washington Bridge for our trip to Atlanta. I took a whiff of fresh air with the sun beaming through the windshield and thought, *I'll get used to this hot weather*. I rolled down my window and took a sip from my water bottle, watching the people as we drove by. Most of the buildings in Atlanta were about four stories in height except a few tall structures like the Healey Building on Forsyth Street, which reminded me of the New York City skyscrapers.

Joseph turned onto the busy intersection of Marietta and Forsyth Streets, where the tall, bronze statue of Henry W. Grady sat in the middle of a huge pedestal. Grady had coined the term "New South" to describe his vision for a more progressive and industrialized economy after the Civil War. During his editorship of the *Atlanta Constitution*, he allegedly supported white supremacy, publishing racist headlines and stories supporting alleged Ku Klux Klan leader John Brown Gordon for the governorship of Georgia, and he took a stance against suffrage for African Americans. I had seen many statues like this in Mississippi, and I mused that they should be in a museum so people could learn the real history.

As our Impala slowed down for traffic, I looked at my watch; it was 1:00 p.m. I saw the hood lights of a black police cruiser in my side-view mirror as it pulled up behind our car. I knew that if they asked Joseph to get out of the car, the results could be dangerous. I glanced at my husband and said, "I am with you all the way." My stomach churned as I ground my toes inside my shoes. Joseph, with his towering Afro and full beard, had beads of sweat on his forehead; he gripped the steering wheel. I thought back to New York, where Joseph had been stopped and frisked many times by the police. I wasn't sure what to expect in Atlanta, the home of the civil rights movement.

In New York, Joseph had joined the Black Panther Party, a militant Black Power group, in 1968 to help fight police brutality and systemic racism. The movement captured the imagination of young Black men and women and instilled pride. The Panthers set up the free breakfast program in Brooklyn and registered people in the community to vote. Indeed, my husband was an eager participant, helping prepare meals to feed hungry school children. At first, I was thrilled to see him active in our community. However, when the FBI cracked down on the Panthers for their political views and arrested many of them, I became troubled that Joseph might be jailed. I believed in his mission, so after I thought about it, I encouraged him since he was willing to stand up for his beliefs and protest in the streets. Also, I felt exhilarated, and scared because I was too frightened to speak up about injustices myself. While growing up in Aberdeen, I did not say a word because I felt like it was my place to stay silent in our town. Daddy told me stories about friends who were missing for speaking up, and I never forgot those stories. Not only did I fear the police, but I thought my voice did not matter, something that was ingrained in me as a child in Aberdeen.

By then, I was worried; did my husband have his Colt 45 pistol under the seat? I did not want to know. Joseph's eyes darted to my startled face, but he just sat up straight with his shoulders back, looking straight ahead like an eagle, waiting.

The police were there for only five minutes, but it seemed like an hour. After they sped away, I breathed a sigh of relief, unbuckled my seat belt, moved closer to my husband, and laid my head on his shoulder. I thought, "Is this really happening on our first day in the city of Atlanta?"

Joseph turned the dial to WSB Radio to an interview with Hank Aaron, the home-run king, who had just broken Babe Ruth's record. It was background noise to me; all I could think about was how much I wanted to believe that my family would survive, and my two girls would always have a loving dad. Joseph pulled into traffic on Decatur Street, and I never discussed this incident with him. It was just part of our experience because of our skin color.

I took a deep breath and told myself to relax while Joseph continued circling midtown. We drove through Atlanta's historic theater district, and when I saw the fabulous Fox Theatre on Peachtree Street with its large red and silver marquee, my eyes were glued to it. It reminded me of the theater on Forty-Second Street in New York where I saw *Hello, Dolly!* on Broadway.

Even today, when I think of the Fox Theatre in Atlanta, I remember *Gone with the Wind*, the blockbuster movie based on Margaret Mitchell's book about the Old South. The film portrays slaves as ignorant and uneducated and happy during the Civil War. During that time in the US, it was rare to see an African American in a movie, and when you did, the portrayals were usually negative, with characters who had big eyes and a wide grin and used bumbling words like a servant. During the showing of *GWTW*, which premiered at Loew's Theatre in 1939, Black people protested in front of the theater over the less-than-progressive caricatures of African Americans.

Joseph's voice brought me back to the present. "I am going to surprise you, Babe," he announced. I wasn't sure I wanted to know what the surprise was at that point. My stomach growled, but a few minutes later, he turned into The Varsity, loved for its burgers and hot dogs. The drive-in sits with its tall red sign on two city blocks on North Avenue and is a fixture of midtown Atlanta. It is one of the oldest drive-ins in the South.

People sat in parked cars waiting for service, so Joseph maneuvered into one of the parking slots. Walking out of the white-and-red building, a young Black guy wearing a creased cap with red stripes and a name tag that read JEROME came to the car and asked, "What'll ya have?"

Surprised by the informal greeting, Joseph stuttered, "I'll have . . . uh . . . Estell, what do you want?" I ordered a chili dog with mustard and some white onion sprinkled on it and a frosted orange milk shake. Still looking at the plastic menu, Joseph ordered a steak burger with cheese, chili, fried onion rings, two apple pies, and a tall Coca-Cola.

We watched other people in the parking lot as we waited; I thought the high school students in the car next to us were especially interesting as they yelled and hung out of the car windows. About ten minutes later, the young waiter handed us two white bags with grease stains on the bottom. Joseph pulled out his wallet, and the young waiter gave him a bucktoothed smile and handed my husband the check for $1.25. Joseph paid and gave him a five-dollar tip. With an even bigger grin, the waiter said, "Thank you, sir!"

I held the paper sacks with the fries and tore into them. Joseph grumbled, "Aren't you going to wait for me?"

"No, Babe!" I said and ate another handful as we pulled away to the street.

My Brother, Wardell

We headed to Wardell's house in Adamsville, where we would stay for a week. The community, about thirty minutes away on the west side of Atlanta, was segregated with middle-class homes. I hadn't laid eyes on my brother in ten years, and as we drove, I thought about the last time I had seen him. I recalled a time when I was around ten years old, when I picked green okra from our backyard garden on Matubba Street in Aberdeen in the sweltering heat. Of course, my black-and-tan German shepherd, Spooky, who was a gift from my dad for my fifth birthday, was always by my side. Spooky barked at everything, like a car horn or a kid passing by. Usually, Wardell would lean down and quietly stroke him on the head, saying, "You are okay," and Spooky would calm down. Then I would put down my bucket of okra and pull out pork-skin rinds for my dog while he sat on his hind legs and wagged his tail.

My brother will meet my husband for the first time, and I think he will be a little surprised when he sees Joseph, who is tall like Daddy with

From New York to Atlanta

a trimmed beard and an Afro, I thought. The guys I dated in Aberdeen were clean-shaven with neat haircuts. They were quiet, too, while my husband always had an opinion. Occasionally, Joseph could be a little arrogant and cocky. But I felt sure they would get along. After all, we are connected as a family.

At 3:00 p.m., our Chevy Impala pulled into the driveway of a white two-story house on Charter Oak Drive. I stepped out of the car with my shoulder bag and wearing a sweatshirt with the saying, BROWN GIRL FROM BROOKLYN. I knocked on the door, and Wardell threw open the screen door and hugged me tightly. He had the same smile I remembered from our childhood, and he looked to be in good shape in his white shirt and tie and slacks.

He embraced me and said, "Sis, you are skinny! And look at your short, textured hair." When we last saw each other in 1962, my hair was straightened, and I was thicker with wide hips.

Joseph was behind me, and I introduced the two men, who shook hands. The small talk that followed included Wardell asking Joseph about the drive to Atlanta. Joseph responded by nodding his head and announcing that Atlanta was a big difference from New York. Afterward, Wardell told us his family was out shopping at Rich's Department Store and should be home soon.

I asked Joseph to bring in the luggage, and when he stepped out to the car, I told my brother, "You have a cozy living room with pictures of Mom and Dad on the wall."

Wardell mentioned that we would sleep downstairs and added that we would be eating strip steak and baked potatoes for dinner that night at Western Sizzler. "Wow," I told him, "it sounds like a delicious meal. I can't wait to get a nap and take a bath."

For the next week, Wardell showed us around Atlanta and took us to Paschal Restaurant on Hunter Street. After a week, Joseph secured a room at the Holiday Inn. We thanked my brother and his family for their hospitality and headed back to Atlanta.

The Holiday Inn

Once we were settled in our room, where we would stay until we found an apartment or rented a house, I told Joseph I wanted to call the girls in Aberdeen, and he said he had seen a phone booth near the entrance to our room. I stepped inside the phone booth and close the door. Next, I put four quarters into the slots and picked up the heavy black phone receiver.

The first time I called, I got a busy signal, so I stood there twirling my braid for a few minutes. Momentarily, I dialed again.

"Hi, Momma," I greeted her when she answered.

"Hey, Sis, did you make it to Atlanta?"

"Yes, we just arrived. I want to speak to the girls."

A moment later, a sweet little voice said, "Hello?"

"Hi, Fatima, I miss you so much, and your sweet voice."

Fatima said, "Mommy, I want to come home to see you and Dad."

My heart wrenched with pain, and I began to cry.

"Fatima, I got your pink teddy bear with me. I am in Atlanta, and I am coming to Aberdeen soon," I promised her. "Put Rabia on the phone."

Afterward, I heard, "Hi, Mama, I love you, and I want to see you."

I struggled to get the words out. "Rabia, how are you? I miss hugging you." I could no longer speak to them because it was too painful, so I beckoned my husband to the phone. He talked to our daughter for five minutes.

After Joseph hung up, I stood tight-lipped by the hood of the car clutching my purse. As he hugged me, I fell into his arms, weeping, "I need my daughters." He rubbed my back, and I wiped my nose with my handkerchief.

Joseph told me calmly, "I know that your mom and dad in Aberdeen are taking good care of them."

"But I need them here, beside me," I said between sniffles.

"Babe, I will do whatever it takes to get our daughters home soon."

"Joseph, I did not realize that this was going to be so painful."

We ended up living at the Holiday Inn for three weeks. I really missed our brownstone in Brooklyn on Halsey Street where I walked our dog, Buddy, with my girls on Saturday mornings, so I was delighted when we decided to find a larger place that felt more like home. Finding a home in Atlanta seemed a bit scary at times, but I knew Joseph and I would work together as a team to get our new lives going in Atlanta so we could bring our girls home.

2
Searching for a New Home

AFTER THREE WEEKS of living in the Holiday Inn, we decided we needed to move to an apartment to save money. After searching the *Atlanta Journal-Constitution* and *Atlanta Daily World* (the oldest Black newspaper in Atlanta), we had a few leads. On Saturday morning, we got into our maroon Impala and headed south in drizzling rain to the Black neighborhood. As we entered the Garden Hills complex, I noted the grass needed a lawn mower and an open trash can. I told Joseph that the place was a little run down, but I wanted to check it out anyway.

The manager, Dizzy, greeted us and grabbed the keys to the first-floor apartment. He was a short man with a button-down orange shirt that was a bit too small. As the door opened, I was happy to see light blue paint on the walls; as we walked through and into the kitchen, I saw two big roaches crawling on the stove like they owned the place. Dizzy announced, "The pest control folks was here, yesterday," which I guess meant the roaches had been disturbed but would soon disappear. After we finished walking through all the rooms, Dizzy asked when we wanted to move in. Joseph quickly responded,

If Grits Could Talk

"We need to think about it." As we returned to the car, I told Joseph, "You know that place needs an exterminator," and we both chuckled.

We looked at a modest duplex in College Park at the Westwood Apartments complex about three miles from William B. Hartsfield Airport. The rent was $150 a month, and the duplex had a big backyard, but as the manager was showing us the apartment, the jets taking off and landing overhead shook the roof. I looked at Joseph with a look that asked, "Why did you bring me here?" I knew the apartment was cheap, but how would I sleep at night with all the noise? The leasing agent asked when we wanted to move in, and Joseph responded, "I'll call when we decide." The agent rubbed his chin and mumbled, "Thanks for coming."

The next place was the Sylvan Hills Apartments on Memorial Avenue. As we drove up, I observed the trimmed evergreen hedges that surrounded the two-story buildings. We met the manager, Mary Lou, at the rental office, and we filled out an application and had to pay the deposit of fifty dollars before seeing the apartment.

"Where y'all from?" Mary Lou asked as we walked to see the one-bedroom apartment. Joseph told her New York.

"I knew it," she responded, "when I saw your wife. She is dressed beautifully in that African print." Then, she opened the door to the apartment. It was clean and smelled like lilacs. I proceeded into the bathroom, where I found sparkling new faucets.

"How do you all like the place, Miss Halliburton?" Mary Lou asked. I told her I liked it, and Joseph nodded his head in agreement. The manager continued, "It requires a month's rent, ninety dollars by check or money order, for a six-month lease."

Joseph stared at the new beige carpet while he told the manager that we were looking for a month-to-month lease. The manager responded, "That's not our policy, but I will make an exception for you nice folks."

"Thank you for your kindness," I told her, and then Joseph asked, "When can we pick up the keys?" We were all smiling when Mary Lou told us we could stop by for them the next evening.

Searching for a New Home

As I strolled to our maroon Impala, I told my husband that I had seen a McDonald's on Whitehall Street, and about ten minutes later, he turned into the drive that led to the Golden Arches. We decided to go inside because the air conditioner in the car was not working. Joseph stood in line to order while I went to the bathroom. As I stood looking into the mirror, I begin thinking about Rabia's tiny hands caressing my neck and Fatima calling me Mommy in her sweet voice. I could feel their spirits, and one tear began rolling down my cheek.

For a moment, I was paralyzed with fear. *When are my daughters coming home? I need a home for my babies.* I gripped the counter, thinking about how I prayed every night to hold them in my arms.

Joseph knocked on the bathroom door and called out, "Estell, come on, get your food, it is getting cold." I wiped my face, powdered my cheeks, and dabbed my lip gloss. When I exited the bathroom, Joseph was waiting.

"Babe, what's going on with you?" he asked. "I heard you last night talking to your sister, Mary, about the girls." Joseph put his arm around my shoulder and continued, "I am committed to keeping our family together and finding us a home." I was worried, but his words made me feel more confident. I nodded my head.

We walked together to our table, but I suddenly changed my mind about eating inside. "Joseph, let's take our food with us."

The server prepared our food to go and added napkins and ketchup. Back in the car, I strapped my seat belt across my shoulder and reached to turn the dial to radio station V-103. The music cheered me up, and I began moving my shoulders and bobbing my head while I listened to Glady Knight and the Pips singing, "Midnight Train to Georgia," a song about not giving up on your dreams.

"Babe, you had me worried," Joseph said as he chewed his burger. "I am happy that you are feeling better. I am going to take care of you and our girls!"

3
Our Place of Worship

AFTER WE MOVED to Atlanta, we wanted to connect with others at the mosque who shared our beliefs and to gather for prayer and worship. Islam was a way to keep our faith in God and a strong marriage.

Before we left New York, we had attended the mosque on Riverside Drive in Manhattan for years, and our imam connected us to our new mosque, the Jama Masjid on Gordon Street in the West End neighborhood, which was about a twenty-minute drive on the expressway. One Friday afternoon, we were headed to a congregational prayer service. Joseph, who was feeling good about driving us to the mosque and looking forward to making friends there, was steering our Chevrolet in heavy traffic.

The mosque was a place to connect with God, and I wanted to connect with others who shared our belief in the sacred scriptures. I also wanted to reflect on our journey in Atlanta and the tough time we were having getting jobs. I was praying daily because being in a new city was lonely, sad, and daunting, but I knew it would take time to feel comfortable.

At first, being in Atlanta felt like an exciting experience until I thought about leaving family and friends behind. Getting a job was stressful, too, especially being rejected and knowing that our money was tight. After three weeks in Atlanta, neither one of us had a job.

Joseph wore a black turtleneck sweater with a black jacket and his loosely braided prayer cap that could barely fit over his thick Afro. I wore a comfortable long yellow dress that Joseph said complimented my brown skin tone and a white headscarf and sandals. I rolled down the window to see the cloud clustering but gazing at the sky elevated my spirit. I wished that my children were with us instead of with my parents in Aberdeen, Mississippi. *At the mosque, I'll say a special prayer for my daughters.*

The Islamic Center was in an Afro American community. It had a large open space for prayer and other adjoining rooms. It is a custom at the mosque to remove your shoes at the door to keep the prayer area clean. As we removed our shoes at the front entrance, we were greeted by brother Daniel and returned the Arabic greeting, *As-salamu alaikum*, which means *Peace be upon you*. Joseph stayed to chat with him, and I went to the separate room for women.

The congregational prayer service, Jummah, which is held every Friday, began in the large room with red carpet. We kneeled and touched our heads to the floor as a submission to God. The imam gave a sermon about strengthening the family. After the service, we met Imam Amir and his wife, Rida.

I first joined Islam with my husband when we lived in Brooklyn, New York, in 1968. The Quran reflects the teaching of God as the word was revealed to the Prophet Muhammad through the angel Gabriel. In the Quran, Allah is referred to as the cherisher and Creator. The first surah (chapter) of the Quran begins with the al-Fatiha, which is a prayer for guidance. I learned about the other divine prophets like Adam, Abraham, Moses, and Jesus. The mosque helped me to stay on the right path with the teaching of God and praying five times a day.

After the service, the men and women socialized in different rooms. I met with the sisters in a small room with a sofa and chairs. One of the older sisters who wore a floral pink dress handed out pamphlets to show Islamic stores that sold prayer rugs, oils, and modest clothing. I settled down with the ten sisters on yellow cushions, nibbling on dates and freshly baked bread. Dates are fruit mentioned in the Quran that help support our immune system and a healthy mind. I was relaxed and felt comfortable.

At the group discussion, I met Lila, who was from South Carolina, and she commented on my dress with a big grin. I told her that I was from Brooklyn, New York, and had moved to Atlanta with my husband and two daughters. She replied that she had been in Atlanta for six months with her husband, Abdul. As we talked, she told me that she went to the mosque every Friday. I asked, "Can I get your phone number? And I like your lilac silk headdress, too."

Lila said, "Could we meet for lunch? I live on Ashby Street about two miles from here." We agreed to speak on the phone the following weekend. Then another sister, Marilyn, told me, "Estell, if you need help with a babysitter, just call me," and I thanked her. After thirty minutes of chatting, we leaned in for a hug.

I was delighted to make friends at the mosque and to connect with others like me.

4
Estell Finds Work

EVEN THOUGH JOSEPH and I had moved to Atlanta from Brooklyn, New York, in May, about two months earlier, I continued to have a problem finding my way around in Atlanta with so many streets named Peachtree. I often waited in the sweltering hot sun for the Marta bus with no shade. I learned how to get around by walking the streets, getting help from friendly shoppers and Southerners just walking up and talking to me. On the contrary, in New York, where the people weren't that friendly, I had to just figure things out when riding the subway.

On many days, Joseph and I rode together in our maroon Chevrolet Impala to go to interviews. For six weeks, I searched for the want ads in the *Atlanta Journal Constitution* and filled out applications. Usually, I am not discouraged easily, but I was fatigued from dressing up daily, staying jovial, and following up with phone calls after an interview.

At 8:05 a.m. on a morning in July 1974, I stepped through the doors of the Equitable building on Peachtree Street and asked the security guard for directions to the fourth floor for K & G Accounting.

The security guard looked at my clothes—I wore a beige dress, a long-sleeve shirt with a tight lace collar, and black heels—and asked, "So you have an appointment?" I was there for an interview and told him I did have a meeting in the personnel department, and then I waited for him to tell me to take the back way. But he just frowned and watched me as I entered the elevator.

I entered the fourth floor where the personnel office was located, and I observed clerks in the offices nearby with adding machines on their desks. I met the manager, who was sitting at a wooden desk with a brown folder in front of her.

"Good morning, Estell." Miss Jane Watson smiled and shook my hand. "Have a seat. The job is as an accounting assistant." She opened the folder and glanced at my résumé. "I am happy to meet you, Estell. How do you like living in Atlanta?" After I said I liked its Southern charm and flowering dogwood trees, she continued, "So, Estell, tell me what skills you can bring to this job."

"When I worked for Gilbert Carrier in New York on Thirty-Fourth Street," I said with more confidence than I felt, "I paid attention to details, got along well with my coworkers, and was voted employee of the month three years in a row by the staff."

"And what are your weakness?" Miss Watson asked.

"Sometimes, I took on too many tasks, which slowed the pace of my work."

Her green-framed glasses rested on her nose. "Do you have any children?"

"Yes, I have two daughters."

"Have you ever been fired from a job?"

"No, I haven't been fired."

She sipped on her coffee as I answered her questions. "I see that you did well on the math aptitude test for accounting." I was feeling optimistic about being offered the job when she said next, "You meet the qualifications for the job, but the company is not hiring now. I will keep your resume on file, though."

I tried not to look as disappointed as I felt. I replied, "Thanks for the interview, Miss Watson."

I walked slowly out her office after receiving this stinging rejection. As I passed the offices again, this time on my way out of K & G Accounting, I did not see anyone in the office who looked like me. I was furious that this woman wearing a fake smile had just wasted my time. I could see that whether I was in New York or Atlanta, merit and qualifications did not matter. I believed that my skin color was the deciding factor. For a moment, I walked with slumped shoulder. On the corner was a phone booth. I called Joseph and explained that I got rejected for the accounting job. He reassured me that I was going to be fine.

I put on my sunglasses to hide my tear-filled eyes as I walked to the Marta bus stop. I thought about growing up in Aberdeen. I was told that I should know my place, and where I could only be hired as a maid in 1959. And in New York City, I walked the streets of Manhattan many days seeking employment until I was hired at the Guerlain Perfume company. Even then, I was not welcome there because of my dark skin. And there were the "jokes" that I needed to return to Africa, like I was a stranger in the country of my birth.

When I arrived home that evening, I could barely talk to Joseph because I could not shake off the prejudice I experienced. I gritted my teeth and tightened my lips.

"I guess that I don't fit in at this company, just like in Aberdeen," I told my husband.

Joseph held my hand tightly and did his best to calm me down.

"This company is not ready for diversity," I continued. "But the bitter taste of rejection gives me fuel to keep going."

I had thought that K&G was following the guidelines for affirmation action, which was a set of procedures under the Civil Rights Act of 1964 designed to eliminate discriminatory hiring and increase hiring of Blacks and women who were marginalized in the workforce.

I knew that not hiring me because of my color was illegal, but I didn't feel like the civil rights laws would ever protect me from this hate. I was not seeking preferential treatment—I was qualified; I had been a dedicated student in business school in New York; moreover, I had two years of experience in accounting. I got the lead for this job from the NAACP, which was helping young women like me find jobs that were free of racial bias in the workplace. I told myself that even though moving forward was painful, I would pretend this incident had not happened.

Meanwhile, Joseph's job at Woolworth's as part of the security crew did not last long. The supervisor asked him to sweep and mop the floors while his white coworker left for home, and Joseph told him, "No, I read the job duties in the handbook, and they do not include mopping the floor." Joseph was terminated after one week after refusing his manager's orders. This was subtle discrimination, yet my husband was determined to find work so that our family could buy a home.

After three weeks of looking for something else, Joseph got a job at the Sheraton Biltmore Hotel with the help of a friend. The hotel, at the northeast corner of the intersection of West Peachtree and Fifth streets, was a five-story building with a doorman at the entrance and decorative lighting fixtures in the lobby. It reminded me of the Hilton Hotel in New York where Joseph and I had dined out to celebrate becoming parents. Joseph got a position in the maintenance department with a friendly crew. His duties were replacing light fixtures, making plumbing repairs, and painting the interior. It was just what he had done when he worked beside his dad, Joseph, who was a supervisor for a four-story apartment building in Manhattan.

I was still job hunting when my husband invited me to lunch one day and told me about a position that was opening at the front desk. He wanted me to apply and offered to check with personnel about it, which excited me.

Estell Finds Work

About a week later, I went in to fill out an application. I got hired immediately as a reservation clerk and clerical assistant, which required good speaking skills. Working in this beautiful hotel with polished door handles and meeting interesting people would be a new adventure.

5

Trouble in Paradise

OVER THE NEXT WEEKS, I met guests from diverse backgrounds at the reservation desk. They often wanted to know about the sites to see in the area, like Stone Mountain, Six Flags Over Georgia, and Underground Atlanta. Black guests were interested in Black landmarks like Sweet Auburn Avenue and the Alonzo Franklin Herndon home, which had been built by the first Black millionaire in America. During my lunch hour, I sat with Joseph in the employee dining room to eat beef ribs with sweet and sticky sauce, Idaho baked potatoes with a side of spicy collard greens, and fresh yeast rolls. The meals were always enjoyable and cheap. Occasionally, I brought bologna sandwiches on Wonder Bread with mayo and mustard and dill pickles. Joseph and I always sat together and shared fresh Georgia peaches.

During work hours, Joseph kept hanging around in the lobby like he was repairing the door handles. Sometimes when he'd see me talking to a hotel guest, he would call me on the phone and ask, "Is that guy bothering you?" "No," I told him, and stop calling me."

The manager overheard these phone calls and said, "The calls are disrupting your work, and I want them to stop." I explained this to

If Grits Could Talk

my husband, yet he continued coming into the lobby. I asked him to stop calling me at the reservation desk, and he promised to stop.

When Joseph and I first met and were getting to know each other, I soon realized that he was assertive with a bossy attitude. But I liked so many things about him that I was unconcerned about his possessiveness. Later, I found him committed to our marriage, and he made me feel important. He made it clear that he really cared for me, and when he got bossy about my work, I just assumed he thought I needed to value myself more.

I thought Joseph had changed over time, but I saw his behavior at the hotel as a part of his personality and his tendency to hold me too close.

I received two warnings in the four weeks I worked at the Biltmore. On Friday morning after I got my third paycheck, I was fired. I grabbed my handbag and rushed out of the building. I left the hotel gripping my purse. As I made my way home on the Marta bus, I thought about how much I liked working at a beautiful place with a good salary. We needed the money, and with my income, we could ensure that our children would be coming home. I was flexing my fingers and unsettled for a while that afternoon. However, I wrote down my thoughts in my journal, and it allowed me to shift my negative energy.

Joseph called me on the phone to apologize. When he came home that evening with a fresh-baked pizza for me, I told him, "You eat it." With his lips tight, he looked at me with a sad expression and immediately went into the kitchen.

It took a few days for me to calm down. We decided to carve out time to discuss our feelings. When we finally discussed the situation, Joseph said, "I take responsibility for my actions."

I wanted our marriage to grow and for us to learn to trust each other. But this wasn't the first time that Joseph had been overprotective. In New York, when I worked as a model on Fifth Avenue, Joseph had come home from Vietnam and thought that I was allowing other men to exploit me or treat me unfairly on the job. He wanted me to quit. I did eventually, but we worked out a compromise in the meantime so I could continue to earn money to help us get ahead financially. Nevertheless, it happened again in Atlanta with this job at the Biltmore.

⁓

Joseph had joined the military like his dad, and he thought his service would change his life and give him respect. But in fact, nothing changed for him as a Black man, and this affected his self-esteem. When Joseph came home from Vietnam in 1967, he seemed different because he had lived to stay alive and protect his country. The war left invisible wounds that Joseph did not share with me. Like so many of those young men, my husband had a difficult time resuming the life he left behind, especially since he had been a soldier in the jungles of Vietnam for fourteen months. Many employers assumed that he used marijuana and alcohol in Vietnam. And so it was difficult for Joseph, as head of our family, to transition to a new, meaningful life as a civilian.

Black men have been looked at as second-class citizens and portrayed in the media as absentee fathers and criminals. While Joseph lived in Harlem, New York, he was stopped by the police and questioned many times. He was profiled for the color of his skin. I realize now that some of his possessiveness about me came from his fear of losing me and not having control of his life because of racism.

Joseph and I shared the same values in our marriage. When I was feeling self-doubt about being a mother, he would say, "You got this, Babe and you can count on me."

⁓

After I lost my job at the Sheraton Biltmore Hotel, I looked for about a week before finding a job at a brand-new fancy hotel, the Hyatt

Regency on Peachtree Street. I was a waitress in the breakfast café for about a month, but I continued looking for a higher-paying job.

In August, I was hired at Southern Bell Telephone Company in Midtown on Peachtree Street. I was excited about this job. When I grew up in rural Mississippi, there was no telephone for me—I first talked on the telephone when I moved to the small town of Aberdeen, Mississippi, in 1953 when I was eight years old. It was a thick, green, rotary phone that had to be plugged into the wall at my home. Now, in 1974, I thought this was a good opportunity to learn a new skill.

I wore a uniform with black pants and a white shirt with a badge to enter the building for work. I trained for three weeks and used a headset to connect to the switchboard. Most of my customers were rude, yet I was polite and kept my tone friendly. I got paid $5.15 per hour, a better wage than most places in Atlanta, and the job came with good benefits.

I ate my lunch every day at tables with metal chairs in the company break room near the bathroom. Often, I listened to nostalgic music in the background like "Moon River" by Louis Armstrong. In the corner, there were two vending machines, one with Diet Coke and Pepsi, and Oreo cookies. I brought my brown-bag lunch every day: red grapes, a Velveeta cheese sandwich with sliced tomatoes, and a Little Debbie cake.

After being on the job for a month, I wanted to quit because the supervisor, Miss Charlene, was always chewing gum and hassling me. She sat beside me during my phone calls for training, and she made comments like, "You are snappy with the customers," and "I don't like that mean tone." I gritted my teeth each time, but I needed this job for my family. Later, I met Susie, who was tall and wore bright green fingernail polish. She kept flipping her long fingers as we chatted in the lunchroom. When I explained Charlene's rude comments, Susie said, "That's my supervisor, too. She had the nerve to joke about my braids. That skinny-legged woman is annoying." When I told Susie that I was thinking about quitting this job, she said, "No, Estell. Did you know that we can get overtime, Honey? We are about to get paid . . . and forget about that mean woman, we've got families!" After that day, Susie and I took our lunch break at noon. She loved to gossip about the citrus perfume smells in the bathroom and women not washing their hands. I replied, "Can we talk about something else?"

Susie lived on Campbelltown Road with her mother and her son. I told her, "I just moved to Atlanta with my family, and we are looking for a place to live." Susie offered to drive me in her old Pontiac to view a couple of apartments.

Another day, while sitting alone and snacking on pimento cheese and Ritz Crackers, I met Josefina, who lived in Snellville, about a forty-five-minute commute to Atlanta. It was hard to understand her Spanish, but that did not stop us from getting together. She taught me to say *buenos días*, good morning. She was from Mexico and had been in the United States on a green card for about six months with her husband, Jose. Josefina, who had long black hair and a gold cross around her neck, was saving money for her sister, Rosa, to come to the US. Often, she shared her lunch with me. I enjoyed it when she brought an enchilada, a corn tortilla covered with spicy red sauce, serrano pepper on the side. My mouth was on fire after I tasted it, and Josefina quickly got me a glass of water. I kept eating and sweating anyway.

6

Welcome Home

WHILE WE LIVED in the apartment, we continued looking for a house with a yard for the girls. At that time, there was residential segregation, and we were told by our realtor that the area where we could buy a home was limited. On Saturday morning at ten o'clock, we met a real estate agent in southwest Atlanta in the segregated Rue Royal neighborhood, which was a few miles from Greenbriar Mall. As we pulled up in front the house with its neatly cut grass, I felt that this might be my new home.

We greeted the agent, Shirly, as she exited her blue Plymouth. She was from Jamaica, and she wore tall red heels with a gray suit and dangling gold earrings. We followed her to the front door, where she fumbled in her purse for her big key ring and then opened the door.

When I saw the shiny hardwood floor and the sun beaming through the blinds, I grinned and looked at my husband. We walked through the freshly painted living room and followed Shirly to a cozy bedroom with wide windows and a walk-in closet. Then we looked at the second bedroom, where I could imagine my daughters sleeping in their beds after I told them a bedtime story. We strolled to the kitchen, which had a new refrigerator, a gas stove, and a small window over the sink.

Shirly asked, "Estell, what do you think of the house?"

Turning around and smiling, I said, "I really like this place," and Joseph added, "I think my wife is happy, and I go along with whatever she wants."

"The owner is out of town, but he is pretty agreeable," Shirly told us. "The rent is $126 a month with the option to own the place in six months."

"My new home!" I hollered.

Joseph put his arms around my shoulder and asked Shirly when we could move in, and she responded, "Next week. The utilities are already on, so just call Georgia Power and change them to your name." Then we arranged to speak with her the next day.

After thanking Shirly, we strolled to the car. Before we got in, I stood in front of it just looking at our new home with Joseph. I wondered if we had enough money to move into our new place *and* travel to Aberdeen. I had started a savings account at Citizen Trust Bank on Panola Road with eighty dollars.

"And Joseph, do you still have those savings bonds for the girls?"

"I still got those postal money orders from friends in New York that I use to pay the rent," he answered.

"Joseph, I am thinking of getting a part-time job and getting a babysitter for the girls."

"Estell, I need you to stay home as my wife."

"Joseph, can you stop being selfish?"

Making a House into a Home

I knew this was our home and a place of comfort and love. Once we got over the excitement of finding a house, our next step was to make a checklist of the things we needed. The place had a strange smell after being closed for months, and it needed painting and new carpets. It would take a lot of work to make it habitable, but I didn't care—I was thrilled that we would no longer be living out of boxes and suitcases. The agent gave us the keys about two weeks before we moved in, and we immediately began to fix up the place. I jotted down a couple of things; on the agenda was cleaning on the weekend and getting our house ready for our daughters during the weekend.

I knew how to clean from my childhood days in Aberdeen. Momma had insisted that I scrub the walls with lye soap, which had a pungent smell, and get on my knees and mop the linoleum floor with soapy water. For our new house, I decided I would clean the kitchen cabinets and sink with a paste of baking soda and white vinegar. Then I would scrub the bathroom sink and toilet bowl and use an old toothbrush to scrub the small spaces. And I'd probably make the girls pink curtains for their room.

We'd have to put the utilities in our name and submit a change of address for our mail, check the inspection reports, and locate the fuse boxes. Then we'd need to check for stores like Big Star and look for elementary schools in the areas. Then, I thought about our finances and buying our appliances on credit. I told Joseph that he needed to bring in more money with a side job.

On August 10, 1974, we moved into our new place. Some of our furniture had been lost during the delivery to the storage, including our daughters' twin beds, our wedding pictures, and photos of our friends Jasmine and Anya from Brooklyn. I was upset with my husband for not filing a claim and getting our money back for the lost furniture and heartbroken that our precious photos were gone forever, but I believed that my husband just got overwhelmed by our move to Atlanta and couldn't deal with the claims process. Joseph promised to buy more furniture from Rich's department store. Before our trip to my hometown to collect our daughters, he found an outlet store to buy beds and a living room set.

Joseph oversaw the household budget and paid the bills. I got my own savings account at Citizens Trust, and I still hid money in a shoebox just like my mom in Aberdeen. I had put money in mason jars in our apartment on Halsey Street in New York because I had watched my mom hide money under the mattress and sew it into the hems of her dresses.

7

Reunited in Aberdeen

ON AUGUST 22, 1975, on Friday morning at 7:00 a.m., we grabbed the small suitcase we had packed the night before, jumped into our Impala, and got on the I-20 to make the trip to Aberdeen, Mississippi.

My handmade curtains were hanging in my daughters' bedroom, a new, light-green leather couch sat in the living room, and a new yellow GE refrigerator had replaced the old refrigerator in the kitchen. Our porch lights were bright as we drove away.

I called Momma and Daddy a few days before to let them know we would soon be on our way, and they had the girls' clothes packed. As we pulled away from our house, I was smiling and clutching Joseph hand—we couldn't wait to hear little feet running inside our home.

As we approached the expressway, Joseph rubbed his chin, and I asked him what was wrong. "Our Impala has been overheating," he said. I paused. Then, I said, "I am sure that we are fine!" He smiled and kept steering the car. I drifted off to the sound of a rumbling engine as the car accelerated.

After six hours on the highway, I was in the city of Aberdeen with my husband. Our Impala climbed the hill on Commerce Street and passed the historic city hall with its marble steps and a median reserved for magnolia trees with leathery leaves. As the car turned the corner on Matubba, the Trailways bus station sat on the left side of the street. I recalled boarding the silver-and-red bus to New York City in 1964, with ninety-eight dollars in my pocket. I was tired of the painful indignities of segregation, so I packed my light blue suitcase. I left Aberdeen and embarked on the beginning of a new journey.

Before long, Joseph pulled into the driveway of my parents' white house with its black shutters. My face lit up when I saw Momma sitting in the green chair on the porch with my baby, Rabia. I watched as my five-year-old daughter began running from the gray porch. In her squeaky voice, she called out, "Mommy is here!" I unbuckled my seat belt, opened the door to a ninety-five-degree day, and rushed from the car. Tears rolled down my cheeks as I scooped Rabia up in my arms. I grinned while I squeezed her tightly. I loved the sweet sound of her voice. Momma, trailing behind my daughter, wore a pink apron and a sun hat. Joseph embraced her when she got to the car. Then Joseph grabbed Rabia, clasped her, and lifted her into the air. Rabia giggled, and he cuddled her in his arms. "I am so happy to see you, Rabia," Joseph told her, his voice cracking.

After wiping sweat from her brow, Momma hugged me and kissed me on the cheek. Luckily, I did not see any stuff on her lips. And she used the name my family gave me as I was growing up in Aberdeen when she uttered, "Sis, you are home!" Momma put her arm around me and said, "Sis, you are all right, and the girls are fine." I smiled because I could tell she was right.

"Gosh, where is Fatima?" I asked.

Momma said, "She's in the backyard with your daddy, they've been feeding the chickens in the hen house." I rushed around to the side of the house with its peeling paint, and then I tiptoed to see Fatima sitting with my dad in the swing with Old Mount, Daddy's cat with pale, lemon-yellow eyes. When Fatima saw me, she began

Reunited in Aberdeen

screaming, "Mommy!" and I ran to hug her. With her arms around me, she said, "I missed you, and I am ready go home."

"Oh, big girl, I've missed you," I told her, and I kept squeezing her small hands. Suddenly, Joseph appeared wearing a big grin and picked up Fatima. She said in a soft voice, "Daddy, I love you," and laid her head on his shoulder while he patted her back.

I turned back to embrace Daddy, who now stood in front of the swing. He was taller than Joseph, light-skinned, with black-rimmed glasses on the bridge of his nose and was wearing his ever-present overalls. I felt his wide hand grip around my shoulder, just like when I was a teenager.

"Sis, you look good with your hat," Daddy greeted me.

"I know that you spoiled the girls with those frosty lemon cookies," I scolded him, but he just smiled.

Daddy turned to Joseph, shook my husband's hand, and said, "I am not ready for Robie and Fatma to go home." I just shook my head because my mom and dad never pronounced the girls' Arabic names correctly. Their names were unfamiliar, not Southern names, but Joseph and I didn't mind because we knew their deep love for their granddaughters. Daddy and Momma had accepted my family joining the Muslim religion years earlier.

In the meantime, Momma asked Joseph to drive her to Fred's Drug Store on Meridian Street to pick up her blood pressure medication. Joseph agreed, telling me, "Babe, I am taking the girls with me."

Momma was a short, dark-skinned lady, just a bit over five feet tall, yet she always spoke her mind, which annoyed Daddy. Besides, Momma really liked Joseph, and she was close to him ever since she visited us in Brooklyn. As I watched her over the years, she was always skeptical of our relatives and even her church friends, so I was a little surprised (and very happy) that she liked my husband so much.

I grabbed two Coca-Colas from the icebox in the dining room for Daddy and me after Joseph drove away. As we sat together and chatted, I asked him, "So, what's happening in Aberdeen, Daddy? When I talked to Momma on the phone last year, she said, 'Sis, I can't pick up medicine because of the picket lines in front of McDuffie Drug Store on Hickory Street.'"

Daddy just shook his head. "The boycott to integrate the stores just increased tensions. Eventually, stores like Mair Jewelry and the hardware store did hire Blacks." Daddy remembered that the Elkin Theatre was segregated in 1958, with Blacks upstairs and whites downstairs. But he never set foot inside, and he knew he did not belong there because he was colored. Rather, he just read his Bible for strength when he faced not being accepted.

"I never knew that Aberdeen had a grassroots movement with local Black citizens protesting for their civil rights," I answered. "I am sure folks got tired of drinking from COLORED ONLY water fountains and picking up take-out bags from the back door of Tony's Café because they weren't allowed to eat at the lunch counter. It is disturbing to feel less than human."

Our talk turned to other topics, and around 4:00 p.m., Joseph returned with our daughters and Momma . . . and more toys. I told her, "Momma, you know the girls got enough bears and balls. As a grandma, you are spoiling my girls." But I couldn't be mad.

In the company of my family in the backyard, it seemed like a reunion with my parents laughing and my girls running after the gray cat. I sat in the swing next to Joseph, who had his arm around my shoulder while I swatted at the mosquitos biting my ankles. When I'd had enough of being a snack for insects, I hollered at Momma, "Can we go inside?" She responded that dinner was on the table.

As I walked through the kitchen room, I showed Joseph the old Maytag ringer washing machine in the corner. He asked, "Does it still work?" I said I thought it did. Then, we strolled into the dining room; Momma had set a fine table with a mustard yellow linen tablecloth. Our dinner included browned beef chuck roast with thick gravy, small red potatoes, turnip greens, and fried green tomatoes with homemade rolls. And for the girls, roasted hot dogs, ketchup, a side of sweet pickles and a Jell-O mold. Mommy poured Daddy a glass of buttermilk. Then he said, the blessing: "Heavenly Father, bless my family!" I couldn't wait to stuff my stomach; Momma was the best cook! Then, I fixed Joseph a plate and poured strawberry Kool-Aid for the girls and made their plates, too.

More Reminiscing

While we ate and I listened to my family's happy chatter, I watched my parents, who were getting noticeably older and now had more gray hair than black. I thought back to how difficult their lives had been when I was young. Daddy had been a sharecropper on the Thompson plantation where I was born in 1945; we lived in a shack and pumped our water from the well. Momma cooked our food on an iron stove in the small kitchen, and we ate off tin pans. I was often barefoot and wore raggedy clothes. I picked cotton, my fingers bleeding from cotton bolls, and carried a sack on my back as I worked with my family in the sweltering sun. I cried many days while picking cotton from dawn to sundown because my stomach ached from being hungry.

My family was fortunate that we were able to pay off our debt. Sadly, the source was a payment from a life-insurance policy when my oldest brother, Alfred was killed while on active duty during the Korean War.

In 1952, we moved to our home on Matubba Street, and Daddy began working at the city hall as a janitor and washed windows as a second job. Momma worked as a maid and a housewife. In Aberdeen, life seemed like an adventure for a while . . . until I saw the signs hanging everywhere: COLORED ONLY. It meant that I was different, and I couldn't enter the front door of a restaurant because I could be arrested. It made me dislike my skin color and my textured hair.

The sweet sound of my daughters chattering with their daddy about their time in Aberdeen brought me back to the present.

We all finished eating, and I helped Momma with the dishes. We were just sitting around and visiting when around 5:00 p.m., my sister, Mary, knocked on the screen door. I screamed when I saw her standing there wearing a pink blouse and matching skirt. I leaned in to hug her and invited her inside. We sat on the green, plastic-wrapped couch that brought back memories of my teenage years.

Mary asked excitedly, "Sis, how is your new home in Atlanta? I am so excited for my family! So, tell me what is happening with you? I just got off work and finished cooking dinner for Gregory and Christopher."

"Maybe I can see my nephews tomorrow," I said, and then remembered that I would be leaving in the morning. By then, Fatima and Rabia had run in to hug their Aunt Mary.

"Sis, you know that the girls called me momma," Mary told me with pride.

"Wow, they love your kind voice," I said. "Of course, I like how you braided their hair and didn't straighten it." I was remembering how, when I was a little girl, Momma straightened my coiled hair from the roots with a heated hot comb. Often, I hid in the backyard to keep her from straightening my hair, but it just delayed the painful Saturday evening ritual. Momma assumed that straightening my hair would help me fit in and be accepted as a good Christian girl at a time when coiled hair was considered ugly. Neither Joseph nor I wanted our daughters' hair straightened.

Joseph walked into the living room to greet Mary with a warm embrace, telling her, " I will never forget your visit to our home in New York." Trailing him were Momma and Daddy, who invited her to join us for dinner.

Forks knocking the plates, chewing, and laughing were the happy sounds around the red metal table that evening. Fatima and Rabia only nibbled on their food because they were waiting for Aunt Mary's dessert: banana pudding with sliced bananas, vanilla wafers, and whipped creamed topping. Once it was served, everyone dug in for big helpings. I wanted another bite, but by the time I was ready for more, the bowl was empty.

After dinner was over and we'd put the girls to bed, I invited Mary into the bedroom, and I surprised her with a gift from Rich's in Atlanta. She untied the white ribbon and opened the box to reveal a black leather purse. She unzipped it and rubbed the shiny leather. Then, I thanked her for sending the box of goodies with pecans and brownies from Kimmel's to me in Atlanta. We sat there together and talked until about 10:00 p.m. Even though we were separated by miles, I shared a bond with my sister like no one else.

Mary and I shared many memories of our childhood. I recalled walking home from town on Canal Street with Mary while eating Sugar Babies and giggling. Then a red pickup truck with the Confederate flag pulled up beside us with three young white boys inside. They hollered profanities and threw rocks and bottles at us and began chasing us. Mary and I ran like two rabbits, screaming because we feared for our lives. We hid behind the bushes until they drove away. Mary told me, "Sis, you are going be fine."

Afterward, I held tightly to my sister's hand and lost one of my scandals as we ran home. We never stopped until we got home and locked the doors. Mary seemed so strong and protected me. I never talked about this incident; I just pretended it never happened.

During our childhood, we did so many things together, going to Pilgrim Rest church on Sundays. Mary carried a small Bible in her purse, and I enjoyed singing in the choir and dressing up with my big sister. Mary would allow me to wear her makeup and earrings. I was so happy being with my sister and watching her smile.

When I moved to New York City, I wrote letters to my sister and telephoned her when I could. I told her that I was mesmerized by the dazzling skyscrapers and the vibrant energy of the city. Besides, I was surprised that I could sit on the subway with the white people; I knew this was different from the South. When I met Joseph and was impressed with this tall army soldier from Harlem, I confided in my sister because she always told me the truth. Mary encouraged me to pursue my dreams.

We hugged again before she left that night. I stood on the front porch and waved so long as she descended the steps.

There is no one who knows me better than my big sister, Mary. And I know that she will always be there for me.

Homeward Bound

The next day was Saturday, and we were up early packing our clothes into suitcases sprawled out on the linoleum floor. Our daughters were sad to leave Aberdeen, but they were ready to see their new home in Atlanta. I dressed them in new light-blue dresses and sandals for the drive back to Atlanta. While Momma packed a cardboard box with fried chicken wings and rolls for us and cheese sandwiches for the girls, I went to talk to Daddy. I found him in his bedroom with his Bible beside him, and I asked if he was all right.

"I am getting old, Sis." Daddy pointed to the dresser. "I put fifty dollars on the dresser for my grandchildren's school clothes." As I thanked him, Fatima and Rabia came in and quickly climbed into his lap in the oversize chair. Fatima looked up at him and said, "Granddaddy, we love you." I watched as Daddy's eyes took on a glassy look, then I sat down beside him and held his hand while my eyes got misty too. I hugged my dad because he believed in my dreams and always sent me money orders and peanut brittle candy. I felt like I never grew up when I came home to Aberdeen. Joseph came in next and stood beside me, and Daddy told him, "I want you to provide a good home for Sis and these girls."

"Yes, sir," Joseph answered seriously, and he and Daddy exchanged a strong handshake. I held tightly to Joseph's other hand before I waved goodbye.

It was time to leave, so Fatima and Rabia ran to hug the cat while they held tight to their red and white teddy bears, a gift from their grandma. I put my arm around my momma's shoulder and thanked her for taking care of my girls.

"Sis, I really enjoyed my baby girls," she said. We all walked out together to our maroon Impala in the driveway, with Joseph carrying the suitcases. Momma hugged and kissed Fatima and Rabia before they climbed into the back seat and then again once they were buckled into their car seats. Then she embraced Joseph, and finally Momma wrapped her arms around me, and I became emotional like a little girl, fighting back tears. I will always treasure the memories in my home on Matubba Street!

We pulled away from the house with the girls waving and calling out, "Love you, Grandma!"

8
Our Place on Rex Avenue

WE ARRIVED BACK in Atlanta with our daughters that evening. Once we were outside of the city, we stopped at a McDonald's for hotcakes and eggs with orange juice, after which the girls fell asleep in the back seat, surrounded by their teddy bears and the Disney blankets that their grandma Estell had bought them. Two packs of lemon cookies that my dad insisted they bring back as a snack completed their moving ensemble.

Our 1972 Impala pulled up in front of our home at 231 Rex Avenue at 6:00 p.m. I was smiling, and Joseph seemed to be bursting with energy. Looking at the back seat at my daughters, I hesitated because I did not want to wake them up.

Finally, I said softly, "Girls, wake up. This is our new home, with brick siding and a big oak tree in the yard."

Fatima looked out the window and back at me in confusion. "You mean I am not going home to New York?"

"No, you will be living in the South," I told her brightly.

In the meantime, Joseph had unlocked the door, and soon he waved to the girls, who rushed out of the car and into the house to see their room.

I watched as my daughters disappeared inside, and soon I heard them scream with excitement. They saw the yellow curtains in the living room with a red love seat and our Muslim prayer rug hanging on the wall and the Statue of Liberty that my friend Jasmine had gifted me sitting on the coffee table. Following them, I showed them our kitchen with its small white table and a bowl of apples and bananas and a picture frame of Coca-Cola with its red logo to brighten the room. Then, I told them to close their eyes, and I guided them into their room as they giggled.

I'm not sure who was more excited, them or me. "Now, open your eyes," I told them. They ran to jump on the twin beds with their matching white-and-pink quilts. On the dresser I had placed their pictures from our brownstone in New York with their puppy Buddy. Adjacent to the twin beds were two green beanbag chairs. I pulled open the closet door to reveal new dresses and shoes for school with two small book bags. As they bounced from item to item, Joseph sat down in the rocking chair in the middle of their room, and soon he was holding Rabia, who hugged his neck. Joseph was beaming. I stood close to Fatima with my hands gripping her shoulders. I was thrilled knowing that I would hear their voices and little stomping feet again every day. Of course, I would read *The Very Hungry Caterpillar* by Eric Carle at bedtime and watch them fall asleep.

"Estell, I must fix the sink in the kitchen, and Babe, are you going to help paint our bedroom?" Joseph asked. We both were overwhelmed by how much was still left to do to make the house our home, but I really wanted to make sugar cookies with the girls, so I told him I didn't know. Then, I followed Joseph into the kitchen and gave him a bear hug because it had been so painful to get our home and jobs. Joseph murmured, "We will always be together."

The Girls' New Puppy, Coco

The next morning, Joseph went to pick up bread and milk. When he returned, he called Fatima and Rabia to the front door, and I followed. As they stepped outside on the walkway, a brown box covered in newspaper caught our attention.

Joseph had a big smile on his face. "Girls, I got a surprise for you."

"Daddy, what's in the box?" Rabia asked.

A puppy jumped out of the box.

It was a poodle! It had floppy ears and black eyes. This little beauty had a brown coat of fur and was about twenty-two inches tall. The girls squealed with excitement, and Fatima rushed to rub his curly ears while Rabia wrapped her arms around his neck.

"What can we name your new puppy?" Joseph asked his excited daughters. "It's a boy, so let's name him Mr. Bob."

"No way!" Fatima said.

I chuckled. "What about Coco?"

The girls looked at each other. Two sets of eyes moved from one parent to the other as they nodded. It was a yes by the entire family!

As the girls played with their new puppy between snuggles, Joseph and I moved to a corner of the yard. I told him firmly, "Joseph, we can't afford this puppy."

"I want my daughters to be happy," was all he said.

"I do, too." I replied. "What did you pay for this puppy?"

Joseph hesitated for a moment, and then said confidently, "Just eighty dollars. I gave my friend Jim at work just twenty dollars, and I'll pay the rest later."

Even though I could tell how happy Coco made our girls, I was upset. "Do you know that we have a budget?" I said to Joseph, but he didn't respond. "Anyway," I continued, "you really made our daughters happy." Then I turned to the girls, and in a lighter tone, I asked with mock sternness, "All right, who is going to walk Coco and brush his fur? Girls, you've got to learn to take care of your puppy." Fatima quickly answered that she could walk and feed him. The girls ran around in the yard, and Coco chased them until we all went back inside for dinner.

As I observed the girls playing with their new puppy, I thought back to other incidents of our money issues. Sometimes, I believe that my husband was bewildered by overseeing the household budget. I remembered that in New York, he took me to the fancy Hilton Hotel to celebrate the birth of our daughter, Fatima, when we were on a limited income. In Atlanta, he bought this cute brown puppy as way to show his daughters that they were special. These were times when I got miffed, but I knew that he just wanted to show his love. And so, when he had not filed a claim for our lost property after the move, I knew that he was overwhelmed with moving to the South and finding a job.

I saw my husband's overspending was a way to compensate for things that he wanted for us. In Joseph's family, his mom and dad lived from paycheck to paycheck and struggled to pay the bills, and they were concerned about just holding onto their jobs to survive. Therefore, there was little planning for the future other than a small savings account.

His parents felt invisible because of the color of their skin, and this history was passed down to my husband. As a Black man, he had the burden of being a good husband and keeping a budget, regardless of the bias in his everyday life.

Before I arrived in Atlanta, my brother, Wardell, often called me on the phone, worried about me moving there.

Wardell was twelve years older than me, and I was the naughty little sister who hid his notebooks under the bed when he attended Shivers High School in Aberdeen. He got upset occasionally, but it was just for a short while. Then on Saturdays, my brother played with me and my dog, Spooky, in the backyard.

Wardell had lived in Atlanta since the early 1960s. I visited him in 1962 while I was a senior at Shivers High School. It was fun traveling on the Trailways to see him. I think my brother chose to live in Atlanta because he had big dreams and realized our small town had limited choices.

In 1959, Wardell completed his undergraduate degree in political science from Morehouse College and later earned a master's degree. He was intelligent and always cared for his family. When I look at him now, I see my dad Wardell, who likes to read the Bible daily, too. And years later, my brother became an ordained minister in Atlanta and traveled to Aberdeen to preach at Pilgrim Rest Church in our hometown of Aberdeen. I attended this church with my mom and my sister, Mary, as a young girl. My brother inspired me to attend Tuskegee Institute by taking me to the colored library in Aberdeen.

I did cool things with my brother, too. For example, I went to McKinley Creek to fish with him using my own rod. I did not catch any fish, yet I liked dipping my feet into the muddy water.

My brother worked part-time at Lawn Hardware while attending high school to save money for college. The owner insisted he use the back entrance to enter the store. Since Wardell had lived under segregation his entire life, he knew what to expect. Although it was humiliating, he needed to work to pay his tuition.

Most Saturdays, my brother and I walked to town to shop at Elmore's Dime Store. It was six long blocks from our house, and as we passed the white painted houses on clean streets with neatly trimmed trees, I chewed Juicy Fruit gum. Wardell wore a short-sleeved plaid shirt and jeans, and I wore my straw hat.

When we entered the store on Commerce Street with its ceiling-mounted fan, Wardell held my hand and reminded me not to pick up toys because the clerk might think I was stealing.

I was always thirsty after walking in the hot sun. One time after skipping down the aisle, I began to run to the water fountain. Wardell yelled, "Sis, stop! That's the white folks' water fountain," but I was just thinking that my mouth was dry, and I wanted to drink out of that shiny water fountain.

My brother grabbed my hand and guided me to the colored water fountain next to the back wall, which looked dirty. I bend my head down to the stream of water and took one sip. The water was gritty, and the water basin smelled like dirty sneakers. "I am not drinking this water!" I told Wardell as I stood with my hands on my hips.

He shook his head and told me, "You can wait until you get home for water; let's go." Afterward, Wardell was quiet. His mouth was tight, and he began walking fast. I told him I wanted "that white doll with the pink silk dress that I saw on the counter."

In a deep voice, he mumbled, "Sis, we are going home."

I thought about that for a moment, and then I replied with defiance, "I am not ready go home."

My brother let out a deep sigh. "All right, we'll stop at Jimmy Lee's café on Long Street, and Lula Mae can cook you a catfish sandwich with hot sauce." I was a little riled up, but then I smiled.

We never talked about that day, but I felt ashamed and ugly at the dime store where I had to drink from a decayed fountain, and I wondered why white people hated us.

Months later, I began to hear Wardell and his best friend Guy Ewing talking about leaving Aberdeen to attend college in Atlanta. They were inspired by Benjamin Mays, a pastor and civil rights activist who was president of Morehouse College. Wardell hoped to increase his knowledge and pursue a good-paying job. Further, he wanted to help our parents pay for their home on Matubba Street because they struggled working menial jobs just to keep a roof over our heads. While Wardell was in college, my dad worked as a janitor and my momma worked as a maid, and they sent postal money orders weekly to pay for his tuition and food. Looking back, I can see that we were hungry to break the shackles of systemic racism. So, I believe each one of us in the family took a different path to breathe and feel free.

◈

I invited Wardell to visit after we bought our new home. At 9:30 on a warm Friday morning, he rang the doorbell. I threw open the door in excitement and said, "Come in!" My brother held two big yellow-and-white teddy bears for his nieces, who he was meeting for the first time.

"Come sit down," I said, pointing him to the red love seat. "I want to thank you for allowing us to stay at your home for a week and offering financial assistance while we were looking for a place to stay. I enjoyed those home-cooked meals, especially the cream cheese pound cake."

Once we were seated, I looked him over. "Well, you look healthy, neat haircut, creased pants, and ironed shirt, just like you dressed in Aberdeen."

"You know Momma taught us to look our best," he responded. "I think about the suits that I wore to church on Sunday with a white shirt and tie."

I nodded my head. "You and Daddy had blue suits that were alike." Wardell just smiled.

We made small talk for a while, and then he remarked, "I can't believe that you left Aberdeen and moved to New York and married a soldier."

I was ready to leave that small town with its one stoplight after graduating from high school. When I got to New York, I fell in love with the city, and I fell in love with Joseph. In Aberdeen, I was distressed over being labeled as unequal and having to work as a domestic worker. So, when my cousin Elizabeth offered me the chance to visit New York, I quickly packed my suitcase and left Aberdeen. In New York, I could eat and shop at any store, which gave me a real sense of freedom. Certainly, there was racism, but it was less visible in New York.

A few minutes later, Wardell asked me, "Sis, where are my nieces?"

I strolled to the door and called to my daughters. The girls rushed into the living room with smiles; I had dressed them in matching white ruffle-trimmed blouses and blue short pants. I announced, "Girls, I want you to meet your Uncle Wardell. You talked to your uncle on the phone in New York and now you get to meet him."

Wardell smiled at me over their heads as he shook their hands and hugged them. Fatima reached out her hand and then hugged her uncle, but Rabia was a little shy; yet she leaned in for a hug.

"I am Fatima," my older daughter said proudly.

"And I am Rabia," her sister said.

"Sis," my brother said, "I don't see much resemblance to you, but they are cute with those thick braids. You have two beautiful daughters." Wardell gave them the big teddy bears wrapped with pink ribbons, and my daughters said in unison, "Thank you, Uncle Wardell."

After Fatima and Rabia returned to their room to play, Wardell asked, "What kind of names are those?"

"They are Islamic names," I explained. "And I told you that I had joined the mosque in New York and became a Muslim. I like that Islam encourages kindness and compassion toward everyone."

"Sis, I did not realize how much you changed your ideas and beliefs. I don't really agree with the teaching of Islam. Besides, I am Christian, and I have put my faith in Jesus Christ and his teachings since I was a young boy. But I do respect your views. Even though we have differences, I will always look out for you because you are my family."

We continued chatting for another five minutes or so, and then I said, "Excuse me, Wardell." I knew that Joseph was in the bedroom listening to Miles Davis on the record player. I hollered, "Joseph, my brother is visiting us."

Joseph walked into the living with a smile and our poodle, Coco, following behind, wagging his tail. Joseph's hair was a neat Afro, and he wore a beige striped shirt and gray pants.

"Hello, Wardell," he said, greeting my brother with a handshake. "I had a great time at your home, and finally, I got to know you after listening to your sister talk about you in New York."

"After meeting you, I think my sister married the right guy," Wardell replied excitedly.

With a slight smile, Joseph said, "I appreciate you showing us around Atlanta and meeting your wonderful family. Indeed, you made me feel welcome at your home."

"I am glad you are here in Atlanta," answered Wardell.

"When we arrived in Atlanta, I did not know what to expect in the South," Joseph said. "Estell told me about eating grits and fried trout on Sunday mornings." They chuckled.

With a big grin, Wardell said, "Listen, you are part of the Sims family."

Wardell sat on the corner of the love seat looking at the yellow curtains as he continued. "I saw in the *Atlanta Journal Constitution* in 1970 about the Black Panther mission for social justice," he told Joseph. "Are you still doing party work in Atlanta?"

"Yes, I am in the Bankhead area with my Panther brothers."

"Stores like Rich's were boycotted in Atlanta a few years ago, which gave us the right to sit at the lunch counter and get decent jobs," Wardell offered.

Joseph nodded. "I am looking forward to meeting the first Black mayor of Atlanta, Maynard Jackson, and others civil right leaders like Ralph Abernathy and Hosea Williams."

Suddenly, Coco jumped onto my lap. I patted his back to calm him down.

Wardell asked me, "What is the name of that frisky poodle?"

"This is Coco."

My brother rubbed the dog's paws and said, "I know those girls have fun with their brown puppy."

I beamed at my brother. "I talked to Momma and Daddy on the phone yesterday, and I love that they are always sending me those Kimmel's fudge bars from Aberdeen."

"Well, you know that you have always been spoiled by them, and even by me," Wardell said with a chuckle.

"They always looked out for us, and you pulled me in my red wagon," I reminded him. "I know that you visited Aberdeen during the Christmas holidays. How were Momma and Daddy?"

"Mom is still growing her peace lily in the living room, and Daddy is complaining about his knees, but he still gets up at five in the morning and goes to work at city hall."

Joseph looked at his Timex watch. "I'm sorry, Wardell, but I am working this morning, so I must leave. I'm glad you stopped by today." Joseph grabbed his tools, took his dark-green jacket out of the closet, and said, "Estell, I'll see you tonight."

Wardell and I talked about our family in Aberdeen for another thirty minutes. Then, he told me, "I got to go meet my friend at Paschal's Restaurant on Hunter Street." He turned and yelled, "Girls, I'll be back to see you." Next, he said, "Sis, I still can't believe you are a housewife and cooking meals in the kitchen."

"What do mean?" I asked.

"You did not know how to cook in Aberdeen."

"Well, I've burned up a few pots," I said, laughing, "but Joseph and the girls love my cooking!"

Wardell just kept laughing. He turned toward me quickly and gave me a warm embrace before he left.

9
Ben Hill School

WHEN WE ARRIVED back in Atlanta in August, I took advantage of early registration at Ben Hill Elementary School on Greenbriar Parkway, which was three miles from our home. Joseph had awakened us at 5:30 a.m. like he was still in the army. I received the girls' shot records and their transcripts from their schools in Brooklyn. Eight-year-old Fatima would be in the third grade, and six-year-old Rabia in first grade.

While the four of us had breakfast at the dining table that morning, I talked to the girls about meeting their teachers. I wasn't sure Fatima was paying any attention; she stared at the ceiling like she was miles away.

"Fatima, what is wrong?" I asked.

"Mama, why do these Southern people speak so slow?"

Rabia chimed in. "Yes, Mom, why do they say our names differently?"

"Girls, let's keep an open mind. Culture is a blending of English, Afro-American, and Native American," I explained. "Also, the culture in the South is considered backward by some people. I know that my education in Aberdeen was mediocre, and I talked with a southern drawl." I told them how, during my childhood, I ate boiled chitterlings (hog intestines), which smelled so bad you needed to open the windows. Often, they were seasoned with onions, red hot peppers, and white vinegar. They tasted pretty good, so I ignored the smell.

"You do know that I was born in Mississippi, and I changed my tone of speech in New York," I reminded them. "Girls, let's concentrate on breakfast."

I prepared scrambled eggs with biscuits and grits and glasses of orange juice. Rabia stirred her spoon around in the grits and asked, "Are these mashed potatoes with butter floating on top?"

"No, they're hominy grits," I answered.

"And why do people eat this, Mom?"

I thought back to when I was eight years old in Aberdeen, sitting at the dining table. I was so happy when Momma made grits with butter floating on top. I munched on hot cakes with sorghum molasses, thick pork sausages, and hominy with my sister, Mary. "I am sure that you will learn to enjoy this Southern tradition," I said.

Fatima nodded and said, "We never had these grits in New York."

"In the North," I told them, "People like steak, baked chicken, clam chowder, and bagels. On the street corners, cart vendors sell fresh pretzels and hot dogs with warm buns and condiments from cart. And in restaurants, I drank unsweetened tea with my meal, but I never got used to it."

Joseph stopped eating for a moment. "Listen, girls, I just want you to pay attention to your mother," he told them with a serious look on his face. "You remember our talk at the table while playing chess last night, and you need to learn how to think before asking questions."

The previous night, my husband explained to our daughters that they wouldn't see but a few pages about our history in the textbooks. "There are two rules for you," he told them." First, to read *The Black*

Book by Toni Morrison, who is a celebrated novelist. She wrote this book in 1974 to show Afro American art, music, baseball, and politics. Your mom and I are committed to helping you embrace your heritage. And you are expected to get A's in school because as Black girls, you need to work twice as hard to succeed in America."

The girls paid attention to their dad but still did not eat the grits.

At 8:30, Joseph drove us to the school, a wide, brick building with clean sidewalks and doors with glass windows. He waited in the car while we went in. The girls wore matching blue striped shirts and long-sleeved white blouses with black-and-white loafers.

We entered with other parents who were walking into the building. The girls were a little nervous and concerned about having to make new friends.

The entrance hallway was decorated with cutouts of the alphabet hanging from the ceiling and signs welcoming everyone. We made our way to Rabia's classroom first, which was in the middle of the building. I met Ms. Roberts, a middle-aged lady who wore a black suit with a pink shirt and black lace-up shoes. She shook Rabia's hand and told her, "You are going enjoy reading and helping to plant the sunflower seeds in our garden," which made Rabia smile.

Fatima's classroom was on the other side of the building. There, we met Miss Amara, who was a short lady with black-rimmed glasses and a squeaky voice. She asked Fatima, "What do you like to read?"

"I enjoy reading rhyming stories and poems, and walking my furry dog, Coco," Fatima answered without hesitation.

The teacher said to me, "Mom, I see that Fatima is a bright student. The curriculum at Ben Hill includes science, math, and geography." She gave me a warm smile. "Miss Estell, I'll keep you informed about upcoming tests and the PTA meetings."

I was happy to meet both teachers and see who was teaching my children. I asked for their phone numbers. Again, I asked to be put on their calendar for after-school meetings.

Although Ben Hill was segregated, I believed that African American administrators and teachers would a provide a good education and help my children learn about their history.

Classes started the next Monday, and the girls were excited to ride the yellow bus with new friends from the neighborhood.

10
My Neighbors on Rex Avenue

I WAS HAPPY LIVING in a new neighborhood with neat trees and flowers. It was segregated, and the neighbors took pride in their property. Even so, I found it challenging to make friends. I really missed the friends that I left behind in New York.

I think the neighbors who were unfriendly were like that because our family came from New York, so they perceived us as strangers. But during my second week in the neighborhood, I saw the lady who lived two doors down the street in the white house walking her dog, a black-and-white boxer. I waved at her, but she bowed her head. After a week, I walked to her home and greeted her with a fresh-baked apple pie. I was thrilled to meet her but unsure of what to expect. She wore a square-neck tunic shirt and bell bottom pants with open-toed shoes. I was somewhat shy, yet I decided to introduce myself and share my phone number. I was a little surprised that she was warm and kind.

"Hi, my name is Estell, and I live in the house with the burgundy door with my husband and two daughters."

"I am Rose," she said. "Wow, I haven't seen this kind of welcoming since I was in Alabama with my grandmother." She smacked her lips.

"I can't wait to eat this flaky pie. I guess I will have to share it with my family." She looked at me, and then we both laughed.

"So, Estell, where are you from?"

"Brooklyn, New York, and I just moved here," I responded excitedly.

"I've lived in this area for three years," Rose said. "I have two children, a boy named Andy, and his sister is Candy, and they attend Ben Hill Elementary." We chatted about our children and the school, and then our conversation turned to local politics. "I am excited about our young mayor, Maynard Jackson, who is the first Black mayor in the South," Rose shared.

I added, "I saw him on *WSB Evening News*, and he looked confident. He was speaking for inclusion at city hall. Plus, he knows how to organize across party lines, and it's about time." We chuckled.

While we talked, her husband pulled into the driveway in his blue Ford pickup truck. "Hey, Tony, come here," Rose called to him. "This is Estell. She and her husband bought the home on the corner."

Tony had a receding hairline and walked with a slight limp on his right side as he slowly made his way toward us. "Hello," Tony greeted me and smiled at Rose. "I think I saw your husband unpacking the boxes on the porch. I am happy to meet you." He shook my hand.

I babbled about shopping at Greenbriar Mall just a few miles away. I asked Rose, "Is it a safe place to shop?"

Shaking her head, Rose replied, "I would advise you to shop in the daytime because the parking lot is dark."

"All right. I have enjoyed our chat, but I need to get home to my girls."

Standing next to her husband, Rose thanked me again for the pie. "And I want you and your family to come over for dinner next Saturday."

"I'll check with my husband and give you call," I replied. "So long!"

Rose became a good friend, and I learned that she had lived in the Bronx with her family in 1965. She was the first neighbor I met. Then, I met Dixie, a working mom with a two-year-old baby, and

Viola, who grew cayenne peppers and tomatoes in the backyard. I met them during our yard party, which we had around the middle of September, about a month after we moved in.

After a few weeks, I was walking Coco, who was smelling the leaves and jerking his leash when I saw Daisy, who lived across the street. She was tending her pink hydrangeas. I said hello, but she kept digging in her plants like she was ignoring me. I suppose when Daisy saw my clothes, her perception was that even though we were all Black, I was different with my head scarf and my long African print dress. Perhaps she was rude because she didn't trust me as a new neighbor.

One day after work, my tall neighbor who wore a red wig knocked on my front door to complain about my husband playing his music too loud, like John Coltrane's "A Love Supreme." I wanted to tell that biddy to get off my porch and that she needed to mind her own business.

But weeks later, Joseph and I were invited to a cookout at Rose's house which was two doors away. I was ready to get to know my neighbors, and I picked out a yellow dress with a black belt; I felt well-groomed and confident.

Rose's husband, Tony, grilled the meat over charcoal—thick, greasy barbeque ribs and juicy hot dogs. The sweet smell of the meat and the smoke filled the air, and I couldn't wait to take my first bite. Joseph carried a big bowl of hot wings and wore his white shorts, red sports shirt, and sandals. I carried the Doritos chips and an onion dip, and other neighbors brought watermelon and sweet tea. I rushed to get my tea with ice cubes because sweat was dripping off my forehead. Tagging along were Fatima and Rabia, who joined the kids grabbing popsicles. The music was loud, with a DJ playing Motown music and Sam Cook's "Having a Party."

Obviously, the aroma from the grilling meat made me hungry. I fixed Joseph a plate of hot dogs with beans while he talked to Tony, and then I filled a plate for myself. While chewing on the ribs, my fingers were dripping with red sauce, which got on my yellow dress, yet I kept talking to Rose and Dixie. My daughters ran around and jumped rope with their new friends, Candy and Andy. That day, I think some of our neighbors had a few beers because they were friendly while dancing and twisting and shaking their hips to the music. Even Daisy from down the street came over to say hello.

After sharing conversations with our friends, I learned about Grant Park and the two-mile trail. It is one of the oldest parks in Atlanta. I suggested that Joseph and I join the group's next outing. While living in New York, we hiked at Central Park many times with its green trees and small streams of water. It felt like home at the time, but now it was time to make this new city our home. I looked forward to a brisk walk in a new park.

11
A Big Change for the Halliburton Family

AFTER OUR FIRST CHRISTMAS in Atlanta, the weather turned cold. I felt more tired than usual, so I spent the last weekend of the year lying on the couch and watching television. My favorite show, *Good Times*, was the first TV sitcom that showed a Black family with strong moral values. I was hungry for my girls to see a show with faces that looked like theirs, so Fatima and Rabia watched *Good Times* with me.

Often, Black men were stereotyped as simpleminded and lazy, but on this show, the dad was stern and had rules for the family. He represented stability and emotional support, and the family depended on him. Yet he was always looking for a job, and they struggled to pay the rent.

Good Times was in sharp contrast to *The Adventures of Ozzie and Harriet*, which was in reruns at the time. It features America's fictional "first family" in the 1950s and early '60s. This family lived in a colonial-style home in a middle-class area and had only minor problems with their boys. But *Good Times* depicted an uneducated family who lived in a broken-down apartment and barely had any food to eat. The show got high ratings from the white audience. Again, I saw the negative images of a Black family living in poverty compared to the white middle-class family that was stable with no worries. There was a stark difference between these sitcoms, with the Black family living in the projects and the white family in *Ozzie and Harriet* enjoying "the good life."

One of the things I loved about our family was making sugar-cookie dough on Saturday mornings with Fatima and Rabia. The girls used cookie cutters to make hearts, and they loved sticking their fingers in the sweet mix. When they thought I wasn't looking, they added red and blue sprinkles on top of the cookies just before we slipped them into the oven. Afterward, the kitchen was a mess, so I told the girls to wash the dishes, "and don't break the glasses this time." Often, this led to some squabbling, but the girls scrubbed the counters and pots and pans and swept the kitchen. I gave them big hugs and praised them when I checked their work. Even though they were young, I was teaching them to work together as a team.

On the first Monday of 1975, I was up in time for Fajr, "dawn prayer," one of the five Islamic prayers. I had a profound sense of peace. Before I got ready for work at Bell South, I called Dr. Crumpler, my new gynecologist, and made an appointment. Two weeks earlier, she had examined me. I took a blood and urine test at her office near our home. I had complained of fatigue, and that hadn't changed. Joseph had come to the appointment with me. I had gained a little weight, too, but after two weeks of feeling run down, it was time to boost my energy.

After hanging up the green telephone in the kitchen, I yelled for the girls, and they came running to the table. "Rabia, did you brush your teeth?" I asked, and Fatima shook her head no. I tapped Rabia's shoulder and said sternly, "Let's go, young lady."

A Big Change for the Halliburton Family

When we returned to the dining table, Rabia wore a matching yellow floral vest and pants with a white blouse and a barrette on each of her two braids. I poured low-fat milk into their bowls for their corn flakes, and I put strawberry Pop-Tarts on a side plate. I asked Fatima, who was dressed in a lime green dress with a matching sweater if she had finished her math homework to solve multiplication problems, and she replied, "Yes, Mama."

The clock started beeping, letting us know it was almost time for bus #2048. As we scurried around getting ready to leave, Coco knocked over his bowl and spilled water on the linoleum floor.

"Rabia!" I shouted. "Stop calling the puppy! Okay, Fatima and Rabia, grab your backpacks, and let's hurry to the bus stop." While we walked to the bus stop on the corner, I reminded them, "Girls, I want you to speak up in class, and pay attention to the teacher."

Soon, I was alone and back home. I was washing the dishes when the phone rang. It was Joseph, asking how the morning had gone so far. Before we hung up, I told him, "I forgot to buy dog food. Can you pick up Purina Dog Chow at Kroger?"

"Yes, no problem," he said. "I love you, Estell." I liked hearing him say that at end of our phone calls because that meant he felt secure and passionate about our family.

Coco hopped onto the bed while I was getting dressed for work. I massaged his back. "You are naughty," I scolded him as I rubbed him back and forth. "You are sweet with those brown eyes." He followed me back into the kitchen, where I gave him a doggy bone.

Shortly, my new neighbor Rose, who had offered to take me to my appointment before work, was blowing her car horn. I picked up my brown shoulder bag and my hat, stepped outside, locked the door, and hurried out to the car.

When we arrived at the doctor's office, Rose dropped me off because I planned to ride the Marta bus to work. Once I was in the waiting room with its small Zenith TV and pictures of bright purple flowers on the wall, I asked the receptionist how long the wait would be.

"Maybe an hour," she replied.

I nodded my head; however, I was worried and thought, *I can't be late for work again.* I sat on the metal chair and read *Jet* magazine about actress, Pam Grier. She was in the hit movie *Coffy*. I was happy to see a black female in the lead role. When I was finished, I opened my makeup bag where I had stashed my lipstick and powder and thought about my days in New York working in Manhattan and going to lunch near the Empire State Building with my friends. I closed my eyes and smiled.

Finally, my name was called, and the receptionist said, "The doctor will see you, ma'am." A few minutes later, I strolled into the exam room, and Dr. Crumpler entered wearing a slight smile and dressed in white scrubs. I had been a little skeptical of doctors since I was twelve years old in Aberdeen. I still recall that the nurse in Dr. Carson's office did not want to touch my skin while I sat at the edge of the exam table. I stared at the blades on the fan, and when I looked at my skin, I felt ashamed and not good enough. Momma stood beside me clasping her hat and bursting with anger. She finally yelled at the doctor, saying, "You damn, ignorant fool."

I was terrified for Momma in that moment, afraid that the doctor might call the police because in 1957, speaking up like that meant she might go to jail. We quickly ran out of the office, and I lost one of my sandals. The deacon from Pilgrim Rest was waiting in the car and he drove us home, "Momma, what is wrong with my dark skin?" She reassured me that I was special and explained that some people are just hypocrites and mean. Even today, I can still smell the bitter odor of that exam room.

But this day, I was seeing Dr. Crumpler, who I liked because she looked like me, with brown eyes and a wide nose.

"Good morning, Dr. Crumpler."

"Did you find a new home?" the doctor asked. I had told her about our home search the first time I met her.

"Yes, and we got a new puppy, Coco," I shared.

Dr. Crumpler invited me to put my purse in the chair and sit on the table. While I did, she continued the conversation by saying, "I am surprised that your husband is not here with you this time." Joseph had made a fuss over me by asking the doctor questions about my swollen feet. He often came me with to the doctor's office for moral support.

Once I was settled on the exam table, I saw a flash of a smile. "Miss Estell, I looked over your tests, and you are going to have a baby."

"Really? I never thought that I was pregnant," I said in surprise. No wonder I had been feeling so tired for the last few weeks.

"Congratulations, Mom!" the doctor continued. "I know that you are in a hurry to get to work, so I'll be quick. I called in a prescription for prenatal vitamins, and I want you to eat lots of vegetable and fruits." She asked if I had any questions and then announced, "I will see you back in six weeks."

In January, Joseph and I started a to-do list and made sure to include the essentials for our baby's arrival. Our newborn baby would be in our room for the first month and would move to the girls' room afterward. I knew I would be spending day and night with our baby. I wanted to create a quiet space for our baby's journey from the bassinet to a crib in our daughters' bedroom. And I planned to make space for a changing table, baby clothes, and two white fluffy teddy bears. On the wall, I planned to hang a white and yellow picture with the words BIG DREAMS over a photo of clouds and stars. But I felt overwhelmed thinking about decorating the bedroom to make it into a nursery. During this time, Joseph painted the ceiling beige and I decided on wallpaper. I picked the color white with a tinge of green, and I made short yellow curtains with ruffles on my Singer sewing machine.

In February, we bought a white chest with drawers. To further adorn the room, I purchased a short wicker basket and added two Raggedy Ann dolls and a white teddy bear with a yellow ribbon to sit on the dresser. Last, we purchased the crib with dropdown side rails and a safety mattress.

I planned on updating the girls' room when I put the crib in their room. I would rearrange the room with cozy throw pillows and colorful blankets. The room needed to show the unique personalities of Rabia, who liked blue and white round pillows. Fatima liked lime-green and pink throw pillows. I'd keep their preferences in mind when I upgraded the room with flexible colors for the beds.

On our limited budget, we shopped at Bob's Furniture Outlet in Forest Park. Fatima and Rabia were truly excited and began drawing pictures of our family with the new baby.

I was very proud of my two daughters. Rabia, who was five years old, liked to read *The Cat in the Hat* by Dr. Seuss. She was rather adventurous and liked helping her dad with his toolbox. She usually wore her jeans and was always asking questions. When Rabia came home from school, she ran to hug Coco, and she taught him to run after the Frisbee with her.

Fatima, who was seven years old, liked brushing her hair and polishing her black-and-white shoes for school. Ever since she was three years old, she said thank you and sat gracefully in her chair rocking chair. One year she got a blue sketch pad for her birthday, and she would sit on the side of her bed after school drawing trees of our yard and her puppy, Coco.

As the big sister, Fatima liked to tell Rabia what to do. Obviously, Rabia thought she was just as smart as her sister, and she didn't like to be ordered around. The girls bickered about their room a lot because Rabia would sit on her bed reading her library books with Coco beside her when she should have been tidying up the room. I encouraged them to get along and hug each other.

One day, I came home from shopping with the girls, and Joseph surprised me with a brown rocking chair with armrests from Rich's, which I promptly sat in.

"Did you pay cash for it?" I asked.

Joseph responded no. But he seemed genuinely unhappy that he'd spent beyond our budget.

"You know that we are trying to stay out of debt," I scolded, but then I got up and embraced him because it was a comfortable chair.

———

On the morning of March 3, 1975, I was nine months pregnant. Though it took what felt like hours before I fell asleep the night before, now I was awake and ready for my green tea. I turned on our portable radio that sat on a nightstand next to our bed and the music of Glen Campbell singing "Rhinestone Cowboy" began blasting.

I was disoriented for a moment. *Oh yeah, I am living in Atlanta*, I remembered. I missed the warm, soothing jazz and Broadway tunes I listened to on the radio in New York. I kept turning the dial to find an FM station, pausing to listen to a few bars of KC and The Sunshine Band singing their disco hit, "That's the Way I Like It." I could feel the vibes from this song. Even though I was uncomfortable, I was happy thinking about holding my new baby. *I wonder if it is going be a boy. Regardless, I can't wait to cradle my baby in my arms.*

I thought back to the night before when I spoke to Grandma Carrie in New York. She was excited and talked first to the girls. Then it was my turn.

"My son is calling me every day about you," she told me.

"I am fine, and ready to have our new baby," I told her excitedly. Then I reminisced about our time in New York. "I can't tell you how much I miss living in my brownstone home in Brooklyn, and you baking the rainbow cake for my family. I can still smell the coffee at Chock full o' Nuts restaurant in Manhattan."

"Estell, you are going to be fine in Atlanta. Kiss my girls for me!"

After I hung up the telephone, I thought about Carrie. Often, she told me stories about her mother and Joseph. Helen Hunter was from North Carolina and had lived on 138th Street in Harlem in a small apartment on the first floor. Joseph had fun with Grandma Helen, who started taking him to amateur night at the Apollo Theatre when he was ten years old. They wore their Sunday clothes; Joseph wore his blue suit and shined shoes. They went several times until he moved to another neighborhood when he was sixteen, and they always stopped for chocolate ice cream cones after the show at the Sugar Hill Creamery. Helen was so proud of her tall grandson. I missed those stories from Carrie.

I smiled as I thought about how much love there was in our family.

Promptly at 7:30 a.m., Joseph walked into our bedroom and announced, "Breakfast is ready!"

Joseph wore his white T-shirt with striped lounge pants. "Hi, Big Momma!" he greeted me. I couldn't remember seeing my husband smiling and so animated in a while.

I chuckled and mumbled, "Thanks, Dad!"

Joseph carried a tray, which he held while I propped myself up with two pillows. He set the tray on my lap. It held a circular plate filled with my breakfast he had prepared for me: an English muffin with blueberry jam, two scrambled eggs, and a glass of water. "Thank you, Dad!" I gushed, even though my eggs were greasy and my muffin was burned on the edges. The single yellow rose was a thoughtful touch, though.

After I finished my breakfast, Fatima and Rabia ran into the bedroom, both hollering, "Good morning, Mom!" They quickly crawled into bed with me, and we shared lots of warm hugs. Following behind

A Big Change for the Halliburton Family

them was Coco, who hopped into the bed and licked my face. All the commotion made me forget that I was worried about having a baby.

I noticed the girls wore their hair twisted in strange-looking braids with barrettes. I asked Fatima, "Did you do your hair?"

"No, Daddy braided our hair," she said proudly.

With a big smile Rabia said, "Mama, he braided my hair, too."

"Um, he did," I murmured. "Oh, wow, you girls really look cute this morning."

I was proud that my husband spent time playing the board game Simon Says with our daughters and walking our poodle, Coco, with them. I was sure that this would give them a healthy sense of who they were growing up, and they could see how much their dad loved them.

After a few more squeezes around my neck, I told them, "All right, girls, it's time to catch the bus, and I want one more hug . . . and take Coco with you."

After our daughters left for school, Joseph got dressed for work. While grabbing his car keys, he leaned in to kiss me on my forehead and mumbled, "I'll call you when I get to work."

As he walked out the door, I turned on the Zenith television to watch Monica Pearson, the first African American journalist to anchor a local news program. I skipped over the other channels on my remote for WSB-TV to see Monica talk about current events. I enjoyed watching her because she had a pleasant smile and looked like she belonged in front of the camera.

I got out of bed and lumbered to the kitchen after the news ended. When the wall phone started to ring, I answered it, guessing it was Joseph. Instead, I heard my dad's voice.

"Hello, Daddy!"

"Sis, how are you doing?"

"I am so big and barely able to put on my house shoes," I told him.

"I am worried, and I am praying for you," Daddy continued. "Did you get the postal money for a one hundred dollars and a box of baby clothes we sent?"

"Yes, thank you! I was excited!"

"How is Joseph . . . and the girls?"

I told him that my husband was fine and had already left for work, and that the girls were fine too. As I listened to Daddy, I wished I could visit him.

Then, he called Momma to the phone. "Hey, Sis, do you want me to come to Atlanta to be with you?"

"Oh, no, I have friends, Laila from the mosque and my neighbor, Rose, who are pitching in to help me. Momma, thank you for the boxes with a pink knitted blanket, white baby shoes, and a box of diapers. And please thank Mary for the white Winnie the Pooh jacket."

"Sis, you are my baby. Just call if you need anything."

"I love y'all, and thanks, Momma." I sighed as I hung up.

After I put down the receiver, I grew teary-eyed because my parents stuck with me and always made me feel loved. Although I attended Tuskegee, which was far from home, and married my husband in New York, they continued to send me gifts and letters. I recalled when Momma made my first corduroy dress for school at Vine Street Elementary in 1953 on her Singer sewing machine, and Daddy brought me peppermint candy from Hussey's. That made me smile, and I wiped away my tears. *I am grateful that I will get more hugs and probably more dishes to wash and staying up late at night after my baby is born.*

12

How Sweet It Is!

ON MARCH 14, 1975, I sat on our red love seat drinking my green tea and reading the *Atlanta Journal-Constitution*, trying to relax between contractions that Friday afternoon. I wore my white-and-black maternity dress that Joseph bought for me from JC Penney. I could hear the wind blowing outside; it was a typical windy spring evening. Joseph had stayed home from work that day because I was in pain the night before. Earlier in the day, I had called Dr. Crumpler, and she reminded me that the baby was not due until the next week. *I guess the baby forgot to look at the calendar,* I thought.

As I sat there feeling so uncomfortable, I just knew it was time; I had been daydreaming about this moment. *I don't think I can possibly get any bigger*, I'd thought the week before. *I feel like I am carrying around a ten-pound ball inside of me.* My packed tote bag sat in the bedroom with my toothbrush, Afro comb, and makeup bag.

Joseph had picked up our daughters after school because my contractions were getting closer together. Along the way, he stopped at Wendy's and bought snack boxes of chicken fingers, fries, and two Sprites for them.

When the girls got home, they ran into the living room where I waited; Joseph had told them I'd be going to Grady Hospital soon to have the baby. Fatima laid her head on my shoulder while gripping my neck and said, "Mom, I'll miss you." Rabia curled up in my arms and clung to my waist, though there wasn't much waist by then. I told her, "I love you, Rabia, and remember to brush your teeth."

I didn't want to let go of my daughters; when I saw them again, a new member of the family would be with me, and I knew how different things would be with a baby in the house. Soon, Joseph was calling to the girls, "It's time to go, and Rose is here." Rabia cried, "Mommy!" Joseph picked her up in his arms and rubbed her back. He held Fatima's hand too; when Fatima looked back at me, her eyes were watery, and she was waving her small hand.

"All right, girls, Mommy is coming back soon," Rose assured them. I trusted her to take care of my precious babies. She was kind, and I enjoyed drinking Lipton tea and sharing a blueberry croissant with her at my dining table.

I am so lucky to have wonderful daughters, I thought, but I was sad to see them crying. *And I will miss the warmth of Coco lying beside me on the sofa. I am happy that I can trust Rose to take care of my precious babies.* Rose was always smiling. I could talk to her about my dreams, like Joseph and me walking on the beach in Cancun, Mexico. She would place her hand on my cheek and say, "You have big ideas."

While I thought about how I knew Joseph would look out for the girls and me, Joseph kept asking, "Babe, are you all right?" I wanted to tell him, "Hell no, I am not all right. I am having contractions!" Around 5:00 p.m., we decided it was time to head to the hospital, so Joseph searched for his car keys.

"Did you see them?" I shook my head no.

He continued, "Where is the baby bag for the hospital?"

"It should be in our closet in the bedroom."

Joseph's frantic movements were so unlike him. "You are getting nervous," I told him, "but I am the one having the baby."

Thirty minutes later, I was finally walking to the car for our trip to Grady Hospital. Joseph put his arm around my shoulder while we walked to our Chevy Impala. Quickly, he turned the key, and the engine began sputtering. I held my breath, and it finally cranked up. Joseph pulled out of the driveway like he was turning onto a racetrack.

"Babe, I want my baby to be born at the hospital!" His eyes had a wild look when he turned to me.

"You need to calm down," I told him. I closed my eyes and gripped my purse.

Before long, I was in the parking lot at Grady Hospital, and Joseph was lifting me out of the car. As I walked to the front of the hospital, I saw a barefooted homeless man sleeping with his belongings adjacent to the brick building. I felt sad for him, and I wondered, *Where is his family?* Even though I was in so much pain, it was hard to look away. I was distracted for a moment as I thought about all the low-income people who had no other choice than to come to this hospital for medical care.

While Joseph gripped my arm and I held my gray purse, I thought, *This is the moment that I have been waiting nine months for.*

With another glance at the homeless man, Joseph said to me, "Babe, I told you that you shouldn't be at this hospital."

"Maybe, you can save your complaint until I have our baby," I snapped.

Shortly, we entered the front lobby of the hospital with its linoleum floor and dim hanging lights, wide hallways, and discolored paint, where a bunch of people waited in line at the desk. The smell of antiseptic and the odor of sickness and pee made me feel Joseph was right.

I still had a lack of trust for doctors, and I felt my health was less important to them because of the color of my skin. Generally, Black women have a higher risk factor for diabetes or high blood pressure, which can result in premature labor or death during childbirth, yet they often received lower-quality medical care. I was born on a plantation in the 1940s in the dark of the night in a slave shack with a midwife in attendance. Neighbor women boiled water on an iron stove and wrapped my tiny body in a raggedy sheet. These women hummed the African American spiritual "He's Got the Whole World in His Hands" and prayed for me. Indeed, I was blessed that Momma survived. Back then, my momma did not have access to a doctor, and things hadn't changed much in many Black neighborhoods. Then, I thought about when Rabia was born five years earlier at the Brooklyn Jewish Hospital in New York that has flowers in the lobby and pearly white walls; Grady was a step up from a slave shack and a midwife, but it wasn't Brooklyn Jewish Hospital by any means.

I couldn't think about that, though; I needed to focus on our baby and the miracle coming that night.

The labor and delivery department and the baby nursery with bright pictures of babies smiling were all on the second floor. But first, we had to get checked in, so Joseph marched up to the desk and greeted the nurse, who had a shiny gold tooth and wore a red wig.

Joseph looked at her name tag. "Hi, Sarah. My wife is having contractions that are about five minutes apart," he announced.

"Can you sign her name on the sheet? Oh, yes, Dr. Crumpler is waiting for her," Nurse Sarah told us. She pulled the wheelchair over from the back of desk.

Once I sat in the wheelchair, I was relieved to grip one of the handles because my legs were getting weak; Joseph guided my feet onto the metal footrests.

"I am taking your wife to her room, and I am giving you the clipboard to fill out the paperwork," Sarah told Joseph.

My husband placed his hands on my shoulder and told her, "I can push my wife in the wheelchair." By that point, Joseph was wildly excited and anxious.

Sarah told him firmly, "Sir, you are not allowed in the delivery room."

"I am going to be with her when she has our baby."

"The rules are you must remain in the waiting area."

The two stared at each other for a moment. Suddenly, six-foot-tall Joseph said in his deepest voice, "I'm going to be with my wife, she needs me."

The petite nurse was agitated and pointed her finger at my husband. "Mr. Halliburton, I am calling security."

"No!" I hollered. "Sarah, my husband will wait for me." I pulled on Joseph's sleeve to get him to look at me. "What is wrong with you, Joseph? Settled down, it is fine."

He mumbled, "Okay." Then he leaned down and hugged me and uttered, "As-alamu alaikum," which means Peace be upon you.

The nurse pushed me to room #421, where I exited the wheelchair and changed into a hospital gown. Then I crawled onto the bed, sweating and in so much pain that I yelled out. *I must remember to breathe.*

By this time, Dr. Crumpler had entered my room. She rubbed my shoulders while saying the baby was coming early. After she checked my vital signs, she said, "You are ready!"

"Doctor, can you make sure that you talk to my husband?" I asked.

She assured me that she would, and then added, "I already heard that he is a bit anxious."

My doctor gave me a shot in my backside and said, "You'll be able to relax now." Moments later, I was rolled to the delivery room with big glaring lights and nurses in gray scrubs waiting for me. Slowly, I just dozed off.

༄

At 2:00 a.m., I heard Dr. Crumpler tell me to wake up. I heard my baby crying, and the doctor saying, "It's over. You have a baby daughter." All the nurses stood around me smiling. I watched as they cleaned up my baby's body, and I could see that she looked pink with a reddish face. Someone told me "She weighs eight pounds."

I was quite uncomfortable afterward, but also proud because I had carried around another human being. *I am truly blessed,* I thought. I felt teary-eyed and a little nervous for a short while. By that time, it was 6:30 in the morning. I shared a room with another woman who had just had a baby; there was a sliding curtain between us.

About an hour later after I was back in my room Joseph strolled in wearing his black leather jacket, and his eyes were puffy like he had not slept in a while. Along with a bouquet of yellow roses, my husband carried a huge balloon that announced, YOU ARE MY QUEEN. He touched me gently and kissed me on my forehead. "I am so proud you, Mom," he told me with a big smile. Then he looked a little more serious and said, "Estell, I am glad that you aren't angry at me. I got so worried about you. I can't stand the thought of anything happening to you."

"It's okay," I reassured him.

"I'll call the girls," Joseph said. "They are going to be so happy with a little sister."

The nurse brought the baby into my room and laid her in my arms; the bassinet was near my bed. Even though I'd had two newborn babies before, I was nervous; I wasn't sure about touching her. She looked like a brown doll with a full head of curly hair and tiny fingers and black eyes, and she was dressed in white swaddling clothes with a light blue rim on her little cap.

Joseph stood by the bed just staring at us and grinning. "Do you remember the name that we picked out for our baby if it was a girl?" I asked.

"Yes. I was thinking it might be a boy who we'd name Aziz or Isaiah. I am thrilled to call our daughter Aisha," my husband replied. Together we had chosen an Islamic name that means alive and happily living.

Finally, Joseph asked, "Can I hold my daughter?" His hands trembled a bit while he picked her up, and then he was cradling baby Aisha in his arms. He studied her face for a long time and then told me, "She's got my cheekbones and a cute little nose." As he looked down into her eyes, he said softly, "Welcome, my sweet daughter! I will do my best to protect you, and I will be present to see you grow up and continue our legacy."

Aisha seemed hungry. I breastfed her, and she fell asleep in my arms. I felt a special bond with my mother because I knew that was how she took care of me in Prairie, Mississippi. Still, I was ready to go home to make pancakes with syrup in the morning for Fatima and Rabia and hear Coco bark out the window and show off my baby girl. At about ten o'clock that morning, Dr. Crumpler checked on me, and I told her, "I am ready to go home and see my children." But she said the policy was that I needed to stay for five days. She added, "This is just a precaution."

Finally, I settled down. It was just Joseph and me with our new baby. I was a little overwhelmed thinking how my life would change, so he brought my red bound journal. I felt lonely for a while, so I planned to write in my journal with my red felt-tip pen about being grateful, and I nursed my little angel, Aisha, every three hours.

The phone kept ringing with lots of phone calls from Aberdeen and New York, which really warmed my heart. On Wednesday morning, I packed and headed home with Joseph and our bundle of joy in her car safety seat.

13

Bringing Home Our New Baby

JOSEPH DROVE at the speed limit as he brought me home with our new baby. When he pulled into the driveway, I was elated. I felt an overwhelming sensation that life had changed. I saw a sign in our yard that read "Welcome Home, Mom," and I observed a few of my neighbors waving at me. I was teary-eyed at this unexpected homecoming.

Joseph hurried out of the vehicle and opened the car door for me. Our baby sat in a rear-facing car seat, dressed in her pink stretchy onesie.

I unbuckled baby Aisha and cradled her in my arms. Joseph asked if I needed any help with her, but I shook my head no. While my husband grabbed the small suitcase and my yellow roses from the trunk, I looked around the yard for my daughters. *Why aren't Fatima and Rabia waiting in the yard? I can't wait to hug them and see Coco flapping his ears.*

I walked slowly to the front door with Joseph trailing behind. As I opened the screen door, I saw balloons with pink streamers hanging from the ceiling, and I heard two little girls scream, "Mom is here!"

"Girls, keep it down, you are going wake, Aisha," I scolded, but I wasn't angry, especially when the girls ran to hug me. "Just a minute," I told them, "let me sit down on the love seat."

Fatima squeezed in beside me with her baby sister, and Joseph held Rabia in his lap. It was magical moment because I knew my family was special. In the meantime, Coco rubbed his fur on my legs and wagged his tail. It was a blissful moment.

Rose, who had stayed with the girls while Joseph picked me up, was sitting in the sofa chair. She got up and walked over to see Aisha, peeping at her under the blanket.

"Girls, you got a cute sister with curly hair," she told Fatima and Rabia, who giggled and touched the baby's tiny hands.

"Rose, I want to thank you for taking care of my babies," I said, my voice filled with emotion.

"Listen, Estell, your daughters are so well-mannered and polite," she replied. "And, I fixed egg sandwiches on wheat bread with slices of cantaloupe for you and the girls." A little later, as Rose prepared to leave, she tapped me on the shoulder and said, "Your husband loves these girls." Rose leaned over to grab my hand and told me she'd be back in the afternoon. I said, "Thanks, girlfriend."

From the kitchen, Joseph brought in pink cupcakes decorated with plastic hearts and sat them on the coffee table with plastic plates and forks. He took pictures as the girls reached for cupcakes and licked the icing from their fingers, and I enjoyed the celebration. By this time, Aisha had put her tiny fingers in her mouth. Soon after, I took baby Aisha to the bedroom, and as I left the living room, I announced to the girls, "I am going to need Mommy helpers to put away the clothes and sort the diapers." They jumped up and helped me with those tasks while I fed Aisha and put her into the bassinet.

After taking a short rest, I returned to the kitchen to make the formula as prescribed by Dr. Crumpler. She had assured me that it was safe and said it was nutritious. I mixed a twelve-ounce can of

Bringing Home Our New Baby

Carnation evaporated milk with eighteen ounces of boiled water and two tablespoons of Karo syrup. After I finished stirring it with a fork, my formula was ready. Next, I sterilized three bottles and the nipples before I poured the milk into them. When Aisha was ready for her bottle, I sprinkled a few drops of milk on my wrist to test the temperature. As I fed Aisha, I thought about how much I enjoyed watching her clench her tiny fist while she drank her bottle.

Joseph came into the room after I put her into her crib. I stood over it, just gazing at Aisha, and Joseph held me close in his arms. "I love my daughters and baby Aisha," he mumbled. "I am running you a warm bath, Babe, and adding coconut oil. And I got a surprise for you," he said, handing me a gold chain engraved *UMI,* which means "mother" in Arabic. "You are the star of our family, and we will always be together."

Joseph reached down and picked up Aisha. After a minute, he sat down on the bed with her, and I sat next to him. "I am not sure that you will like me when my hair is gray and I get wrinkles," I teased.

"I am sure that we will grow old together."

After we had been home for a few days, I was holding Aisha in my arms in the living room, with my other daughters sitting beside me, when suddenly, Fatima told Rabia, "You are no longer the baby." Rabia held her head down looking ashamed.

"Fatima, that was impolite," I scolded. Then I pulled Rabia close to me and hugged her and whispered, "You are so sweet." Soon, Rabia was kissing her baby sister and rubbing her tiny fingers.

Later, while Aisha was lying in her baby rocker, Fatima held onto her blanket and told her, "I can't wait until you start crawling." Then Rabia quietly sang a lullaby to her baby sister. I felt so proud of my girls, and I loved seeing their bond grow.

For the next weeks, I continued to exercise and tried not to fret about those stretch marks. I was seasoned as a mother, so I was ready to settle down to sleepless nights. I set up a calendar to manage my time. I got up early to fix breakfast, and Joseph was always up at 5:00 a.m. like he was in the army, and he wanted things neat and in place. I was kind of messy, like leaving my toothbrush on the counter and my clothes lying in the chairs. Joseph would pick them up and fuss a bit.

Our adorable baby girl, Aisha, brought so much love and laughter into our home. In this picture, she is a chubby-cheeked 12-month-old, wearing a bright red-and-white striped shirt, which fit her personality. She liked eating animal cracker cookies. She captured my heart when she called me "Mama" at 9 months old. Her arrival represented a new beginning for our family and filled our home with love and laughter.

My favorite thing to do, though, was spend time with my baby. While Aisha was sleeping, I gazed at her chubby cheeks and just watched her for hours. Other times, I liked brushing the tiny curls around the edges of her head. She was sweet . . . except for those potty diapers.

The days flew by, with Aisha waking up about every three hours. Often, I could catch a nap while she slept, but other times, I wanted to be nearby and ready to swoop her up as soon as she woke up. I enjoyed watching two-weeks-old Aisha wake up because I knew that after a three-hour nap, she would try to raise her head and whine a bit. Sometimes Aisha woke up with a smile, and I knew when she wanted her bottle.

After six weeks, Aisha was lifting her head while lying on her back and cooing. She was following my face, and she listened to the sounds of her rattle. I sang "London Bridge Is Falling Down," and sometimes I hummed as well. While she napped, I read Dr. Benjamin Spock's *Baby and Child Care*, which offered the most current practical advice. I was loving every moment of being a mother.

Every weekday afternoon, Fatima and Rabia arrived home from school on the bus. The bus arrived at three-fifteen, and most days, I looked through the window to see them running and swinging their arms with their book bags.

Every day, within six minutes of arriving home from the bus stop, the first thing the girls did was open the screen door to the living room and run to their baby sister, who was sitting in her pink Minnie Mouse rocker on the sofa. The girls would stand there just looking at Aisha with expressions of love and affection. Rabia liked to lean close to her baby sister and whisper, "I missed you today, and I told my friend Edna that I like rubbing your curly hair."

Fatima would sit next to her baby sister and tell her, "I am so happy that you came into my life. I love being with you every moment." Both had stayed close to their baby sister from the day she came home from the hospital.

One afternoon, Rabia asked, "Mom, can I call my sister 'Sissy'?"

I nodded and told her that was fine. At that moment, I felt so much love as I watched my daughters bonding with their baby sister. Finally, I announced, "All right, girls, go wash your hands, and your snack is waiting on the table. I'll bring Aisha—Sissy—into the kitchen." I had poured each of them a glass of cold milk and set them next to a Twinkie and a box of Cracker Jacks.

As Aisha got older, I allowed Fatima to hold her sister in her lap while she sat on the couch with her hand tucked tightly around the baby. Aisha sucked on her thumb as their heads rested close together. At first, Fatima looked a little nervous, but she had the brightest smile. Then, I placed Aisha in Rabia's arms while she sat in the comfy chair, and Rabia smiled as Aisha sucked her fingers. Other times, I put Aisha in her stroller, and we took walks in the neighborhood with Coco running beside us.

Chess

When Aisha was four weeks old, I was dusting off the blinds one afternoon while she slept in her crib. I bumped into the ivory chess set that sat on a stool in our living room. I remembered how much Joseph treasured this chess board from his mom, Carrie. I sat down in my chair to think about our home in Brooklyn.

When Joseph came home from serving in Vietnam in 1968, he wanted to teach me how to play the game. I thought it was just a game for white people because it was slow and boring, and unlike the physical action in a basketball game.

Bringing Home Our New Baby

I was eager to learn to play chess with these sixty-four medieval pieces on a square checkerboard. I knew that some of the pieces moved horizontally and vertically, and I practiced for weeks to memorize the moves of each piece. One Friday night, I sat down to play our first game with Joseph, who had his tall cup of Maxwell House coffee sitting next to him. He smiled while rubbing his chin and boasting, "You think that you are ready to beat me?"

As the game proceeded, I moved my pieces slowly, which ticked him off. After we had played for an hour, I got anxious because my bishop could only move diagonally, and my knight only vertically, and I knew I was losing. He kept reminding me, "It's your move." In the meantime, he checkmated me. I frowned and grunted because he was able to figure out my moves from the beginning. I wanted to push his pieces off the board because he blocked me at every move with his pieces. I was determined to beat him, so I read books and practiced. Finally, three months later, I did beat him!

When Fatima was seven years old, Joseph began teaching her to play chess. She was excited to learn the moves. After practicing with her dad for three months, Fatima captured his king. She shouted gleefully, "Checkmate, Daddy!" meaning his king had no escape, and she began bragging. Joseph just stared at his chess pieces and smiled, and told her, "You're pretty good."

Joseph believed that chess would give Fatima and Rabia analytical and math skills in school. I told him I thought they were too young. Then I recalled that when I was growing up, my teacher told me that math was too hard for girls at Shivers High School, and I changed my mind; I wanted my daughters to have strong math skills.

When Joseph began teaching Rabia how to play chess, she was distracted and preferred to play with her Raggedy Ann doll in her bedroom. Once she saw Fatima playing chess, though, she decided that her sister was not smarter than she was, so she soon began practicing with her dad and focusing on the moves of each chess piece.

In a short time, she was practicing with her sister. Before we left New York, five-year-old Rabia could beat her dad at chess.

Chess always seemed kind of complicated to me, and I was just an ordinary player. My seven-year-old daughter, Fatima could beat me, and five-year-old Rabia couldn't wait to play with me. When we played, she smiled like she was thinking, *Are you ready for me to take your queen?* Nevertheless, it was a fun way to connect with my daughters and see that they developed a real skill in learning the game.

On Friday nights, we had a tradition of playing chess as a family in our home. We started this in New York and continued after we moved to Atlanta. One Friday when Joseph came home from work, we were waiting to start the game. Fatima was ready, wearing her yellow turtleneck sweater with her bare feet on the floor. She sat down to face her dad and the sixty-four chess pieces on the square board. First, she moved her pawns slowly because she knew her dad was aggressive. She used her skill to get him off guard. Still, she looked him in the eye while slowly moving her pieces. After an hour, she called out, "Checkmate." Fatima, who watched the entire game, mumbled, "I figured out your moves."

Shaking his head, Joseph just replied, "You beat me!"

Meanwhile, Rabia pulled up her chair. Joseph said, "All right, let me see what you got, Rabia!"

She moved her pawn and then quickly moved her bishop with her eye on the chess board. She sat straight in her chair, her long ponytail swishing as she leaned forward and back to play, her feet in penny loafers flat on the floor. Within five minutes, she said casually, "Daddy, how was your day?"

"I am feeling tired and ready for dinner," Joseph replied. As they talked, she was thinking about her next move. After about thirty minutes, she knocked over his queen on the board and announced in delight, "Checkmate, Daddy!"

Joseph leaned back in his chair and said in mock exasperation, "I can't beat you either." We all laughed at that.

Chess bolstered my daughters' math skills and gave them confidence in their ability to learn. As my daughters grew up, they could master any skill in math. They were patient and excited to learn anything new. Fatima did not talk much, but she knew the concepts in biology and algebra. Rabia loved to write stories, but she also excelled in physics and science. They weren't intimidated like I was.

When I went to Vine Street Elementary in Aberdeen, I struggled in math class. When I told my mom, she said, "You don't need math because you are going to be a wife." In my classroom, my teacher just passed me to the next grade even though I received Cs and Ds in math. I just assumed that being a girl, I wouldn't really need that stuff. Years later, I realized that I missed out because I felt that boys were better at math than me.

My daughters would need to be more than just housewives. I wanted them to have academic success and be fiercely competitive. When I was growing up in Aberdeen, I thought my education was less important because I was a girl. I felt that I needed to depend on a husband to lead and make decisions for me, like my momma. When I went to Tuskegee in 1964, I changed my beliefs about my value as a woman. I began to believe in myself, knowing that I was free to decide my future, and I set goals to achieve. I had big dreams of wearing fine clothes and living in a big city. At the time, I felt uncertainty and fear, but I had faith and began writing down my thoughts.

Even with their education, I knew my daughters' race and gender would deprive them of many opportunities.

14

Bus Ride to Visit the Doctor

1976

TWELVE-MONTH-OLD AISHA had an earache, and I was up late one night making a list of the things I needed to take to the doctor the next day. Joseph wanted to take off from work to drive us there, but I reminded him that I wasn't working and we had bills to pay.

I took my girls to Grady Hospital on Butler Street because they had good pediatricians, and it was cheap. And I was eligible for the blue card, which meant I only paid two dollars to see the doctor and the medication was free. Grady was different from other hospitals because they treated uninsured patients like me.

Grady was a hospital for low-income people; many times there was sick patients in the hallways who were bleeding and groaning for help. Inside, the garbage cans were overflowing, and the entrance outside was littered with beer cans and wine bottles. I just pretended that I did not notice any of it. Even when I did not have any money,

I was never turned away. As the girls got older, I continued to see the doctors there who were from Emory Hospital to treat patients who couldn't afford the other hospitals. They were friendly with so many patients waiting in the halls.

I woke up Fatima and Rabia for morning prayer with their dad. Afterward, he prepared a breakfast of hot Cream of Wheat cereal. The box featured a happy black man with a big smile showing his white teeth, and he wore a white chef's hat. When I bought this cereal, I thought, *This is a stereotype with the Jim Crow image of a happy Negro.* Fatima asked me about the picture on the box, but I just shook my head.

By 6:45 a.m., the girls were dressed in their light blue sweaters. I braided their hair and attached pink and yellow beads on the ends. They wore their flowered dresses and Vans Era checkered sneakers; I dressed Aisha in a lime-green jacket and silver sandals. She did not eat her mashed banana and drank only a four-ounce bottle. I rushed around to grab my tote bag with disposable diapers, two plastic baby bottles, and some teething biscuits. I added snacks for the girls, which included Goldfish crackers, peanut butter sandwiches without the crust, and an apple. Then I put Aisha in her umbrella stroller.

I checked the Marta schedule, and bus #25 was scheduled to arrive at 7:15 a.m. I told the girls to hurry because the bus stop was three blocks away. As I was closing the front door, Coco tried to sneak out. I knelt to hug him and said, "I left two doggie bones for you."

Luckily, the weather was cool, and it was breezy. As we hurried to the bus stop, I reminded the girls to stay on the grass because the sidewalk was cracked.

The bus was thirty minutes late, and the traffic was heavy with cars swerving close to the sidewalk. Then, Aisha began to whine. I picked her up and laid across my shoulder, rocking back and forth while holding my baby bag.

Bus Ride to Visit the Doctor

"Girls, I want you to stop talking and pay attention to your library books." Rabia replied, "It's Fatima who keeps talking about that movie *Peter Pan*, and she likes this magical story."

At that moment, the white bus with blue and yellow stripes pulled up. My daughters climbed on first, and I lifted the folded stroller onto the bus. I dropped twenty-five cents into the slots by the bus driver. who wore a white shirt and black pants. The driver said, "Good morning, ma'am." I told the girls to sit in the metal seats behind the driver.

The bus was full and smelled like mildew. Passengers were heading to work and holding onto the handgrips, and the ride was bumpy. I observed a waitress wearing an ironed blue dress and holding a creased handkerchief in her hand, a young disabled man who wore a Vietnam cap, and a grandma holding a bag of groceries. By this time, my daughters had opened their library books and were reading.

Fatima asked, "Mom what time are we getting to the hospital?"

"I think we have about three more stops," I told her. Aisha was still sleeping in my arms, and I glanced at my journal, which was decorated with flowers and pictures of places where I wanted to go in the world, like Egypt, Brazil, and France.

Once we arrived at Grady Hospital, I was anxious to see the doctor. At the entrance near the glass door was a rusty garbage can with a nasty smell, and next to it, a man with a portable radio playing loud music and. I pushed Aisha in her umbrella stroller, and the girls walked beside me. First, I went to the front desk to register for my Grady Card, and I stood in a line with about thirty other people. By this time, I was holding Aisha on my hip saying an Islamic prayer, "God, please shower blessings on me and my family."

Once I was registered, I was sent to the clinic for young children and told to wait in a crowded waiting room with other mothers and babies who were waiting for their number to be called. I was number forty-eight. I enjoyed chatting with a mother named Josephine, who had driven forty miles from Kennesaw, Georgia to see about her three-month-old baby who had asthma. The waiting room was noisy, with babies crying and coughing, and the air was stuffy, but there was sunlight shining through the window. I barely had any space to move my chair, and I kept my daughters close to me and washed their hands several times.

About 1:30 in the afternoon, I was called into the doctor's office. Dr. Kathy Dudley examined Aisha, who was squirming and kicking. She diagnosed her with an ear infection and prescribed an antibiotic and aspirin for the fever. She told me, "Aisha is going to be fine after a few days." I felt really happy.

Later, I would need another card for the pharmacy to pay for my medicine, and I stood in another long line. Aisha was crying and tugging on her ears, and the children were begging to go home because they were hungry. I stopped at the snack bar, and I bought chocolate moon pies, which had a graham cracker crust and marshmallow in the middle. When I handed Rabia her moon pie, she pulled off the wrapper with a joyful smile. Fatima took her time to peel the paper off her moon pie and then ate it slowly. I decided on the small pecan pie with a pastry crust and the taste of buttery, sweet pecans for myself. I loved the way my mom made this pie, and the taste reminded me of home.

Once we got the prescription, we collected our things and walked to the Marta bus stop. While waiting, the girls sat on the grass because they were exhausted. Aisha slept on my shoulder as I pondered what I wanted to fix for Joseph's dinner. Finally, the bus arrived. We'd left the house at seven in the morning, and we finally walked back in at 5:00 p.m. Aisha kept tugging at her ears, and she had a slight fever. I put her in her Winnie the Pooh nightshirt and rocked her while holding her close in my arms. She cried until 2:00 a.m., when she finally drifted off to sleep. Shortly after, I climbed into my comfortable bed.

Years later, I found this online:

> If Atlanta is the birthplace of greatness, Grady is the bassinet. It's a badge of honor in this city to be called a Grady Baby. Grady Babies have changed the world, secured civil rights for all, and achieved educational success. Music moguls, super stars, and world class athletes all started as Grady Babies. If she's a Georgia Peach, chances are she's a Grady Baby.[2]

Aisha was a Grady Baby, and she is proud of that. Grady treated Black people when other hospitals turned us away, and it helped us keep our families healthy.

That night, I smiled as I drifted off to sleep.

---

[2] https://www.gradybabyco.com/about

15

Fun Days at School

ONE OF THE FIRST THINGS Joseph and I did when our daughters began attending Ben Hill Elementary in 1975 was purchase the *World Book Encyclopedia*, all twenty-two volumes from A to Z. I did not own these books growing up because my family couldn't afford them; they cost around eight hundred dollars. When Rose mentioned that she'd purchased these books, I talked to Joseph about getting a loan to buy a set for our daughters. We knew they would help the girls get better grades because they covered topics like science, biology, and history and included a research book with key terms. Joseph took out a loan for eighteen months to pay for the encyclopedias, and we purchased them right away.

Since the girls were going to a segregated Black school, I was happy to see teachers who looked like them. In addition, the school was allowing the children to sing "Lift Every Voice and Sing," the Black national anthem, during pep rallies.

First Day of School

I remember the girls' first day of school on Monday, August 18, 1975. I could barely sleep thinking about their beginnings in a new school in the South. The girls were a little scared about going to Ben Hill Elementary, and I was somewhat anxious but also excited.

I walked with my daughters to the bus stop; they were the best-looking girls there. I had braided their hair the night before. Fatima, who was tall like her dad, with thick, wavy hair, wore a light-blue polyester knit blouse and skirt and a beige head scarf, and she carried a striped book bag. My sweet girl Rabia was so cute with a pink turtleneck dress and tights. Of course, she gripped her pastel lunch box, and at lunchtime, she'd find the note I had slipped inside that read *Be kind to your friends.*

Promptly at 7:15 a.m., a big yellow school bus pulled up. I hugged Fatima tightly and then knelt down to kiss Rabia on the cheek. They got in line with the other children and climbed onto the bus. I stayed to waved goodbye with a smile on my face, but I had a knot in my stomach. Would they be all right at their new school? Tears streamed down my face as I walked home.

The first week of classes seemed to go well. On Wednesday, Fatima enjoyed the cafeteria lunch of pizza and chocolate milk with a peanut butter square for dessert. And she could get an extra serving of pizza because the line lady liked her. Rabia liked the grilled cheese sandwich and fries. She squeezed lots of ketchup on her fries. On Friday, it was show-and-tell, and Rabia carried her plush Mickey Mouse toy to school that day.

There were a few things at the school that made my daughters uncomfortable during the first few weeks. The girls were both lonely at first because they didn't have many friends, but I assured them that their classmates just needed time to get to know them.

Rabia was in the first grade and sat at a metal desk in the second row of the classroom. In the back of the room was a play area with lime-green and blue bean bags. A display of sight words and math symbols decorated the walls. The class started at eight o'clock sharp with Miss Roberts greeting the children with "Hello, class." The morning routine always began with exercise: the children twisting their bodies while swinging their arm back and forth. Next, Miss Roberts announced, "Let review the homework."

The new lesson for the day was to learn about the value of coins and how to count money. The children sat in a circle on the floor. A side table held labeled cups filled with quarters, dimes, nickel, and pennies. The teacher turned to call on my daughter and said, "Robbie."

Rabia corrected her with, "My name is Rabia." Her classmates giggled. Rabia told me she was thinking, *How could anyone get those five letters wrong?* Then, while her classmates slowly added their coins, Rabia added hers quickly. Rabia was bored and asked, "Could I read a book?"

Miss Roberts said loudly, "No, because you are disrupting the class, and you need to follow the curriculum of this class." So Rabia just sat quietly playing with her shoestrings.

At lunchtime, Rabia stood in line with the other students, and they marched to the cafeteria. They waited to be served by the cafeteria lady, who was always friendly. At the table, with the clanging of dishes all around, Miss Roberts told the children to eat quietly. Rabia began to nibble on her blueberry pie. Her friend Edna asked, "Rabia why you are not eating your corn dog?"

"I am Muslim, and I don't eat pork."

Edna asked, "What kind of religion is that?" The other children began to give her strange looks.

Finally, Miss Roberts said, "Just eat your food." Rabia just bowed her head and nibbled on the apple she had brought from home.

Fatima's third-grade class was in a big room with forty students. The wooden desks had pencil marks on the sides, and they were close together. She sat in the third row with her notebook and yellow lead pencils. While students were arriving before the official start of class, Miss Amara walked the aisles in the classroom and stopped at Fatima's desk. "Is your mother from the South?" she asked Fatima. "Because she asks a lot of questions about the curriculum."

"Yes, ma'am," Fatima answered.

Promptly at 8:00 a.m., Miss Amara said, "Let's turn to our assignment for today."

Fatima's assignment was to write a one-page essay about an historic person and present it in front of the class. She decided on Shirley Chisholm, the first African American woman in Congress. Fatima talked about how her mother had met Miss Chisholm in Brooklyn during her 1968 campaign. Then Fatima asked, "Does anyone have any questions?"

From the back of the room, Jimmy, who had a bald head, asked, "Why are you wearing that silly headscarf?"

Fatima tightened her lips, and her teacher said, "Go sit down, Fatima."

As she walked back to her seat, Fatima stopped at Jimmy's desk and said, "You are a knucklehead." The students began mumbling and staring.

The teacher rang a bell at her desk and ordered the class to settle down. "I added a negative mark to your sheet for poor behavior, Fatima," she announced. Next, the teacher scolded Jimmy, saying, "I am disappointed at your behavior today." Then she told the class, "We will skip recess and do more reading."

Poor Fatima! Her classmates blamed her and Jimmy for the loss of their free time, and several told her, "I can't believe I'm missing recess because of *you*!"

When we talked about it that evening, I asked her how she felt about this situation; her eyes filled with tears, and she was angry because she had high expectations for herself. She calmed down. and I fixed her a Nestle's hot cocoa with whipped cream. That put a little smile back on her face.

On a Saturday morning in March, I sat with my daughters in their bedroom to check on their homework. As I opened their folders,

I saw a red check mark next to the behavior column for Fatima. I waited a few minutes and thought about what I wanted to say. Seeing these poor grades was alarming. I recalled my own schooling, and I thought, *I need to help them.*

I believed education was a necessity for Fatima and Rabia. From the first time I laid eyes on them, I decided they were going to college. Not only would a good education keep them from falling into poverty, but it would give them access to jobs that pay a decent wage. I knew from my own experiences that my daughters would face gender and race bias; I was angry for years because I was overlooked in the workplace and offered limited choices. However, I was determined to use their energy to help them thrive and foster a better outcome for my daughters in school.

I asked Fatima, "What is going on at school?" She looked down at her hands in her lap and told me that her classmate Jimmy was talking about her headscarf in a loud voice, so she got in his face.

"So, you were impulsive!" I accused.

Fatima looked up at me. "I saw that smirk on his face after he criticized my headscarf," she said. "And other children were grinning. I tightened my lip and got angry. I just wanted to wipe that look off his face."

As we talked, Rabia swayed in her chair and looked uncomfortable. I opened her folder.

"Rabia, you got 'U' for Unsatisfactory," I admonished. She could tell by my voice how displeased I was.

"Mom, the teacher mispronounced my name, and I waited while they counted those silly coins in math class." Rabia looked at me and then continued, "It was dull. I already know all that stuff. I didn't mean to be impolite to Miss Roberts."

"Girls, I did not get these folders last week."

Fatima answered, "I was afraid to tell you because you are going to tell Daddy." I looked at her expectantly. "That's right, Mom,"

Fatima mumbled. "I don't want to hear him ask what we're thinking like he always does."

I chuckled inside because she was right—Joseph loved to ask our daughters to use their critical-thinking skills, and he would often ask them things like, "Did Columbus discover America or were Native Americans here first?" They'd often use an encyclopedia from the library and do some research, then report back to him.

I told her, "He just wants you to do your best." By this time, I was worried that they were struggling, and I wanted to help them. "Come here," I said, and they both leaned into me. With my arms around their shoulders, I said, "I am sure that you will make lots of friends." I squeezed them tightly.

I had met my daughters' teachers in August, and I kept in touch with them by phone. I went to the PTA meetings to volunteer my help with raising money for school supplies; I was an involved mom. Here it was March, and I was still seeing my daughters having issues.

About a week later, at a Ben Hill School's parent-teacher conference on a Thursday after school, I visited Fatima's teacher, Miss Amara, for thirty minutes. She had recently moved from Virginia to Atlanta with her family, and her son was in the fifth grade. Miss Amara mentioned that Fatima was getting A's in class but that she seemed assertive.

On the wall of the classroom were rules of discipline for infractions like fighting and disrupting the class. I saw that paddling was used on the buttocks or outstretched hands (this practice was later outlawed) for discipline. I remembered that my teacher used a wood paddle on my hands in Aberdeen when I was ten years old. I thought that teacher never liked me. I was concerned, but Miss Amara assured me it was the principal who decided on punishment.

I met Miss Roberts, Rabia's teacher, who had been teaching for eighteen years. Miss Roberts was bubbly and kind, but also strict about the children saying "Yes, ma'am." We discussed the goals she set in her classroom for her students' reading and math levels. The teacher showed an interest in Rabia and provided a supportive environment to give her a sense of belonging. At the conclusion of our meeting, she told me, "Rabia is smart, but she talks too much. I am learning your daughter is above average, and I will give her different books to read than the other children." She also told me Rabia could read in the library.

The school assumed all the children were on the same academic level, and they weren't prepared for children like Fatima and Rabia, whose parents valued education so highly and worked with them at home. The school they'd attended in New York had more resources for Black children than this school in Atlanta. Another thing I didn't realize until we moved was that the Black schools had more students than the white schools.

I was a little nervous that afternoon, but after discussing my daughters' grades and behaviors with Miss Amara and Miss Roberts, I was pleased. I came away knowing these were caring teachers.

I continued to meet with both teachers regularly. As the months went by, Fatima became a line leader in her class, and Rabia oversaw a small library in the classroom. On Teacher Appreciation Month, I sent notes to both teachers that read,

I appreciate you spending the long hours helping my daughters, and they enjoy the lessons in class. Thank you for being kind, and I admire your dedication.

16
Daughters and Discipline

I DID NOT KNOW how to raise daughters, except I thought I was supposed to keep them dressed up in pretty clothes and smiling. My three daughters are energetic and lively. I was told many times that girls are a handful. That does not bother me. I liked spending every minute with them. I wanted to set a good example for them and to share my values. I had to watch my words because I would say a few curse words when I got flustered.

One of the things I knew would help my daughters was discipline. In fact, I decided to teach them responsible behavior and self-control by setting an example in our home. I set rules for them to follow, like being kind to friends and saying good morning to our neighbors. I wanted them to be loving sisters as well. If I saw Fatima stomping around in the kitchen and feeling frustrated, I would sit down and talk with her. I wanted to help her solve problems and follow the rules of respect at home.

Just as important was education. I knew it would help them become lifelong learners and would give them coping skills, mental stability, and financial success. They would face barriers to their braided hair, their brightly colored clothes, and their body shapes. This implicit bias in school and the workplace could affect their self-esteem, and I wanted to do everything I could to counter that. Indeed, I wanted them to have a better life than I did.

I wanted them to be able to express themselves with words. To enforce their use of proper grammar, I kept a mason jar on top of the counter in the living room, and they had to put fifty cents into it each time they used poor grammar. Their allowance was one dollar a week, so they had to be careful to speak properly, or they could lose their entire allowance. On one occasion, Fatima said, "I love to draw, I like my pencils." After she uttered this run-on sentence, she shook her head; she knew what she'd done. "All right, I'll put money in the jar," she said as she walked over to the jar and dropped in two quarters. "And it's not fair, Momma," she added. Then Rabia wrote a paper for school, and she did not capitalize the name *Minnesota*. I turned and looked at her. Sighing, she put fifty cents in the jar. "You are getting like Daddy with these rules," she said. Later, they received A's in English.

Joseph would often lecture the girls for hours about getting good grades. He would talk to them about their homework and their behavior. We both spoke with them about other important subjects, too, like not allowing anyone to touch their bodies without their permission and that they could say no if they felt uncomfortable when someone touched them.

Joseph never spanked our daughters, but I did spank them from the time Fatima was eight years old until they were each around fourteen years old, and I used Joseph's old leather belt. Today, I regret using a belt on them, which I did in frustration, but it didn't seem wrong at the time because spanking had been part of my upbringing. My mother whipped me many times and left welts on my skin while I was growing up in Aberdeen. The first time was for being naughty when I was six years old. Another time, I remember telling a lie about my new sweater at Vine Street Elementary School, and Momma told me to bring a switch from the oak tree in our backyard. She whipped my legs and my butt. My legs burned for days. But I never did that again. I know spanking helped me follow the rules, so I used it for discipline, too.

I only gave them a few spankings over the years, and it wasn't the only form of discipline for our daughters. If they did not say thank you in places like restaurants, I tapped them on the hand to remind them.

One Friday night, Joseph took me to see the movie *Jaws*. It was a little scary when the killer shark was unleashed on a beach. We had a lot of fun hanging out together that evening, just the two of us.

When we came home, we saw burned papers in the trash, and I knew the girls had been playing with matches in the kitchen. Immediately, I got my belt and began whipping Rabia and Fatima, who blamed each other. They each got three licks on the butt. Just the thought of a fire at our home on Rex Avenue scared me.

The family table talk started in Brooklyn after Joseph was discharged from the army. He was strict, like a drill sergeant, firm about things like the family eating together and keeping our home neat and clean. This startled me because he had been flexible and laid back when we were first married. But I accepted his behavior because I saw him as a strong leader. He was loving and kind, and I felt safe with him.

Our Friday night talks later became a ritual for discussion between the girls and their dad. When I think of the table talks, it was like him holding court. At a typical Friday evening family table talk, Joseph sat at the head of the table and began in a solemn voice, "Family, we need each other." He expected family loyalty, which to him meant a strong family bond and sticking by each other no matter what—through good times and bad. He believed taking care of each other served as self-protection against racism. He remembered the hard times his family had and how they'd lost their home in Harlem. He taught the girls things he had learned from being a member of the Black Panthers, especially that everyone deserves to be treated with respect. He told seven-year-old Fatima and five-year-old Rabia, "It took years before I decided to speak up, and the party inspired me to work for our rights."

When the girls' grades slipped in those first weeks at their new school, it was a big deal, and that warranted a serious discussion. That Friday evening, Joseph called around six to say that he would be late for dinner. After the girls had cleaned up the kitchen, I told them that their dad would talk to them when he arrived home about their school.

Fatima spoke for both. "Mom, did you have to tell Daddy? He is going to give us his lecture about focusing."

"Your daddy and I really care about your education," I told her. Education was important to me because I wanted my children to have a better future than the one, I expected as a child living in poverty. As an adult Black woman, I continued to feel small and unimportant. I lacked the education I needed for the jobs I wanted and was rejected for jobs. That hurt and was mentally stressful, and it continued to haunt me as a mother. I deferred to my husband to help keep our daughters on track because they listened to him. I felt Joseph was too pushy at times, but our daughters needed to be strong to live independent lives. With both of us working hard to help them succeed, I believed my daughters could have a better life.

On this evening, I was in the living room with baby Aisha, who was four weeks old, when Joseph arrived home. He greeted me and rubbed Aisha on the head before heading to the kitchen. I remember thinking, *I hope he doesn't get loud with our daughters because his voice is deep, and he is six feet tall and wears a leather jacket.*

I watched him walk to the kitchen; he could barely lift his feet. He was working two jobs, and he looked worried. He poured himself a cup of coffee, sat down at the table, and turned off the radio.

Daughters and Discipline

I hollered, "Girls, your daddy is home!" I knew our daughters were a little intimidated by their dad because he was strict and because he wanted them to excel. I hoped he did not bang his fist on the table that night because that annoyed the girls.

Fatima, who wore cornrows with beads, walked into the kitchen, and Rabia, who wore shoulder-length braids with beads, skipped in. They sat down quietly next to their dad, who had his notebook in his hands. The girls were used to seeing the notebook where he kept track of family things and their grades.

"Hello, my queens," Joseph greeted his daughters. Rabia smiled, and Fatima said hello in a weak tone. I smiled, too, when I heard him call them queens. He loved them and was devoted to their futures, and he called them that to boost their self-esteem and to let them know their ancestors were proud people. Joseph sipped on his coffee before saying, "I warned you that it would be hard switching school from the North. Your Islamic names and your northern accents make some people feel uncomfortable. Did you think your classmates were going to welcome you? They need time to get to know you."

Fatima just sat in her chair and looked up at the ceiling. She did not like how strict her dad was, and she tucked her lip and had a dry expression on her face.

"What do you have to say, Fatima? Look at me when I am talking," her father said.

Fatima answered in a loud voice, "My teacher is not answering my question about my essay. And I got into this boy's face who made me upset about my clothes. He was talking to me like that because I'm a girl."

"This is not the way your mother and I have been teaching you to think and use your mind. So you allowed your emotions to control you."

"No, Daddy. I was speaking up," Fatima exclaimed.

Joseph looked at me. Then he nodded and said to Fatima, "I *have* been teaching you to speak up, to be more assertive." He leaned toward her with his face close to hers. "You are gutsy and bold." Then he smiled. "Next time, Fatima, tell your teacher about Jimmy bothering you."

Joseph then turned to our other daughter and said, "Rabia, what's going on with you in school?"

"Daddy, I told my teacher that I'm bored in class, and I wanted to read a book instead of counting coins as homework. The teacher rolled her eyes at me."

Rabia continued. "Miss Roberts keeps mispronouncing my name. She was annoyed with me."

Joseph looked her in the eye. "So, were you talking during class?"

Rabia held her head down as she answered softly, "Yes."

Joseph softened his tone a bit and said, "It's a lot to handle in school with new teachers in the South. You should have told your mother about the homework."

Fatima responded, "Mom was taking care of Aisha." The girls looked uncomfortable.

"Come here," Joseph told them. "I am proud of you because you like learning. Still, I want you to focus on those grades. Mom and I will work this out."

Fatima and Rabia got up and went to Joseph, who hugged them close, saying, "I love you." Rabia giggled; Fatima was still quiet.

17

Soul Train

March 1975

THE NEXT DAY, after the Friday night chat with our girls about their schoolwork, they seemed a little down. I thought, How can I make them smile? I decided to make it a fun afternoon with pizza for lunch and an hour of watching Soul Train. I never missed a show. Black people on TV for one hour!

The suave Don Cornelius was the host. He was a brown-skinned guy with a neat Afro, and he produced the show from Chicago. The popularity of *Soul Train* proved Black culture had mass appeal. For years, I watched *American Bandstand* hosted by Dick Clark. While this program showcased the latest rock-and-roll hits as well as country and western and rhythm and blues, I do not recall seeing any Black teenagers on the show in the early 1970s. Eventually, it was integrated.

At one o'clock, I hollered, "Come here, Fatima and Rabia!" The girls recognized the whistling train that announced *Soul Train* on the screen. They stood close to the TV, dancing to the music. I told them to sit down, and they did, but they continued to bounce up and down on the couch. On the coffee table, a bucket of popcorn waited for them. The girls huddled together, giggling, in their blue jeans and tunic shirts.

We watched and listened as the smooth voice of Don Cornelius said, "Welcome back, and I got the *Soul Train* dancers." Then, dancers did the "Soul Train Line," a variation of a 1950s fad known as "The Stroll," when the dancers formed two lines with a space in the middle for dancers to strut down the aisle. The couples wore matching red or yellow outfits. The dancers kicked and twisted their way down the aisle and shook their hips to the latest songs. I loved watching the dancers get into a groove. They were letting go and feeling free, by moving their hands and shaking their hips. Dancing in the African American community was fueled by our experience and represented freedom from our daily struggle. We could own our rhythm and be ourselves. Dancing was creative and fun for us.

Each episode featured a guest artist who usually performed twice on each program. That day, the guest was the amazing Stevie Wonder, who sang, "Isn't She Lovely." I knew all the words to this song and bobbed my head to the rhythm while the girls sang along. Later in the program, he came back on camera and sang "Signed, Sealed, Delivered I'm Yours."

As I watched this show, I saw how happy it made my children. I'll never forget how *Soul Train* made me feel, too. At the time, it was the only commercial television program being produced by a Black person for a young Black audience. Don Cornelius celebrated our culture with *Soul Train* for thirty-five years.

18

Joseph's Story

I MET JOSEPH'S PARENTS, Joseph and Carrie Halliburton, in 1964. Joseph Sr. would always say, "Estell, you are just the person my son was looking for." Carrie called me "daughter," and she was kind to me and stayed with me in the hospital when I had my first baby, Fatima. I loved this family.

After Joseph came home from Vietnam, he began telling me stories about his life before living in Harlem.

He told me that he had once lived in Washington Heights, in a good neighborhood with clean streets, and he dressed in good clothes. He remembered his mother humming in the kitchen and cooking Sunday dinner. She worked as a maid on Long Island, and his dad worked maintenance at the apartment building where they lived.

Joseph's dad talked about how proud he was to have been a U.S. Army soldier who fought in France during World War II. He liked wearing his uniform, whether on the field or in the supermarket. Being a soldier gave him a sense of security, and he loved representing his family and his country.

The military was segregated in 1945. Negro soldiers in the army were considered less capable than white soldiers. They received medical treatment in a separate hospital; their segregated barracks were unclean. Yet Joseph Sr. was patriotic and willing to sacrifice his life.

He thought that being in the army and fighting for his country would earn him respect when he got home, but things didn't work out quite as well as he had hoped. He was still called "Negro" or "boy," and he was angry that he was treated as a second-class citizen even though he had fought for his country. He took odd jobs like delivering groceries, pushing racks of clothing around the garment district, and washing dishes to support his family. Eventually, he learned a trade and did maintenance for large apartment buildings.

The family of four—Joseph Sr., Carrie, Joseph Jr., and Herbie—lived happily in their quiet neighborhood with friendly neighbors. After eight years, their landlord raised the rent, and they couldn't afford to stay even though both of Joseph's parents worked long hours. Joseph Sr. tried to borrow money, but his credit wasn't good. Later, he lost his job and was unable to find work. Carrie put in a lot of extra effort at work to make a little extra money, but the family couldn't survive on just her paycheck, and they exhausted their savings.

The Halliburtons had to leave their home in 1957. That's when things changed for my husband, who was twelve years old at the time and had to change schools and leave his friends. The family moved to Harlem to a low-income apartment building where people hung around in the hallway that was unclean and filled with loud music.

Joseph's dad felt ashamed for not being able to provide for his family. His identity as a man crumbled. Sometimes there was barely any food in the house. After months of living in Harlem, he begins to drink cheap wine and Kentucky bourbon to numb his pain, and that was mentally devastating for Carrie. The parents began arguing with each other, and the family was not the same. Joseph loved his family, but he was angry about the move. He began carrying inspirational

Joseph's Story

books with him, like Langston Hughes's *Dream Deferred*, which he related to because they described how he felt.

Joseph attended Frederick Douglass Middle School in the Bronx, which was segregated. He felt unsafe walking to school because of the guys hanging out on the street drinking beer on his route to and from school. He ran home every day at first, but on one occasion, he was stopped by a gang member who took his books and threw them on the ground. He decided to fight back. This resulted in a fight between the two. The guy, who was tall and wore a red bandana around his head, was used to street fights, and Joseph ended up with a bloody nose.

Even though the family moved several times while Joseph was in high school, he continued to visit the Harlem library to read classics like *Othello* that his mother had taught him. Joseph loved learning. At school, he really liked science, and it helped him develop his critical thinking. He dreamed of one day being a teacher.

His American History class had forty-five students, and many of them slept at their desks. The teacher was a white woman named Miss Kelly; she had long gray hair to her shoulders and wore black-rimmed glasses. One Friday, the topic was the Civil War and slavery. Lecturing from her podium, Miss Kelly told the class that most of the slaves benefited from slavery, and they had food to eat and a place to sleep. Joseph spoke up and told her that was not the truth, that slaves were forced to eat animal parts their masters threw away. He told her slaves toiled for eight hours a day in the winter and doubled that in the summer, seven days a week, even if they were sick, and they were never paid for their labor.

The other students hollered, "Go, Joseph!" But Miss Kelly marched over to his desk and announced, "You are out of order! I am teaching this class. I don't like your tone and attitude." Then she said, "I want you out of my classroom, and I am sending you to the principal's office for detention for a week."

Joseph recalled he was sent to a room with a green door that had chipped paint. Four other black students sat with him on hard wooden chairs in the dimly lit room with grimy floors that looked like they hadn't been mopped in weeks. He remembered being scared that day because it was his first time ever in detention. He was only seventeen, and he was stunned that Miss Kelly was so insensitive and reacted so poorly. Joseph could not accept being treated like a criminal for telling the truth, and he shook with anger.

When he got home, he told his mom, "No one cares about my education since I'm a Negro. My teacher is overwhelmed with how many students she has, and she isn't supportive. I don't think she sees much potential in any of us. And she doesn't understand our culture. I am dropping out of school."

Carrie was heartbroken. She worried that Joseph could end up like some of his friends and go to jail. But he promised his mom that he would never quit learning. Later, he got his GED after studying at the Harlem branch of the New York Public Library.

Joseph told me this story about his childhood many times, and he would get riled up and irritated every time he told it.

When Fatima was about seven and Rabia was about five, Joseph shared this story with them for the first time. Two years later, when they attended Ben Hill Elementary, they thought their school was noisy and not a good place for them to learn. When they went to middle school, the girls had teachers with poor attitudes, and they were told things like "Your braided hair is ugly" from the other students. Often, our daughters came home upset. That's usually when Joseph shared his own story with them again; he wanted them to understand that this was normal behavior in the public school system, especially for Black children, but that school wasn't the only source of education.

19
Missing Aberdeen

WHEN I THINK of my hometown in Aberdeen, Mississippi, I have countless memories. Our daughters enjoyed visiting Aberdeen to see their grandparents; they liked shopping at Piggy Wiggly. Fatima always got caramel popcorn, and Rabia got a handful of bubble gum and Smarties candy rolls. I couldn't wait to see my momma and daddy with my daughter, Aisha. My baby was six weeks old and had dark brown eyes. She looked like her dad.

On a warm Thursday afternoon in August, I was in the kitchen. When the green wall phone rang, I answered it, and my brother, Wardell, replied, "Hi, Sis." I had not seen him since my baby was born. He called to tell me that he had visited Aberdeen, and Momma wanted to know when I was coming home because we hadn't visited in eighteen months.

"Maybe next month," I told my brother. "Joseph is taking off from work."

Next, Wardell told me, "I am stopping by after church service on Sunday. I am bringing books for the girls and a baby swing for Aisha."

We chatted about other things for a few minutes, and then he said, "I am wondering how your husband is doing with finding his way around Atlanta."

"Yes, he is getting use to the southern ways of doing things . . . slow."

Wardell chuckled at that.

Then I told him, "Wardell, my baby is whining. I'll see you on Sunday afternoon."

"Love you, Sis."

I hung up, thinking, *My big brother has such a soothing voice.* Shortly after that, I picked up Aisha, who had dropped her blanket on the floor. She settled down when I gave her the pink pacifier. Then, I sat her back in her wooden highchair to play.

It was around 3:00 p.m., and my daughters were playing in the front yard in their shorts and T-shirts. Fatima and Rabia played hopscotch on the driveway with their school friends, Bonnie, and Amani. I allowed them to play outside until the sun went down. From down the street, the girls heard the happy musical sounds of the Good Humor ice cream truck with the Good Humor man who wore a paper hat. I heard the ice cream truck from my kitchen. Fatima and Rabia ran into the house to get money from their room. Most of the cones cost ten cents.

The girls gathered around the truck, calling out for their treats with their friends. Rabia got the Orange Push-Up, and Fatima paid for Oreo ice cream sandwiches. Other choices included cherry bomb ice cream and a waffle ice cream cone with chocolate.

While my daughters were outdoors, I prepared our dinner of chicken soup from my momma's recipes with leftover chicken. It was a simple meal with my fresh-baked biscuits. Usually, my biscuits came out flat and dry, but Joseph and the girls loved them with jelly.

While I prepared dinner, I observed Aisha from the corner of my eye, with Coco lying near her chair. Aisha was six months old and had two tiny teeth. I felt so good hearing her call me mama.

Aisha was quiet eating her Gerber baby food on her plastic plate. As I looked over at her, she smeared banana pudding in her hair and everywhere else. I just smiled at my adorable daughter and thought, *She needs a bath.*

By this time, Joseph was jangling his keys at the front door. I was so happy my husband was home so he could do the bath this time.

Joseph sauntered into the kitchen saying, "Hi, Babe." He still wore his work shirt and dusty shoes. He walked toward Aisha in the highchair.

"Hi, sweet girl!" He picked her up and held her tightly with her sticky face against his shirt, which she tugged on. Then he turned to me and with a smile said, "We are going to Aberdeen tomorrow."

I smiled in delight and shook my head in disbelief. "Wow, I am thrilled," I said, and then I added, "The girls have school tomorrow."

"No, they are out, it's a teacher's workday. And I am off for two days," my husband assured me. I leaned over and kissed him on the cheek. He smiled at me and announced, "I wanted to surprise you."

"Joseph, our car needs new tires," I told him, worried if we could even make it to Aberdeen.

But Joseph just gave me a reassuring hug. "Don't worry," he said, "it's all right."

When my daughters came in for dinner, I told them about the upcoming trip. They screamed and shouted, "I'm going to Aberdeen, I'm going to Aberdeen!"

༄

The next morning, I got my baby ready first. I dressed Aisha in a knitted pink dress with a tiny white cap. Fatima and Rabia wore striped shirts and jeans with T-strap Mary Janes. After rushing to get everyone else ready for the trip, I just threw on my bell-bottoms and a long-sleeved white blouse.

My hometown is about six hours from Atlanta. Before getting on the road with my family, I prayed with gratitude for having such a good family.

At 7:00 a.m., Joseph pulled the Impala into the driveway after getting gas at the service station. Our suitcases were packed for our two-day stay in Aberdeen and waiting on the front porch. He rushed out of the car, calling "Girls, go get into the car." He looked handsome in his green army jacket and dark shades. After he loaded the suitcases into the car, he came inside, scooped up Aisha in his arms, and took her out and strapped her into the rear-facing car seat. I hopped into the car and fastened my seat belt.

When Joseph turned the key and put it into drive, again there was a grinding noise from the engine. I sighed; we didn't have the money to buy a new car.

"Estell, it's okay," my husband assured me. Suddenly, he was backing out of the driveway and heading to the I-20 expressway for our drive to Aberdeen.

After Joseph drove for about three hours, our girls fell asleep. On the radio, Joseph listened to John Coltrane's modern jazz recording of "A Love Supreme." I remembered hearing this song many times on the radio when we lived in the brownstone on Halsey Street in New York.

I leaned close to my husband and said, "Excuse me, Joseph, the music is too loud. Would you turn it down? Our daughters are sleeping."

"Besides, Joseph," I continued, "you are speeding. You remember Daddy told you about the highway patrol and surprise check points."

"I know what he told me," Joseph said in a serious tone. "I am not worried about them."

"Do you want to get locked up in Anniston, Alabama? Remember I told you about my friend who got locked up by the highway patrol for speeding and was beaten in jail?"

"Okay, Babe, I just want to get us there safely."

Missing Aberdeen

Daddy was a tall man who was quiet and did not talk much, but he was wise, and he read his Bible year after year. Momma was a short lady who dressed up on Sundays in fancy hats with matching dress and gloves. She was always telling me about holding my head up and walking with confidence. I attended church with my parents, and we came home to eat Sunday dinner together with my sister, Mary, who always wore pretty dresses for church. Indeed, Sunday dinner was not complete without Momma's four-layer coconut cake for dessert. Daddy was a farmer and worked as a custodian at the Aberdeen City Hall for many years. He got up at 5:00 am and walked to work. My dad and mom sacrificed for our family, and they were an elegant couple who were married for 55 years.

I worried that if Joseph was pulled over for speeding, he could lose his license and get fined . . . or worse. Sometimes Joseph was cocky, and I didn't know what would happen if the highway patrol pulled him over.

Eventually, the humming of the car tires made me sleepy, so I laid my head back on the seat. When I woke up, we were in Montgomery, Alabama.

Joseph said, "I am stopping at Dreamland BBQ. Do you want spicy wings?"

"No, I am fine with my bottled water," I remarked.

"I can stop at Huddle House for a burger for you. You need to get some meat on your bones," Joseph replied.

I didn't say anything. I knew he thought I was too thin, but his statement annoyed me.

At the next exit, Joseph pulled off the highway and headed to Dreamland BBQ. The restaurant's big slogan was, "Ain't nothing like 'em nowhere."

"Are you getting that grilled BBQ again?" I asked Joseph. He replied that one thing he liked about driving in the South was those spicy ribs. When we got to the busy restaurant, he stepped out of the car and went inside to eat his messy barbeque. Soon, he returned to the car smacking his lips.

We drove again for a bit before Joseph announced, "We'll be in Aberdeen in a couple of hours." I looked over at him, gave him a smile, and winked. He reached over and squeezed my hand.

I dozed off for a while. When we stopped again, we were at the Dairy Kream in Tupelo, where Joseph bought fries and Nesquik chocolate drinks for the girls. I fed Aisha her bottle while Fatima and Rabia snacked and chatted.

With full tummies, the girls all fell asleep again, and so did I. When I woke up for a minute, Joseph said, "I am in Amory, Mississippi." I closed my eyes again, and the next thing I knew, we were driving up on Commerce Street with the magnolia trees. I said, "Fatima and Rabia, wake up!"

As Joseph pulled up the driveway at 308 Matubba Street, I saw my old white house with yellow daisies blooming in the yard. It was hotter than usual that day, and Momma was waiting on the porch wearing her pink plaid dress and a straw hat. She rushed down the steps and hollered, "Sis, you are home!" She wrapped her arms around me and looked over my shoulder. "Where is my grandbaby?" she demanded.

"Momma, Joseph is removing her from the car seat." I smiled at her excitement and impatience.

"Hey, Richard, I am so glad to see you," Momma called to him, using his legal middle name. While she waited for baby Aisha to appear, she shared plenty of hugs with Rabia and Fatima. "You girls are tall," she said as she admired them. "Do you like going to school in Atlanta?"

"Yes, ma'am, Grandma," Fatima answered.

By this time, Aisha was crying and licking her fingers, which she did when she was hungry, so I pulled out a disposable Gerber bottle.

"Give me my granddaughter," Momma said. "I'll take care of Ashy." I winced at the mispronunciation, but I knew my mom and dad were stuck in their southern ways with the girls' names, so I just let it go. Then Momma walked slowly to sit on the green porch chair and feed the baby her bottle, just as she had with Fatima and Rabia.

I asked Momma where Daddy was, but she just held Aisha close and kissed her. *I hope she doesn't have snuff in her mouth*, I thought. Momma chewed Days O Work chewing tobacco on the plantation and continued after we moved Aberdeen.

⁂

As I looked for Daddy, I recalled him joining the King David Masonic Lodge in 1958. It was on Vine Street and two blocks from our home in a gray brick building. Daddy went to meetings twice a month on

Monday nights after work. I asked Daddy often about what happened at those meetings, but he never told me.

I learned that Freemasonry is one of the oldest and largest fraternal organizations. It's for Christian men (like my dad) to build moral character and help their neighbors. In Aberdeen, it was one of the ways for Daddy and other men to meet for support and friendship and feel independent during segregation. On special occasions and for funerals, Daddy wore a yellow and gold hat, a white apron trimmed in blue, and white gloves. Daddy also wore a circular Masonic ring that represented the "eternity of the circle of the brotherhood." During this time, my uncles Curly Sims and Jason Sims joined the Masons, too. Years later, Daddy's grandson joined.

Momma joined the Order of the Eastern Star, part of the Masonic lodge. Members met twice a month for meetings and wore white dresses with a lime-green and red ribbon across their shoulders for meetings. The Eastern Star is a sisterhood social gathering for women who are related to Freemasons. I recalled that Momma and the other women members held fish fries to raise money for the needy. They sold plates of fresh fried catfish with potato salad and hush puppies for seventy-five cents to help the needy. Membership was a connection to feel respected, especially during segregation. It meant respect for these women who were housewives and maids.

I rushed into the living room and found my dad. He was a big man with thick hands and long legs, and he wore his khaki shirt and overalls. As I leaned down to hug him, he patted my back.

Daddy said, "Sis," while shaking his head. "I am glad to see you and your family! Sis, can you bring that big fan near my chair?"

"Sure, Daddy," I answered, and I did as he asked.

Daddy continued, "I want to hold my grandbaby." Daddy's shoes were off, and I knew that at seventy years old, he was tired from working two jobs. I sat on the green plastic couch, and as we chatted, I asked him, "Daddy, did you vote yet?"

"Yes, I finally voted at city hall," he said with pride in his voice. "I tried to vote for many years, and I could not pass the test." He bowed his head. "I placed my ballot in the box last year in November."

Just then, the girls ran into the living room and climbed up to sit in his lap. He caressed them, saying, "Fatma and Robia, did you get those toys and treats I sent last week?"

Rabia told him the chocolate was good and that Fatima licked off the icing from the lemon cookies. In the meantime, Joseph brought in the suitcases and was sweating. He walked over to hug my daddy, who told him, "Richard, you gained a little weight."

"Yes, Estell is a pretty good cook," my husband said as he gave me a wink.

I hurried to the porch, where Momma was talking to Aisha, and said, "Daddy wants his grandbaby."

Momma replied, "I am coming." She went into the living room holding a sleeping Aisha to gently place her in my daddy's arms.

He held her tightly with his wide hands and looked up at me. "Sis, you got a pretty baby." Then, looking down, Daddy said, "I am your grandpa," while he shook his head. "Lordy, I am blessed to see my baby girl. Sis, how much does she weigh?"

I told him she weighed ten pounds; Daddy never took his eyes of Aisha. Finally, I mumbled to Fatima and Rabia, "Girls, let's go to see Daddy's cat Misty in the backyard." Joseph stayed to talk to my dad and momma.

In the evening, Momma put her arms around Fatima's shoulder and said, "I have a surprise for you girls." She brought out new jeans and pullover shirts.

"Grandma, can I wear my new clothes?" Rabia asked excitedly.

Next, Momma said, "I got something to show you, too, Sis." I followed her into the bedroom, and Momma gave me the red-feather hat she had worn to New Grove Church for many years. I remembered how she would always wear Charlie perfume on Sundays, and she still had a bottle on the dresser, so I put some behind my ears. Then, with a big grin, I put my arm around Momma, and laid my head on her shoulder.

For the evening, Momma had piled up the table in the dining room with a tray of crispy fried chicken, buttered rolls, and potato salad and a pitcher of sweet tea. Joseph and the girls ate a lot, and Momma took care of Aisha so I could enjoy the meal with the family. Daddy liked a simple meal; he had fried pork chops, turnip greens, and corn bread with a glass of buttermilk. He always ate the same meal, especially corn bread and thick buttermilk. He liked Momma's apple turnovers made with fresh apples from the tree in the backyard.

My sister, Mary, stopped by before bedtime. During our chat, I told her that I was going back to work and leaving my daughters with a babysitter, and I said, "It is so painful." She listened to me just like she did as a little girl. She told me, "Sis, you are a good mother, and the girls will be fine," and she leaned in with a big hug. Her gentle voice was just what I needed to elevate my spirit.

Uncle Curly

In the morning, while my family packed to leave for Atlanta, the aroma coming from the kitchen was the smell of Folgers Coffee and fresh biscuits.

Soon, Joseph poured coffee into his tall cup, and eventually, Fatima and Rabia settled down for cornflakes. I was still in my housecoat with Aisha lying on my shoulder so I could burp her. While I drank my orange juice, Fatima opened the back door when she heard Daddy's yellow short-haired cat, Max, meowing for a treat; he scurried under the table, where she gave him a crumbled piece of her biscuit. Momma strolled into the kitchen and told the girls, "You are spoiling Max," but I could barely hear her voice because of the loud music. Gospel singer Mahalia Jackson's voice rang out from the Victrola in the living room as she sang "How I Got Over."

Soon, I heard a knock on the screen door; Momma bolted to the living room with me trailing behind her. Standing in the doorway was Daddy's brother, my Uncle Curly. He wore khaki pants with tall work boots.

Momma invited him in, and I greeted my Uncle Curly with a warm embrace. Curly was Daddy's brother, and he even looked like my dad, with high cheekbones and vanilla skin. He was always curious, and he talked a lot—not like my dad, who didn't talk much at all. He was a little shorter than my dad, too, and had the ever-present cigar hanging between his lips. Uncle Curly said hello to Joseph and shook his hand, asking him, "How was your trip to Aberdeen?"

Joseph told him, "I came through Tupelo and saw a deer crossing the road, so I slowed down. I'm getting used to these highways in the country."

I hollered for the girls, saying, "Your Uncle Curly is here." They ran to the living room wearing pink T-shirts and knee pants. Uncle Curly took Fatima's hands in his and shook them for a bit.

"You gave me a quarter when I was here last time," Fatima told him, which made Uncle Curly smile. Rabia sat beside her uncle, and he patted her on the head.

A moment later, Rabia told him, "That cigar looks nasty," and she wrinkled her nose as she frowned. The room was silent at first, but then Uncle Curly said, "Yeah, you are right."

"Curly, these kids always got something to say," Momma muttered. Quickly, I grabbed Rabia's hand and took her to the kitchen.

"Rabia, you embarrassed your Uncle Curly," I scolded.

"Mom, I did tell the truth, "She said defensively.

"Okay, I'll explain later," I said.

I returned to the living room where Uncle Curly was standing up and talking to my Momma about going to Fred's Dollar Store before work. "I am so happy that you stopped by, Uncle Curly," I told him, and he replied, "Y'all have a good trip home."

After we packed up for our trip home, Joseph put our suitcases in the car. Daddy and Momma did not want us to leave, but they knew that Joseph had to get back to work. My family got lots of hugs before leaving for Atlanta.

20

Visiting Parks

J OSEPH AND I were committed to making sure our daughters participated in physical activities so they could be healthy, make friends, and explore nature. This commitment came about because we wanted to instill family pride and provide emotional support as a buffer for the negative impact of racism. I never went to a decent park in Aberdeen, Mississippi, when I was growing up, but instead, I went to Newberger, the colored park near Franklin street and the projects.

When I left Aberdeen in 1964, the park was just a small area with swings for young children. Some days, the park was not clean, and the water fountain often did not work. I was excluded from the white park with a new swimming pool because of my dark skin. In September 2022, I visited the park during a trip to Aberdeen, and it was still run down, with no decent playground equipment. Aberdeen's residents have poverty-level income, so I wasn't surprised to see Newberger hadn't changed.

On a warm Saturday morning in September, Joseph drove us thirty minutes from our home on Rex Avenue to Grant Park, the fourth-largest park in Atlanta, which is located in a residential area known for its Victorian mansions and Craftsman bungalows. The park is a 131-acre green space and recreational area with miles of trails. Joseph and I had walked the 1.4-mile trail at the park just months earlier.

We arrived at the playground about 11:00 a.m. I had dressed my older girls in matching red-and-white sneakers and red caps and Aisha in a white dress with silver sandals. The girls quickly hopped out of the Impala and slammed the door. I hollered at them to slow down while Joseph got Aisha into the stroller.

Rabia ran to the slides and yelled, "Hi, Daddy!" as she got on. Fatima climbed the jungle gym with her legs dangling down. Two Black boys played on the swings adjacent to her, and a white girl with brown hair played nearby with a pink ball. With the warm sun beating down on us, I sat at the picnic table with my husband, who held our baby, Aisha, while she drank her Carnation milk. I kept an eye on my daughters.

After a while, I saw the white girl and Rabia playing with her ball. I thought these girls were having fun until I saw the mother of the white girl jerk her away and grab the ball. Immediately, I ran over to see what had happened, and Joseph trailed behind me. Rabia roared, "Mama, that woman called me a nigger. Did I do something wrong?"

I replied, "No; some white parents are mean!" I pulled her tightly to me while clenching my teeth in anger. Joseph shook his head and said a few curse words under his breath. Finally, he tapped Rabia on the head and told her, "You are safe." Fatima stood staring at her sister because she had never seen Rabia so upset or treated in such a mean way. The girls had played with white kids in New York, so they didn't expect this racist attitude on the playground.

I thought back to an incident that took place when I was growing up. When we first moved to Aberdeen, I went to Maier Jewelry on

Commerce Street with Momma. I saw a white girl by the counter and said hi, but she turned her head away, pretending not to see me. That hurt my feelings, but I never told Momma because I was ashamed; I masked my tears with a smile.

"Hey, are we ready to head to the zoo?" I asked brightly.

Holding her long braid, Fatima said, "Mama, I want to see Willie B[3]." I smiled. I replied, "I showed you this stocky animal with big hands from Africa on *WSB-TV News*."

Joseph grabbed our tote bags, and I pushed Aisha in her blue stroller. I smiled as I watched my daughters skipping along the sidewalk. It was one o'clock, and the sweltering sun was on our faces as we headed to the zoo.

Zoo Atlanta had free admission. We were lined up to enter the large wooden building with another family with a stroller and kids crying and running around. Animal spaces in zoos were designed very differently than they are today, and the Zoo Atlanta animal displays were all inside at that time.

I picked up a pamphlet and read about Willie B, pandas, and zebras while Joseph warned the girls, "Do not touch the animals." Shortly, we were inside, and I pushed Aisha, who had fallen asleep. Fatima pointed to pandas sitting on a log, and Rabia peeped through the bars while lots of children called out to the panda with white and black fur. Just around the corner was the famous Willie B, the 456-pound gorilla with thick, springy hair covering his body. He was feeding on bamboo. Fatima and Rabia screamed and jumped up and down. Some of the kids threw flowers to Willie B.

---

[3] Willie B. was a famous western lowland gorilla who lived at the zoo from 1961 until his passing in 2000 at the age of forty-two. He was named after the former mayor of Atlanta, William Berry Hartfield. Willie B. was remembered by generations of Atlantans and was the icon for the transformation of the zoo. He lived indoors for twenty-seven years until they built an outdoor area for him in 1988. Learn more at https://zooatlanta.org/animal-legend/willie-b/.

If Grits Could Talk

I stood close to my husband as we watched the brown gorilla. I was exhausted from focusing on my daughters after the playground altercation and from carrying Aisha on my hip.

By then, she was nine months old and weighed about twenty pounds. I leaned on Joseph; my feet were aching. He suggested we grab a bite to eat, and I whispered to the girls, "Let's go."

We stopped at a small food stand, where the girls had corn dogs with a lot of ketchup. Next, Rabia got candy cotton, which ended up all over her face. Next, Joseph ordered hamburgers with a bottle of hot sauce and sweet tea. Once we'd had our fill, we headed to our car.

In October, Joseph and I decided to see the Etowah Indian Mounds State historic site near Cartersville, Georgia. We wanted our daughters to learn about the Native people and their rituals. I looked outside in my purple housecoat after breakfast that morning and saw cloudy skies. I hollered to Joseph, who was checking the air in the tires, and asked if we were still taking our trip that morning. He waved yes!

By 12:30 p.m., we were in heavy traffic for an hour and twenty minutes on northbound I-75. The girls looked comfortable in the back seat—Rabia with her brown teddy bear and Fatima with her Raggedy Ann doll. I glanced at my baby, who was whining a bit, but she soon settled down.

While we drove, I thought back to my high school textbooks; there were no mentions of the Native Americans as the first Americans. Instead, I learned that indigenous people lost most of their land and control of their reservations.

The street in Aberdeen where I grew up, and where my parents still lived, is named Matubba for Native Americans. Other tribes that settled in Mississippi were the Choctaw and Chickasaw. When I watched movies in 1955, I saw white actors portray Native Americans with painted faces. It took years for Hollywood to change this image. Like our history, their stories were lost and forgotten.

Visiting Parks

As Joseph turned the car into the historic area, the Etowah Indian Mounds were close by. Etowah has three main platform mounds and three lesser mounds. Joseph parked near the front, and the girls strolled into the visitors bureau while laughing and chewing bubble gum. Joseph and I follow them, with me carrying Aisha on my hip. After Joseph talked to the attendant, I picked up a couple of flyers. I saw my daughters looking at the brown beads and metal bracelets made by Indian people, which represented their deep traditions and beliefs. I purchased two green bracelets, which meant abundance and hope, for Rabia and Fatima. Quickly, I received big hugs!

Next, I stepped out of the building into the clean-smelling air, and the girls began running on the sidewalk. Then, Joseph led us into the doorway of the tall, coned teepee near the entrance. We learned that another name for the structure was *wigwam*; the tent had a flap at the top to allow smoke to escape. Rabia and Fatima touched the three poles that held up the structure.

Fatima asked, "Daddy, what did they eat?" Joseph said they would hunt fish in the river and grow corn and vegetables. Then we went to Mound A, which is sixty-three feet tall and was the home of Natives American many years ago. The mound seems like it is touching the sky. I walked the long trail by the mounds with Fatima and Rabia, who kept looking at the historical masterpieces. These mounds were rectangular with flat surfaces and had been used for thousands of years.[4] While I took a picture with my Kodak Tele-Instamatic camera at the mound, the girls snacked on potato chips and Oreo cookies.

In the late afternoon, we all headed to the car. As we got close, Joseph said, "I can't believe this; I just bought a new tire!" Sure enough, one of our car tires was flat. "I'll get the spare tire from the trunk. Estell, wait at the visitors bureau with the girls." I stayed in the visitors

---

[4] The Georgia State Parks website says Etowah Mounds is the most intact Mississippian Culture site in the Southeast. Learn more at https://gastateparks.org/EtowahIndianMounds.

center for an hour until Joseph came inside, sweating and with grimy hands, and yelled, "Estell, I fixed the tire; let's go."

Joseph walked back outside with his shoulder slumped. I said, "It's going to be all right, Honey. Despite the flat tire, I learned about the culture of indigenous people with my family."

21
Returning to Work

May 1976

I THOUGHT ABOUT going back to work for months. I had left my job at Bell South for maternity leave in February. Then I had my baby girl, Aisha, and Fatima and Rabia became big sisters. It had been almost a year and a half since I had worked for a paycheck.

At first, I had planned to return to work after eight weeks, but I was not too fond of being away from my children all day. I felt comfortable being home with my daughters and my new baby and watching them play and grow. Plus, Joseph always mentioned the girls needed me. Just thinking about going back to work made me feel guilty about leaving my girls with a stranger. It was difficult for me to trust someone with my fourteen-month-old baby and my young daughters. Still, I wanted a stable income for our family.

Most important, I wanted to spend quality time with my children to reinforce positive behavior. As a stay-at-home mom, I made sure they were eating right and brushing their teeth. Other times, I enjoyed giving Aisha a bath in the evening, with yellow ducks floating in the water. Afterward, Fatima and Rabia liked taking a bubble bath with its fruity smell and splashing in the water. It was messy in the bathroom with towels and toys, but then we worked together to clean up.

When I was growing up in Aberdeen on the plantation, my momma, Estell, picked cotton in the field. She worked to put food on the table. Even in the winter, when Momma was not picking cotton, she was canning peaches, sewing quilts, and scrubbing clothes in a washtub to provide for our family. I spent my childhood in poverty on a plantation and picked cotton at six years of age. I wanted things to be different for my daughters.

On a Monday morning in April, I was preparing breakfast before school. Fatima and Rabia sat with their Mickey Mouse bowls as they waited for cereal. I grabbed for the tall box of cornflakes from the cabinet, but it was empty with just crumbs and the carton of milk had just a half cup left.

Rabia looked at me and asked, "What are we going eat?" Fatima chimed in with, "I am so hungry, Mom!" Not knowing what to tell them, I grew nervous. I opened the refrigerator; it was bare, with only a can of red fruit punch left over from the night before.

"You can eat a couple of biscuits from dinner last night," I told them. The girls looked gloomy. I continued, "I forgot to go shopping, and Daddy will pick up food this afternoon." They chewed on dry biscuits while I worried about their next meal. Soon, they hugged me before grabbing their book bags and heading to school.

Afterward, I just wanted to kick something; I felt angry like I did as a child in Aberdeen when my family was hungry. I couldn't deal with seeing my daughters hungry; I couldn't deal with our financial

Returning to Work

situation anymore. We had been struggling like this for a month, but I kept hoping things would change. My dad often sent me money orders to help. I received fruits and vegetables from our mosque; I clipped coupons from Kroger to save money on groceries.

I worried all week about our finances and how we could improve our situation. By Friday evening, I knew things must change. As I waited for Joseph to get home from work, I sat on the red love seat, gripping the handle and wondering about his reaction to my decision to return to work. I was not ready to argue with him.

When I had talked to him about three months earlier, he was adamant about me staying home. But I was struggling, and not just because money was tight. I never changed out of my pajamas many days, and I did not remember whether I had brushed my teeth. My routine was the same every day: cooking, doing laundry, ironing my husband's shirts, cleaning the bathtub rings, and changing diapers I felt like I had stepped out of society and had a different identity. I was not sure who I was anymore.

On weekdays, the yellow school bus pulled up to the bus stop at 2:48 p.m. to drop off the children. Each day, I waited patiently with Aisha in the stroller holding her brown teddy bear and our puppy, Coco, on a leash. The girls would hop off the bus with their book bags, yelling, "Hey, Mama!" Then they would run to hug their baby sister. Of course, Oreo cookies and milk were waiting for them at home. I was grateful that they'd made it home safe again. I felt my world was complete with my daughters.

At 6:00 p.m., I heard the engine of the Chevrolet Impala in the driveway. I checked my makeup in the mirror to be sure I was ready for this conversation; I knew I would tell Joseph in a moment of my decision to go back to work. I sat on the love seat in my light-blue dress with hoop earrings and flat brown shoes and waited for the door to open. I wanted to change my way of thinking; I had been down in the dumps because of our financial uncertainty. For a while,

If Grits Could Talk

I had been eating chocolate and drinking sweet tea all day because my spirits were low. I finally decided that I needed to be productive if I wanted to improve our home life.

When my husband opened the screen door, he said, "Hi, Babe," and then reached over to kiss me on the cheek. I liked the sound of his deep voice, and he looked handsome with his toned muscles showing through his beige zipped jacket and khaki pants. He was holding a bag from Walmart with toys for our daughters. Joseph asked, "Where are the girls?" I told him the baby was with our neighbor Rose, and Fatima and Rabia were playing in the backyard.

Joseph went to wash his hands, and I poured a cup of Folgers Coffee for him and returned to the couch. As he sat down, Joseph said with a smile, "You look lovely tonight."

I mumbled a thank you. I asked him how he liked the bologna and mustard sandwich I'd made for his lunch, and he said it was just right.

Joseph and I had been married for ten years. We'd had some rough times, but we always worked through things together as a team, and I hoped we would be able to do that again. I took a deep breath and said, "Well, Joseph, I decided to go back to work."

That smile just disappeared from his face. He put his right hand on his face and looked at me for a second. Slowly, he uttered, "I want to see you when I get home. Did you think about our daughters?"

"Yes, I did," I said curtly. "But our family can no longer live on just one paycheck. You need to eliminate that pride and see that we are broke." I added that our mortgage had been late the previous month. "And you still owe Big Mike's Repair Shop for the tires."

Joseph reached over to squeeze my hand. "You are right, Babe; I have been stubborn. It is your choice; I'll make sure our girls' needs are met and there's a roof over their heads. With you working, we can increase our budget."

I was happy that we were in this together. "Surprise," I said in a whisper. "I made stuffed peppers for dinner with garlic mashed potatoes and string beans. We'll eat soon. Do you want to watch the news with Walter Cronkite?"

"Yes," Joseph responded, "I trust that guy."

I dreaded talking to my daughters about returning to work. On Saturday morning, I went to their room and watched them for a minute. Their bedroom had short yellow drapes and twin beds with light-green pillows for the older girls and a crib for Aisha, though she sometimes slept with her dad and me when she was fussy. Aisha played with her torn brown teddy bear and pushed around the red toy Ford truck her dad had bought for her. I sat down with my baby and next to the girls on the carpet while they watched Scooby Doo on the square Sony television in their room, which I bought for them after I had Aisha.

I had to tell them eventually. I finally said, "Girls, I got some news. Mommy is returning to work, and I'm getting a babysitter for you."

Rabia asked, "Mom, you won't be home when I get off the school bus?"

"No," I answered, growing nervous.

Fatima gave me a blank stare before asking, "Who will help me with my homework?"

I sighed as I held Aisha close in my arms. I felt torn inside, knowing how much I loved my daughters. But I continued, "I need to help your dad with the bills. Indeed, my schedule will change, and we will figure this out together."

Suddenly, Fatima said, "Daddy already told us that you are going back to work, and he will make breakfast."

A big grin spread across my face. Quickly, I put my arms around my daughters. I treasured every minute with them that morning.

On Monday morning, the sun was pouring through my window. I was cheerful because I had contacted my friend Rose to help me find a job and a babysitter. While I waited for her, I sat on the floor stacking blocks with fourteen-month-old Aisha. I didn't get the chance to just sit and play with her very often; she had been walking for three months, and she liked pushing her shopping cart to show off her skills. She was a little spoiled by her dad, but she was cute in her yellow dress and white tights. With the TV playing a *Tom and Jerry* cartoon, I could barely hear when Rose knocked on the door.

I first met Rose when we moved to Rex Avenue. She was about my age and had loose, bouncy curls. She liked wearing deep-red lipstick and a thick gold necklace. When she wore a miniskirt, her rusty knees drew my attention, and I always thought, *Sweetie, you need to use some Vaseline on those knees.* We became good friends over time, and I visited her often in her home.

"Hi, Rose, come in. You can sit on the big sofa chair."

Rather than sitting down, Rose swooped up Aisha and then held her tightly. "Estell, Aisha is charming with those brown eyes. It was fun watching her when you went shopping. I know you told me on the phone that you are returning to work. How does Joseph feel about you going back to work."

"He plans to take off early from work to help me with the girls," I assured her.

"I am not available to babysit when you go back to work, but I will help while you look for a job."

We chatted for a while, and then I mentioned, "Rose, I enjoyed our lunch last week at your home, especially the pineapple upside-down cake."

"It was my mom's recipe, so thank you," she said with a look of pride. "And speaking of eating, unfortunately, I must rush home to prepare dinner. Anyway, sister Estell, I came over to tell you that you are a fantastic mother, and you should do what's in your heart." Then, she grabbed her shoulder bag and stood up to leave.

As Rose walked to the front door, she said she would call me soon, and then she said bye to my baby girl. Aisha waved and gave her a smile! Wow, my baby is growing up fast!

Returning to Work

A few days later, I was thinking about how my routine at home would change when I returned to work, which worried me a little. But I felt isolated sometimes, and I missed going to work. I sat down at the kitchen table with a cup of green tea and my journal, which had a red binding. Fatima and Rabia had left for school, and Rose was watching Aisha. Adjacent to the table, Coco, our poodle, was gnawing on a meat bone. I thought about how the interview I had, when the employer had asked, "How many children do you have?" I had been so frustrated because, sure enough, fathers do not face the same question. Since I'd started working years ago, employers looked at my gender and decided that I would be less committed to the job.

Around 2:00 p.m., I called Bell South. I spoke to Todd, the manager, who told me I had taken off more than three months, so my job was gone. I wasn't sure what the company policy was for maternity leave, but it was stressful not to get my job back. After working with white women on the job, I was fairly sure I was being discriminated against because I was not white. As a Black woman, my mental health and stability were not worthy of support.

Next, I looked for a job in the Help Wanted section of the *Atlanta Journal-Constitution* classified ads. Finally, I turned to the "Help Wanted: Women" section: listed were jobs for secretaries, bookkeepers, daycare teachers, maids, and servers. Since I didn't have a college education, my choices would be limited. *Nevertheless, I will do my best.*

I hopped on the Marta bus at 7:00 a.m. on a cool Monday morning. Joseph was watching our daughters that morning while I went job hunting. It was tough leaving my sweet daughters, especially Aisha. I hurried out the door to keep from crying and prayed that I would get a job. I brought my peanut butter and jelly sandwich and Lay's potato chips so I didn't have to spend any money on lunch, and I brought my book, *The Bluest Eye* by Toni Morrison, to read on this long trip.

After an hour's ride, I got off the bus at Marietta and Broad Streets and headed to Rich's department store. They had run an ad for a job in the accounting department, but when I got there, I was told the job was already filled. I was disappointed, but I was also determined to find a job, that day if possible. I found a phone booth, put a quarter into the slot, and called two companies I had on my list. Neither was hiring.

I had already been looking for a job for three weeks. A week earlier, I'd taken a math test at the Mason Collection Agency, and when I finished, the receptionist told me I scored a sixty-seven. I had a sinking feeling in my stomach that I had failed. She said that I could retake the test, and I said okay, but I knew I wasn't going back. I felt shame that I dropped out of Tuskegee in 1964. I just wanted to take whatever job that I could get.

I decided to walk to Forsyth Street and apply for the waitress job at Anna Café. As I swung open the door, I observed the walls with pink flowers and inhaled the aroma of fresh coffee. It was a busy café at lunchtime. I approached the circular serving counter, and when the server tried to hand me a plastic menu, I asked for an application. The server told me, "Sweetie, you don't need an application." Then, she turned toward the back of the café and hollered, "Miss Betsy, this lady is looking for a job."

I sat at the counter while I waited. Miss Betsy came out of the kitchen wearing a white apron over a short-sleeved shirt and a skirt that showed her thick knees.

"Hey, I am the manager," she greeted me. "What is your name?" I introduced myself, and then she continued, "I hear that you are looking for a job. It doesn't pay much, but I need help. Are you interested in the job?"

Returning to Work

"Yes, I am," I said, trying not to sound too excited.

Betsy said, "It's five days a week and some Saturdays. You wear a light-blue uniform and white shoes. Hey, Joanna," she called to the server, "give me a pen and paper." Joanna handed both to her, and she passed them to me. "Put your name and address on the pad. When can you start?"

"Next week," I replied.

"I need you to come for a training day so you can learn how to use the cash register and do takeout orders. See you on Monday, Estell."

After I left the café, I smiled. I finally had a job; I felt pretty good.

22

Got the Job—Now What?

I WAS HIRED AT Anna Café. I walked out of the building with my shoulders back and my head up like I had won a lottery ticket. I thought about getting my first paycheck and taking my daughters to Toys "R" Us on Buford Highway.

I stepped out onto Forsyth Street. It was sunny and windy that day. As I walked onto the sidewalk, I paused by a gray flowerpot to check my Mickey Mouse watch because I needed to catch the Marta bus. With the sun in my eyes, I bumped into a young lady with a slicked-back ponytail. She looked stylish in her short leather jacket and silver sneakers. I said, "Excuse me," but she turned her nose up and kept walking; I thought, *What is her problem?*

On my way to the bus stop, I observed two tall white guys wearing cowboy hats and puffing on cigarettes that created a smoky haze around them. The scene reminded me of the Marlboro Man on TV, where the ads for a cigarette featured a man looking rugged and robust. That made me think about my daddy, who never smoked. It's a nasty habit.

Continuing my walk, I observed the street did not have one shred of stray paper, like someone had used a broom to clean the sidewalks.

Soon, I stopped to buy the *Atlanta World* newspaper from a newspaper vending machine. My dime got stuck in the machine, and while I was shaking it, an old lady with thick gray hair stopped and asked, "Honey, do you need some help?"

"No, it just opened." I reached in to grab my paper.

With its bustling downtown traffic and loud car horns, Atlanta was starting to feel like home. However, I missed living in my brownstone in Brooklyn and riding the subway. I shook away that thought and focused instead on how excited I was to tell my husband about my job.

My thoughts raced as I walked. *I will be working and contributing to our family. However, I still need a babysitter, and I'll check with my neighbors at the mosque. Then, of course, I need references. I am starting to feel overwhelmed.* I sighed. *I know I have friends who will help me. I could find a phone booth and call Joseph, but I'll miss the 6:05 bus.*

I crossed the street from Forsyth onto Marietta and joined the other passengers waiting at the Marta bus stop. I wanted to sit down on the bench because my feet were aching from my brown wedge heels, but it was occupied. Nearby waited a mother with a crying baby, a young college student with a ponytail, and a short lady with stylish cornrows and beads at the end of her braids.

About five minutes later, the blue-and-orange bus pulled up, and I stood in line waiting to board behind the other passengers. I climbed on, nodded to the driver, and dropped my twenty-five cents into the slot. When I turned to sit down, I made eye contact with the same lady with the tight curls. I introduced myself with a smile, and said, "Hi, do you ride the bus every day?"

"My husband drove me to work today. Usually, I ride two buses to get to my job at the dry cleaner in Decatur. By the way, I am Isabelle."

"It's nice to meet you," I said. I began settling down in my plastic seat. "You know, Isabelle, it smells like dirty socks with no air conditioner on this bus, but it is a cheap ride." Then, I watched as she pulled out the *Ebony* magazine she had tucked in her handbag. She turned a few pages, and I saw singer and actress Diana Ross featured in a red sequined dress.

"She was in that movie," I commented, and I could see Isabella's excitement as she agreed, "I know, *Mahogany*, and with that handsome guy, Billy Dee Williams, who was her costar." We chuckled.

"When I was young, Momma kept *Ebony* on our coffee table," I shared. "I still read it because it shows Black people working as doctors and teachers and other middle-class jobs, and Black people who are leaders and own their own homes. And celebrities who dress fine," I added, and Isabelle nodded her agreement. "None of the other popular magazines even show Black families, and when they do show us, we have big lips and greasy hairstyles." I continued, chatting about how Black people were called Negroes in 1960, and now we were Afro Americans.

Then, I heard the bus driver yell, "Turn down that music before I put you off this bus." I turned and saw the guy with the ponytail from the bus stop; he sat across the aisle from us and had a square boom box on his lap. He cut off the sound. Isabelle leaned toward me and remarked, "That's a groovy song, 'Don't Go Breaking My Heart' by Elton John with Kiki Dee. Wow, it's good song." It was my turn to nod in agreement.

I noticed Isabelle had some toy trucks with her, and when I mentioned them, she said, "I have a baby boy, Tyrone. He is three years old," and she quickly pulled a picture out of her wallet of a little boy wearing an Atlanta Braves outfit.

"He is adorable," I told her. "I am looking for a babysitter. Do you know if yours is available?"

"I'm not sure, but she is a kind lady."

"Because I got a new job and am looking for a sitter for my three girls," I told her.

"Okay, I will find out for you." Isabelle took out a pad from her purse, handed it to me, and said, "Jot down your phone number."

Suddenly, the bus came to a quick stop and the driver yelled, "Rex Avenue!" I got off the bus, and Isabelle followed me.

"Do you live here?" I asked.

Isabelle said, "Just around the corner. My husband and I bought the house at the end of the block three months ago. I am amazed that you are my neighbor. I live in the house at the end of the street with the other burgundy door." We walked for five minutes down the sidewalk and parted ways at the corner.

Isabelle said, "It was nice talking to you, and I'll see if she, my babysitter, Lucinda, is available," and she waved goodbye.

When I got to my house, I climbed the steps and unlocked the door. The moment I stepped inside, I bumped my foot on Aisha's wooden blocks—ouch! Then our dog, Coco, began barking, so I put water in his bowl. Next, I went to the kitchen and noticed a note Joseph had left on the refrigerator.

Hi Umi[5] I took the girls for ice cream at Dairy Queen.

And he signed it with a big red heart. Then, I circled the living room, thinking about my job and how I needed a babysitter. *Let's hope Isabelle remembers to check with her babysitter. It hurts to think that I am leaving my children with a stranger, but I will feel better if the babysitter is referred by someone I know.*

About an hour later, I heard the car doors slamming in the driveway. Soon, my husband was walking through the front door and into the living room with my daughters.

"I got a job!" I hollered.

Joseph reached out to kiss me on the cheek, and then said, "I am so happy for you." Rabia and Fatima joined by my side holding tall milk shakes and wearing big smiles. At the same time, I grabbed fourteen-month-old Aisha from Joseph and cuddled her in my arms.

---

[5] *Umi* is the African name for mother.

Got the Job—Now What?

She pressed her sticky face onto mine while she mumbled, "Mommy." Soon, everyone settled down, and I told the girls to go play in the living room because I wanted to chat with their dad.

After they left the room, Joseph asked, "What kind of a job?"

"It is a waitress job on Forsyth Street, at Anna Café."

"I thought that you were going back to Bell South."

"No, the company did not hold my assignment for me," I told my husband sadly.

"Babe, you liked dressing up and working in accounting in New York. Are you sure that you want this job?"

"Yes, Joseph, you are getting on my nerves; you know I really wanted a job. I am sorry, but you deserve more money. Anyway, I met this lady on the bus, Isabelle, who lives on this block, and she told me that her babysitter might be accepting new children. I am nervous about these changes."

My husband put his arm around my shoulder and said gently, "So, when will you start?"

"I believe next week. Joseph, do we have enough money to pay for a babysitter?"

"No, but I will borrow money from the payday loan place on Memorial Avenue."

I could feel my heart beat faster. "You know that place is a rip-off. You can borrow the money from your job."

"All right, that's a good idea."

23

Lucinda, the Babysitter

ABOUT TWO DAYS LATER, Isabelle called to tell me that Lucinda was available, and she wanted to meet me. I wrote down the phone number and immediately called Lucinda. I asked if I could come over for an interview, and she agreed.

While I walked to Lucinda's, three houses down the street, I wasn't sure what to expect with a babysitter for the first time. Isabelle told me that she was a kind lady. As I walked to her home, I prayed that she was also a competent one. *What is my next option if she doesn't work out?*

I walked up the faded steps and glanced around to see a fuzzy gray cat lying in the rocking chair. Adjacent to the door was an *Atlanta Journal-Constitution* newspaper, with President Gerald Ford on the front page. I rang the doorbell.

"Hi, Estell, come on in," Lucinda greeted me. She was a big woman with a thick arms, a reddish complexion, and a gap between her front teeth. It seemed like her dress was too small, with the buttons barely latching on her blouse. "Sweetie, have a seat on the sofa."

When we had spoken on the phone, I mentioned that I was looking for a babysitter for my three children. I told her that I'd lived in the neighborhood for two years and had just found a job. Lucinda replied that she could help me. "I pay close attention to each child and keep a clean place," she had assured me.

I sat down on the plastic-covered purple couch and noticed the living room smelled like Lysol. I observed baby swings, colorful animal pictures on the wall, and a bunch of teddy bears sitting neatly in a corner. Lucinda began telling me about the three children she watched during the week, including Isabelle's son.

I watched Lucinda's cat meowing and scratching on the screen door. When she noticed, she said, "That's our cat, Bobo, who sleeps on the porch," and then she yelled, "Be quiet!"

Lucinda then turned her attention back to me. "Anyway," she said, "I have been babysitting for six years and worked as a midwife in Winder, Georgia. I left that small town because they burned a big cross in our front yard. After all, my daddy was a member of the NAACP with a voting rights sign in our yard. I was scared for my life. So then, I moved to Atlanta. Recently, I got divorced, and it's just me and my five-year-old daughter, Lulu. I check with their parents to be sure each child has been immunized for measles and whopping cough. Otherwise, I refuse to allow them to come to my daycare."

As she talked, I thought about my daughters. I wondered about Aisha, who was a toddler. For instance, when I tried to get my baby to eat her green beans, she would refuse to open her mouth. I'd have to promise her a yummy snack, like banana pudding. She could be kind of fussy at times and even throw her sippy cup.

I knew how active and curious Rabia was, and she liked asking questions. I imagined that she would be opening the closets and looking into the refrigerator to see what's inside.

And quiet Fatima liked to wear beads on her long braids, but I would have to warn Lucinda not to touch her hair or clothes because Fatima would think that's rude. "Let's go into the kitchen. I am frying fresh salmon on the stove with onions and spicy peppers." I followed her in as she continued chatting; the kitchen smelled like my momma's cooking in Mississippi.

"Can I fix you a plate?" Lucinda offered.

"No, I've eaten already."

"Pardon me," she apologized. "I've been running my mouth. How old are your children?"

"I have three daughters. Baby Aisha is fourteen months old, Fatima is nine years, and Rabia is eight. I will need you to watch them five days a week."

Lucinda said, "I charge fifteen dollars a week for all three, and I am open from 6:30 a.m. till 7:00 p.m."

We chatted while I sat at the table for a while. I grabbed my small red purse when I remembered that my daughters were waiting for me to make sugar cookies. Lucinda walked me to the door.

"I can see that the place is clean, and you seem to care about children," I told her. "I will talk to my husband about hiring you, and I'll give you a call tomorrow. Have a nice evening."

Lucinda waved as I left to walk back home.

Joseph and I decided to hire Lucinda as the new babysitter. We had a long discussion, and my husband told me he had a gut feeling that made him uncertain, but I was willing to take a chance and pleaded with him to try her. Finally, he nodded, sure.

A few days later, I called Lucinda and hired her. Then, I went to meet her with my family. Joseph was cordial, the girls liked her, and Aisha slowly talked to her. At that time, I set up a plan with Lucinda about dropping off my daughters and Joseph picking them up in the evening.

On my first day of work, my Emerson clock radio woke me at 5:00 a.m. I sat on the bed, thinking, *It is time for morning prayers in Islam at sunrise.* I rushed to the bathroom to wash my hands and face, and then. I grabbed my prayer rug and said the morning prayer, Fajr, in a clean place in the dining room. I was seeking peace and harmony for my family. After I got dressed, I strolled into my daughters' bedroom.

I stood close to the twin beds where they slept peacefully and watched the rise and fall of their chests as they breathed. I leaned down to rub Fatima's thick braids and then kissed Rabia on the cheek. Then, I moved closer to Aisha's crib and picked her up in my arms. I felt her warm face touching mine, and I felt a tightness in my throat. Once I had her dressed, I picked up her brown teddy bear and the white blanket to keep her warm.

Next, I packed the baby bag with her juice bottle and food, which I'd labeled with her name. Before I left the house, I walked into the bedroom to wake my husband but then decided to leave a note for him on the breakfast table instead. In it, I announced, "I am a working woman," and scribbled a heart at the bottom.

At 6:30 a.m., in the visible glow of the sunlight, I left my house to walk to Lucinda's. I rang the doorbell, and Lucinda opened the door.

"Good morning. Come on in," she greeted. I entered the living room, and Lucinda grabbed the beige baby bag with Aisha's blanket, teddy bear, and food. Then she said, "I'll take the baby."

All I wanted to do was keep hugging my baby; slowly, I handed Aisha to her. Lucinda began rocking my baby in her arms, saying, "You got my phone number."

"Of course, I do," I answered in a soft tone. I felt my eyes getting wet so I kissed Aisha on the cheek, said "Bye, sweet baby," and I quickly headed for the front door.

Once outside, I shook off my sadness and rushed to the Marta bus stop, where I said hello to two neighbors who were waiting with me. I carried my shoulder purse with my red bound journal and my book, *The Shining* by Stephen King, so I could work through my fears and get lost in the story. Finally, the blue-and-yellow Marta bus pulled up; it was 6:50 a.m.

As I dropped my twenty-five cents into the slot, I greeted the bus driver with a cheery, "Hi, Jerome." I made my way to the back corner, but instead of opening my book or writing, I pondered how I had decided to get this job and leave my baby with a new babysitter. I was in a daze for most of the forty-five-minute ride. Finally, the driver called out Marietta Street. I followed the other riders off the bus and briskly walked to Forsyth Street until I reached the Healey Building, the last major skyscraper built in Atlanta during the city's pre-World War I construction boom.

It was a cool Monday morning; I entered the Healey Building, where Anna Café was located on the first floor; I was fifteen minutes early. I knew my first day on the job would be fantastic because I had taken the menu home and learned the items over the weekend. I felt like a working girl with my light-blue uniform's creased sleeves and a skirt that hit just below my knees, my white Walmart shoes, and a square apron trimmed in blue and tied in the back. My tight pantyhose itched my legs, though.

I made a quick stop at the bathroom down the hall. I needed to fix my makeup, reapply my pink lipstick, and check my Afro. I had been crying, and I needed to look confident. I knew this was a low-wage job; however, I just wanted to help my family to survive. I was somewhat nervous, but I could bring on a smile.

24

A New Adventure Begins

I MARCHED INTO ANNA CAFÉ, where the slogan "The Best Coffee in Atlanta" greeted customers on the signage as they entered. The circular beige counter was filled with older white folks talking about President Jimmy Carter and his brother Billy from Plains, Georgia. The dim lights hanging from the ceiling illuminated the menu painted on the wall in white and red letters facing the counter: breakfast meals, hamburgers, biscuits, donuts, and drinks. The smell of brewing coffee made me feel like I was home. I sat down on the tall counter stool, and an awkward, uncomfortable silence followed. I shrugged and looked at the Coca-Cola clock on the wall.

I saw Marybelle, the waitress I'd met when I got hired, waiting on a customer. Soon, she greeted me with a smile. Marybelle was tall with dark brown hair, freckles around her nose, and red rouge on her cheeks. She yelled to the owner, "Anna! The new waitress is here." Then she leaned over to me and mumbled, "Do you want a cup of coffee, Estell?"

"No, just a glass of orange juice," I responded.

"I have a customer," Marybelle answered, "and I'll check back soon."

I rested my legs on the stool's footrest while I waited. In front of me sat a napkin holder, a glass sugar dispenser with a metal top, and salt and pepper shakers. While I was taking a mental inventory of things on the counter, a man sitting at the other end who wore a Braves baseball cap yelled, "My coffee is cold. I wonder why I come here before work."

Marybelle ignored his comment and just said that would be sixty-five cents. He replied, "You all have gone up on your prices," and he paid the bill. She smiled politely and told him, "I'll see you tomorrow."

Then, I met Jessie Lee, an older dark-skinned woman with gray hair who wore a hairnet and looked like she had snuff in her lower lip. She reminded me of Momma dipping snuff when I was a little girl in Aberdeen. Jessie Lee's light-blue uniform was starched, and she had a handkerchief in her breast pocket.

"How are you doing, sweetie?" Jessie Lee asked me. I said I was okay. "I will be training you today; you need to make eye contact with the guests," she said, sounding very matter of fact.

Meanwhile, Anna, the owner, had come out of the kitchen wearing her long white apron. "Morning," she said to me. "I am happy you are wearing your uniform. Estell, did you bring your social security card and your birth certificate?" I told her I did. Then Anna said, "I want you to fill out the application. It's just one page." As I took the application and the pen she handed me, Anna continued in a serious tone, "I pay eighty cents an hour plus tips, five days a week. You are allowed three days off a month; if you miss more than three days, you will be terminated." Then she flashed a big smile and announced, "I am a country girl from Ellijay, Georgia, and we are like family here."

Before the noon rush started at 11:00 a.m., Jessie Lee showed me how to use the cash register and brew coffee with the percolator. Then, she stood close and whispered, "Only a few Black folks come in here; this place had rules, and Blacks were not to be allowed to sit

A New Adventure Begins

at the counter for a long time. I had to work in the kitchen for five years because I couldn't serve white people. I advise you to watch your words with the customers."

By this time, office workers had filled the counter and were waiting for service. Jessie Lee told me, "I am training you to take the orders, showing you around the kitchen." Suddenly, she added, "Here is your first guest, Mr. Hall."

I tightened my lips and said, "I'm not ready to take orders," but she just gave me a stubborn look like my momma. Quickly, I walked over to Mr. Hall with a smile.

"Hello, my name is Estell. May I take your order?"

"Where is Jessie Lee?" He sounded more confused than upset.

I told him she was busy and that it was my first day. He looked at me for a second and then said, "I'll have my hamburger with a side of mayonnaise and pickles, and sweet tea." I wrote down the order on the yellow pad. While I waited for my order to arrive, I removed the dirty dishes from the counter.

Soon, Marybelle tapped me on the shoulder and said, "Your order is ready." I rushed to the kitchen and returned to serve Mr. Hall. When he finished his burger, I rang up his check. He left me a dollar tip. Later, I asked Jessie Lee if a dollar was a good tip, and she responded, "Yes, sweetie. You could have gotten a quarter."

By 2:00 p.m., my feet were hurting, and my white shoes had ketchup stains on them.

Jessie Lee told me I got a thirty-minute break, so I went to the kitchen and ordered an egg salad with toast and sliced tomatoes from Big Boy, the young cook with a dark-brown ponytail. I was so hungry that I barely chewed my food before swallowing it. After lunch, I helped refill the condiments and wipe the counters with bleach. At five o'clock, I clocked out and rushed to catch the Marta bus.

I felt so happy when I saw my home with the burgundy door. I climbed up the steps to my front door, my white shoes squeezing my toes. I opened the door, and Coco was waiting inside and wagging his tail. Fatima and Rabia ran to greet me with hugs. Then, I walked to the couch, took off my shoes, and threw them in the corner.

My journey from a small town to the Big Apple was exhilarating and a little scary, but it was an awakening for me. In this photo, I am 25 years old, and I'm wearing a stylish tweed jacket. New York became a classroom when I went to museums, libraries, and diverse restaurants. Other times, I went to Harlem and listened to jazz music from a small shop on the sidewalk on 125th Street. And I enjoyed shopping at Saks Fifth Avenue in Manhattan and buying new purses and heels.

I went to business school, and I got my first job in a tall office building near the Empire State Building. In 1968, I became a mother, and my two daughters were born in Brooklyn. With them, I began to grow up and develop an inner strength. I wanted to teach them about God so they would keep their faith as they grow older. It was so rewarding to spend time with my daughters with Joseph by my side. I thought, *I am following in my mother's footsteps. I have some big shoes to fill.*

A New Adventure Begins

Fatima asked, "Are you all right, Mama?"

"Yes, I am home," I assured her. I sat there and rested my feet, and soon, Joseph came into the living room with Aisha, who hopped into my lap. While I cradled her in my arms, Joseph asked, "How was your day waitressing?"

I told him it was good. Then, he sat beside me and held my hand.

"The girls were smiling when I picked them up from the babysitter," Joseph shared. "Babe, I cooked Hamburger Helper. Are you ready to eat?"

"No, I just want to be with my daughters and rest." I couldn't believe how tired I was after just one shift. After an hour, I devoured my food, helped the girls with their homework, and gave Aisha a bath.

After I read my daughters a bedtime story and tucked them all in for the night, I strolled into the kitchen, opened the door of a light-pink cabinet, and picked up my coffee cup with an image of the Brooklyn Bridge on it. While I waited for the water to heat for tea, I thought about how much I missed city life. I poured the hot water into a cup and made peppermint tea, which I took over to the broken chair near the window. I enjoyed settling into that chair; it reminded me of when Joseph bought it from a yard sale and swore it was an antique. It was just a piece of junk, yet I learned to feel comfortable with the padded bottom.

I took off my beige house shoes and spread my toes on the floor; I could finally take a deep breath and relax. Then, I noticed a pile of pots and plates in the kitchen sink. *Joseph told me he had done the dishes*, I thought, feeling frustrated.

The green wall phone rang, so I grabbed the receiver with its long cord and stood against the sink.

I said hello and smiled when I heard the voice on the other end.

"Sis, how was your first day of work?" my sister Mary asked.

"Girl, don't ask me. I was scared, going from staying at home to working in a restaurant. It's like my identity is changing." Mary made sympathetic sounds on the other end. "My boss, Anna, seems nice, and I've met my coworkers, Marybelle and Jessie Lee. And the cook, Big Boy seems okay, too. Jessie Lee had her Bible under the counter. She looks like Momma's best friend, Sister Kelly."

"Glad you met someone friendly," Mary replied.

"My cheap shoes hurt my feet, but I did serve one customer. Also, when I arrived in the morning at Anna's, it seemed conservative, with primarily white customers, who had a moment of silence when they saw me."

"You can handle those white folk, and you're from Aberdeen." We chuckled together.

Then I told my sister how I'd had to leave Aisha at the babysitter that morning, and how I cried on the Marta bus and sat in the back. "Of course, I won't see Fatima and Rabia when they get off the bus," I added, my voice getting a little shaky.

"Sis, you got Richard," Mary said, using my husband's given name that everyone in Aberdeen knew him by. "And Joseph takes care of you; he love those girls."

"Indeed, I am thankful that my husband loves our daughters," I agreed. I tried to think of something to talk about that wouldn't make me teary. "So, Mary, can you send me Kimmel fudge candy and fresh pecans from your backyard tree?"

"Sure, I'll pack a box and mail it next week from the post office in town."

"Wow, I can always count on you, Mary," I smiled, thinking about how supportive my sister always was.

"Sis, you are welcome, and I'll call tomorrow night," Mary said in her kind voice.

"Love you, Mary."

"Bye, Sis."

After the conversation with my sister, I went into the dining room, pressed my uniform, and got Aisha's clothes ready for Tuesday. Certainly, I was excited for my second day on the job!

25

Oh, Waitress!

AFTER GETTING OFF the Marta bus the next morning wearing my light blue uniform, I felt light rain falling on my head. I pulled out my green umbrella, but the lever was locked. I still had a seven-minute walk to Forsyth Street, so I walked briskly with other people heading to work in that direction. I threw my umbrella in the trash can when I arrived at the building, and then I rushed to the ladies' room because my short Afro was flat on my head.

I opened my purse, sprayed Afro Sheen on it, and used my wide-tooth metal comb for styling it. I was proud of that comb; it was just a regular wide-tooth comb, but on the end was a balled fist, a symbol of unity and resistance in the Black Power movement and the historical link to Black Pride. I remembered buying this comb and my dashiki at Amari African shop on Nostrand Avenue in Brooklyn. That's when I began embracing our culture by wearing my first Afro.

While I reminisced, I opened my shoulder bag with my makeup and pressed powder onto my skin still damp from the rain. Smiling at my reflection in the mirror, I thought, *I still look good at thirty-two years old.*

If Grits Could Talk

Down the hall, I stopped at the phone booth, opened the door, and deposited my dime into the slot to call the babysitter, Lucinda. The line was busy, and my two nickels dropped down into the change slot. As I left the booth, I wished I could see my baby, Aisha.

My shift started an hour after Anna Café opened, so when I entered, people were already there, eating and talking and waiting for their servers. I headed down the hall to sign in on the worksheet and then grabbed my notepad and pencil.

As I walked past the kitchen, I observed Anna cooking bacon and cursing about the student she'd hired who had not shown up. Her face was dripping sweat and flushed with anger. When I got to the main room, Jessie Lee greeted me.

"Morning. You got two guests waiting near the corner wall."

I took a deep breath and adjusted my name tag. I strolled up to the counter and greeted a couple seated there.

"Hello, welcome. May I help you?" I gave them a big smile.

The older woman, who wore a gray tweed suit, responded, "I want my eggs sunny-side up, and don't break the yoke, bacon, and dry toast with a cup of coffee. Okay, thank you."

After I wrote down her order, I turned to the man sitting next to her who wore a bow tie, and I said hi.

He roared, "I want hot cakes, sausages, a side of grits, a frosted strawberry donut, and orange juice." I just stayed calm and smiled. Then he remarked in a normal voice, "You must be new here."

"My second day," I answered. I turned and walked briskly to put my order on the spindle in the hot kitchen. When I returned to the main room, Marybelle, wearing a wrinkled uniform, said hello. I nodded my head.

I began brewing more tea and helping Marybelle with the takeout orders while waiting for my orders to come up, and it wasn't long before I served the lady in the tweed jacket.

As I set her food in front of her, she asked, "Can I have my check, Estella?"

"No, my name is Estell," I corrected softly, giving her a smile. She pushed her lips out without a word and put two dollars on the counter for her bill.

"Marybelle," I yelled, "Can you help me open the cash register?" and Marybelle called back, "I told you yesterday, you have to hit the left key before opening the drawer." I just rolled my eyes at her.

After that, I handed the lady her change, twelve cents. She jerked it out of my hand, doing her best not to touch me. I thought her fearful reaction was ignorant and crude.

Next, the man with the bow tie watched as I placed the warm plate with his order on the counter. He asked for an ashtray, so I grabbed one from under the counter. He quickly pulled a cigarette from a red pack of Winstons and lit up, so I moved away from his cloud of smoke. About fifteen minutes later, he asked for the check, and he paid his two-dollar total and left me a one-dollar tip.

I had been on my feet for five hours, and I was hungry and tired. Even though there was a lunch rush, I got a fifteen-minute break, so I took a seat at the counter. I drank the nasty sweet tea and ate a chocolate donut because they were free. Even though I could have an employee discount while I was working, the food at the restaurant was sugary and greasy—there were no healthy options. Still, I was so hungry, I gulped down my donut.

I removed my shoes and wiggled my toes for a while. As I sat there, I thought about the cockroaches I has seen crawling under the silverware tray that morning when I was serving my first customer. I had continued to smile so customers wouldn't know, but I wanted to smash those bugs. I wondered if they were anywhere near where I was sitting for my break. I had already decided to bring my lunch from home from then on.

After my break, I went to my station at the end of the counter. Three young women wearing name badges from the First National Bank sat there.

"Hi, welcome. May I take your order?" I asked.

One of the women, who wore a green beret said, "Give us a few minutes." When I returned, they had each decided on a BLT with a side of fries and lemonade. I quickly took another order and watched Marybelle and Jessie Lee each carrying two plates with their arms and holding tall glasses in their hands. I wondered when I would feel confident enough to carry so much food at one time.

I served the three sweet teas to the young ladies and put in my orders, and then helped Jessie Lee serve her plates to two young women from Rich's department store. While I waited for my orders to come up, I placed three silverware setups on the counter for the three women, who kept giggling. I had a hard time keeping up, getting into the groove with requests for refills, so I was hurrying.

When the orders were ready, I decided I could save time by being like the experienced servers and carrying three plates filled with sandwiches and fries in my arms. I was showing off a little, too, because I was new and wanted customers to see how capable I was. I didn't see that the floor was wet, and I slipped, bumping into Marybelle; as I lost my balance, the plates slid onto the floor, making a terrible sound as they shattered. Food flew everywhere and splattered sauces onto Marybelle's uniform.

She looked upset and said angrily, "Watch where you're going." I was so flustered and embarrassed that I thought about just leaving the café right then and there, but we needed the money. I muttered an apology, but I just stood there. Jessie Lee told me to clean up the mess, so I found the broom and swept up the broken glass and pottery. When I finished, I told Anna that I needed three more sandwiches.

"I am taking it out of your paycheck the next time you break those dishes," Anna said in a stern voice.

I returned to the three women from the bank and mumbled, "I dropped your food." They had watched the entire incident, so they already knew, but they were kind enough to tell me they could wait for replacements.

I continued to serve customers for the rest of the afternoon, but my smile was gone. I just wanted the day to end, and I kept looking at the red Coca-Cola clock on the wall, waiting for five o'clock. Finally, my shift ended. As I was on the way out, Jessie said kindly, "It was a rough day, but tomorrow, I'll show you how to handle the plates." She tapped me on the shoulder and grinned.

On a warm Friday evening, after my fifth day of work, I climbed off the Marta bus at Rex Avenue. I was thrilled to see my home just a block away, but I strolled home because my feet begged me to remove my shoes. Before long, I was turning the silver doorknob, and as I opened the door, the smell of lavender greeted me, and a feeling of contentment washed over me. As soon as the girls heard me, they came running to hug me.

Aisha held up her tiny hands and said in her sweet baby voice, "Mommy." I scooped her up in my arms, happy that the stains on my light-blue uniform were only from tea. Rabia was right behind her, pulling on my shirttail to get my attention. "Mom, my science class experimented with peeled oranges." Before she could continue, Fatima said, "Stop talking, Rabia. Mommy, I want you to sign my paper for my field trip to Piedmont Park."

I reached down to rub Coco's ears, and he licked my hand. I stood back up straight and looked at my two older daughters.

"All right," I said softly, "I got time to listen," and we sauntered to the dining table. As I looked around the dining room, I saw the red and green Muslim prayer rug on the wall, and I felt God was watching over us.

The front door opened, and Joseph walked into the living room and pulled up a chair. Even as tired as I was, I couldn't help but admire how handsome he was in his camouflage jacket and a well-shaped beard.

"Babe, how was your day at the job?" Joseph asked.

"I'm getting into the groove of waiting tables," I told him, "and I am tired from walking."

"Don't you want to relax with a bubble bath?" my husband asked, and I nodded yes. "So, girls, I bought pizza for us tonight."

The girls' faces lit up with smiles. We headed to the kitchen to eat, and I laughed inside as I watched them, Rabia smelling her slice and Fatima choosing the triangular slice with meat sauce. Baby Aisha kept sticking her fingers into the gooey cheese.

"Joseph, thanks for getting dinner ready." I was so happy that I didn't have to cook after being on my feet all day.

Finally, I thought, *I can take off this uniform and brush my teeth.* I headed to the bathroom for my bath. I turned on the portable radio to an FM station and listened to the disco music of Chaka Khan singing "I'm Every Woman." It was just the right song to keep me moving.

My family and I soon settled into a routine. After my Marta bus ride, I greeted my family when I got home. Then, I rushed to sit on the couch with them in the living room. My legs and back would ache from standing on my feet for eight hours. After I rested for a bit, I fixed dinner, like meatloaf with a brown glaze sauce, garlic mashed potatoes, fresh green beans, and nutty fudge brownies for dessert. Afterward, I washed the dishes in the sink. Sometimes, Joseph prepared dinner after shopping for groceries at Kroger. While preparing dinner in our tiny kitchen, I would carry Aisha around on my hip because she wanted to cling to me. She weighed about thirty-two pounds and had long legs, but I wanted to feel her close to me since I missed my baby.

Fatima and Rabia talked to me constantly while I put two loads of clothes in the washing machine. When the garments finished washing, I ironed my husband's uniform for work and made tuna fish for his lunch. When that was done, I sat down to help my daughters with their homework, and I made sure all three girls got a good bath. I squeezed in a quick bath in there somewhere, and afterward, I scrubbed the tub rings. Before bed, I prepared my uniform and a bag lunch for myself and packed the baby bags for the morning. Then, I crawled into bed and slept for about five hours. At 5:30 a.m., my alarm let me know it was time to start my day.

26

Working Mom

THROUGHOUT THE FIRST WEEK at Anna Café, I learned to write down my orders, ring up the checks, and make eye contact with the guests. I practiced remembering the pies and croissants on the menu, and I was happy to be part of a team that worked efficiently together. I broke a few plates, but I was keeping this job. On Friday, I got my first paycheck, which was for fifteen dollars plus my tips. I kept looking at my check because it felt good to see my name on a paycheck again.

One Saturday after I had been working for about two months I decided to work in my garden. It was a warm afternoon in August, and I enjoyed being surrounded by trees and roses. I decided to teach Fatima and Rabia how to plant turnip green seeds in our little garden in the front yard by digging their hands in the dirt. I wore my straw hat and garden gloves, and the girls wore their own garden gloves while they worked beside me.

We hadn't been working for very long before Fatima mumbled, "Why do I have work when I could be watching *Popeye*? I already know about plants; Grandma in Aberdeen had us water the flowers."

I stopped digging for a minute and looked at my oldest daughter. "I want you to develop good working habits as I did with my mother," I told her.

She stared at me for a moment before saying "You have too many rules like working in the garden, Mommy."

"I am teaching you to grow your own food," I replied. "And I know that you complain, but you are a good role model for your sisters."

Fatima beamed at the compliment. "You think so?"

We heard Joseph's Chevrolet come down the street with its loud engine. As he pulled into the driveway, the girls stood waiting with excitement. Their dad hopped out of the car holding bags from KB Toys. Because I was working now, Joseph had money to buy toys for the first time in a while. I never saw so much giggling and laughter from our daughters.

After the girls went inside to play with their new toys, I sat on the steps with my husband and hugged him because I was happy. We finally had a little money in the bank, and I had shopped at A&P that morning for food.

"Joseph, I am taking the girls shopping at Davidson's in the Lenox Square Mall to buy white leather boots for Aisha and dresses for Fatima and Rabia. And I am stopping at Hazel's Beauty Salon for a manicure with pink nail polish."

Joseph kept his eyes on me as I told him my plans, and he listened until I finished. Then he said, "Babe, I have a surprise. You know that stereo I showed you in the newspaper? I rented it. The Fisher stereo and record player in a mahogany cabinet will look good in our living room. Big Man's Rental had a billboard on Buford Highway advertising it for ten dollars a week." Joseph's eyes were bright. "Babe, I want to listen to Miles Davis and John Coltrane, just like in New York."

I became tense as he uttered those words. "Joseph, you are being duped at ten dollars a week. Tell them that you don't want it." I couldn't believe my husband would be so frivolous when we were finally able to live within our means again.

"I can't," Joseph told me. "I signed the contract."

"Well, you didn't say anything to me."

"So, Estell. I see you are planning to shop at that upscale mall," was his response.

"Joseph, I am tired of us being broke. Even though you are working two jobs, it still is not enough."

In bed that night, my thoughts turned a little dark. *Housework is still considered a woman's responsibility in the home*, I thought, *just like it was for my mother in Aberdeen. I am still doing most of the work around the house.* I was frustrated that Joseph watched the Braves games on television after work while I helped my daughters with their homework and cleaned up behind my husband. I asked Joseph to take out the trash, and it would still be sitting there the next morning.

On a Thursday several months later, a steady drizzle of rain kept me inside during my lunch break. I pulled my egg salad sandwich with tomatoes and a bag of Doritos chips from my brown bag. I was thinking about my paycheck just one day away. While I ate, I took off my white Walmart shoes to relax my feet and thought about my earlier conversation with Anna about the roaches under the counter; she told me not to worry about it. "I'll spray some Raid this weekend," she said, and that was the end of that conversation.

When I returned to the dining area, the three girls from the First National Bank who usually sat in my section were there and waved hello. Marybelle, wearing a dirty apron with grease stains on it, waited on them while popping her chewing gum.

With the heavy rain, the restaurant was slow, with just a couple of guests at the counter. Anna, the manager, had a list of things for us to do to keep occupied. I pretended to work hard, but the chores were trivial, like filling the ketchup, mustard, and sugar containers.

While I wiped down the counter, Jessie Lee whispered in my ear. She complained that Anna allowed her to take home leftover donuts but always made her scrub the walls with Pine Sol and never gave her a raise. I nodded my head, and we both kept working. But as I continued, I pondered how some people lacked values of fairness.

Finally, Anna announced that we would get off early because of the weather. I smiled and wiggled my shoulders; I could pick up my daughters soon. Then, I mentioned to Jessie, "I am taking a taxi home."

"Oh, no, sweetie," Jessie Lee said, shaking her head, "you are riding with me."

At 3:30 p.m., I signed out, and Jessie Lee followed me to the door. "I'll bring the car around to the front of the Healey Building near the front steps," she said, so I waited under the building's eaves to stay dry.

Soon, Jessie Lee drove up in a large-body, red, four-door Ford sedan with chrome wheels. The paint was peeling, and the engine roared. I sat down in the comfortable front seat. Jessie Lee held on tightly to the large steering wheel covered with a fluffy pink cover, like a blanket. I quietly rolled down the window because her perfume had an overpowering musty odor.

"Excuse the mess in the car," she told me. I carefully moved my feet away from the Coors beer cans and an empty Burger King bag stashed on the floorboard. Jessie Lee drove through the city streets until she hit the heavy traffic on I-85, when she turned up the music. On the radio, the gospel song of BeBe and CeCe Winans singing "Up Where We Belong." The music was relaxing as well as uplifting after a stressful day.

About thirty minutes later, we passed the Greenbriar Mall, and soon Jessie Lee pulled onto Rex Avenue. "This is a nice neighborhood," she said. As we continued down the street, she continued, "Sweetie, I met your husband last week when he came to drive you home. He is a fine-looking brown-skinned man and looks so happy to see you. If I was just a little younger . . ." Her voice trailed off, and she gave me a sly smile.

"Jessie Lee, slow down; that's my home with the toys in the yard," I said, pointing. She pulled into the driveway and I grabbed my purse, thanked her for the ride, and said, "See you tomorrow."

The sun was shining, and I was happy to be home. For dinner that night, we would have Hamburger Helper, which could easily feed our family, and strawberry Jell-O for Aisha. At eight o'clock, we would watch *Star Trek*, the science fiction show whose slogan "Where no man has gone before" always excited us. The beautiful Ohura was played by Nichelle Nichols, the first African American actress on American television in a leading role. It was the first time I had seen a Black woman on the TV screen who wasn't a maid. Not only was she a role model for young girls, but my daughters loved the show. Rabia liked Dr. Spock, and Fatima's favorite was Captain Kirk.

I smiled as I thought about the nice family evening that lie ahead.

27
Hold Your Head High and Keep Going

AFTER I PICKED UP Fatima and Rabia from school, I walked up the steps to Lucinda's home and stepped over her sleeping cat to knock on the front door. Almost immediately, the door swung open to reveal Lucinda standing there wearing a wrinkled dress and white house shoes; pink hair rollers covered her head. I greeted her, and we all stepped inside. I walked into the living room, where two little girls were watching Bugs Bunny cartoons and eating Goldfish crackers that had spilled onto the floor. Fatima and Rabia headed to the kitchen.

"You came early today," Lucinda said, following behind me.

Nodding my head, I asked, "Where is Aisha?"

Lucinda told me to follow her to the bedroom, which I did. The room felt overly warm to me. At first, I didn't see Aisha, and then suddenly, I spotted her. She was asleep on a dirty mat on the floor with another child beside her. Her shoes were off, and a blanket covered the middle of her body.

"Why is my child sleeping on the floor with a dirty mat?" I asked the babysitter in a loud voice, trying to control my anger. I knelt to pick up my child and realized she was dressed in too many layers. I called softly, "Aisha. Wake up. Mommy is here." I felt her pants, which were wet; she had crumbs around her mouth, and her little face was damp from sweat.

I stood up quickly, hugging my baby to my chest, and I pointed my finger in Lucinda's face. "You did not change my baby's clothes today?" I demanded.

"I did change her clothes at lunch, and I got busy with another child," she said. Her tone was defensive, and she fidgeted with her hands.

"That's no excuse!"

"I am sorry, and this will never happen again," Lucinda assured me. She looked embarrassed.

I clenched my teeth and tripped over toys in my hurry to get away from that woman; I just wanted to slap her. By then, the girls had heard my angry voice and came into the room.

"Mommy," Fatima asked, "what happened with Aisha?"

"Just grab your book bag, and let's go."

I headed for the door, grabbing my baby bag by the fridge on my way, and my other daughters followed close behind. Lucinda brought up the rear, saying, "Please, I am sorry. Will you be back tomorrow with the girls?" I just ignored her and kept walking. Rabia, trailing behind me with her sister, said, "Mommy, are you going to tell Daddy?"

I didn't know what I would do, but at the moment, I couldn't speak because I was so angry about seeing my baby neglected.

During the short walk home, Aisha clung to my hip. I kept thinking, *What is the best way to explain this to my husband?* When I hired Lucinda, I remembered, she was kind, seemed to genuinely care for children, and her home was clean, with a Bible on the night table. But over the past few months, little things had started to bother me. I noticed that Aisha's hands were dirty when she got home, and Lucinda had braided the baby's thick afro without my permission. I complained, and Lucinda promised to do better. So far, she had been reliable as far as being available to take care of my daughters. But the way I found Aisha that afternoon made me wonder if I had completely misread the situation. Had Lucinda been taking good care of my baby or neglecting her?

I was still fuming when we got to our house. I told the girls they could play in the yard. Once inside, I headed straight for the bathroom and immediately gave Aisha a warm bath in the tub, with rubber ducks to play with. Afterward, I dressed her in clean, dry clothes, all the while trying to calm down because I didn't want my baby to know how upset I was. Finally, I did settle down and sat in the living room with Aisha, holding her brown teddy bear, in my arms.

Shortly, I heard the engine of my husband's car, and soon he walked into the living with a smile on his face. "You picked up the girls early," Joseph said, scooping Aisha into his arms and kissing her on the forehead. When my husband looked at me, his face changed.

"Babe, did something happen at work?" Joseph sat down beside me with our daughter.

"Lucinda had our baby sleeping on the floor, and her clothes were wet," I told him, feeling overwhelmed by the situation.

Joseph's mouth tightened, and he pounded his fist on the coffee table. "You know, this is the second complaint; last month, I went to pick her up, and Aisha was drinking from another child's sippy cup. I told you that the babysitter was always talking on the phone. I am going to talk to her."

"No, don't talk to her, Joseph!" I pleaded. I believed I should oversee this situation, especially because he was angry and would get so emotional over our girls.

We sat there looking at each other for a moment before he said firmly, "You should stay home, Babe, and quit your job."

I felt my heart beat faster. "I just started this job less than two months ago, and I want to keep my job, Joseph. I want to bring home a paycheck; I want to buy clothes for my children." I blinked back tears and stared at the floor with my head bent down. "But I feel so much anxiety over the babysitter. Just the thought of her leaving baby Aisha alone for hours on that mat . . . I can't bear the thought of her touching my baby." I tightened my fists just talking about the situation.

Joseph put his arm around my shoulder. "I apologize for getting so upset. You can keep your job and look for another sitter."

Suddenly, I knew what I had to do. "Joseph, I decided to quit tomorrow and get my last paycheck. I don't trust the babysitter, and I don't like her."

"Babe, are you sure that this is what you want to do?"

"Yes, I can handle being out of work for a while." I watched as Joseph stood up with Aisha, who was sleeping in her dad's arms, and laid her near the corner of the couch.

"Joseph, I was so happy coming home today, and I don't understand how this could happen to me."

Joseph held my hand, looking sincere. "Babe, I will figure this thing out. I know you are worried and tired; I'll pick up dinner from Captain D's. I'll get your favorite fish sandwich with hush puppies and corn on the cob." He paused and grinned. "I knew that would make you smile."

On Friday morning, after a night of tossing and turning, I hugged my girls before leaving home for work; Joseph stayed home to watch our daughters. The birds were chirping in the hazy sky as I rushed to the Marta bus.

I watched as the 6:45 a.m. bus arrived, but the driver did not stop, driving right past me. I just saw a silver and light-blue bus zooming down the street. I was upset; I took a deep breath. I gazed at the sunshine rather than think about that foolish driver. About forty minutes later, another bus came, and this driver stopped. I climbed on, said hello to the friendly driver, and paid my fare of twenty-five cents. Then I marched to the back of the bus, trying not to inhale the cigarette smoke that permeated the air, and I sat down in a seat near the window.

Once I was on Marietta Street, I moved with the crowd of workers who marched to the beat of honking horns. Before I walked into the Healey Building, I just pondered that this would be my last day. Although I complained about my sore feet and the low wages, I was bringing home a paycheck. As I reminisced about my happier days at Anna Café over the past weeks, I did not realize that I had walked through traffic and was opening the door.

As I entered the small café, the smell of roasted coffee and burnt toast from the kitchen greeted me. I saw dirty dishes on the counter and giggling customers at the counter, which I walked past to sign in by the kitchen door. Next, I headed to my station without even saying good morning to my coworkers.

One of my regulars, a guy with a greasy army cap and tattoos on his arms, was waiting for me at my station. "Hello," I greeted him politely but without my usual smile. "I'll put in your exact order and get your coffee." He nodded, and then he began reading his *Sports Illustrated*. Sitting next to him were two guys wearing yellow hard hats and Georgia Power uniforms; when I asked, they told me they just wanted glazed donuts and coffee.

After I served them, I had a few more customers, but nothing like the usual steady stream. I continued to mope around until lunchtime, but then I couldn't eat because my stomach felt tight. I decided to call my friend Rose. I stepped into the hallway to use the pay phone and put ten cents in the slot.

"Hi, Rose," I said when she picked up. "I must quit my job." I told her what had happened, and without asking any questions, she replied, "I am coming to see you tonight, and remember, I am here for you, my sister." I thought about how we shared everything about our feelings, and I was so grateful for her friendship.

I returned to the restaurant and was greeted with the sound of breaking dishes. One of the other servers had dropped several plates, and I remembered how that had been to me just a few months ago. I headed to the kitchen to speak to Anna, who had a burger on her plate but had stopped eating to pick her nose. I waited for her to get up and wash her hands when she finished, but she just sat there and looked at me, so I said, "I am quitting today."

Anna looked confused. Finally, she simply asked, "Why?"

"I can't find a babysitter for my children," I said in a flat tone.

"Can you work another week?"

"No," I said. Anna's attitude tended toward negativity, and she had been uncaring, even unkind to me while I was there, so I didn't feel any obligation to help her out.

Jessie Lee stood nearby, listening. When I returned to the café, she followed me and leaned in when I turned to her.

"Sweetie, I can't believe that you are quitting," she said in a loud whisper. Then she told Marybelle, who seemed startled.

"You can't leave because I'll have more work to do," Marybelle whined.

Jessie Lee put her hands on her hips and said, "Marybelle, I've never seen you work hard except to stuff your mouth with biscuits." The tall, lanky waitress tightened her red lips and walked off.

By this time, Jessie Lee had put her arm around my shoulder. "Do you plan to stay home with your girls?" she asked kindly, and I nodded yes.

"Excuse me, sweetie. I got to pick up my order. Remember I am driving you home after work," Jesse Lee told me. I smiled.

At five o'clock, I signed out, and Anna gave me my last paycheck, which made me feel sad. Marybelle hugged me. As I began walking to the door, Anna exited the kitchen.

"Hey, wait, Estell. I can hold your job for thirty days," she called out.

Jessie Lee mumbled, "That witch was finally kind to you," and we both smiled. I got into the red sedan, rolled down the windows to air out the smell of rotten eggs, and looked out the window in silence for the entire drive home. Soon, she was turning into my driveway on Rex Avenue.

"Estell, I want us to get together next Friday for lunch at Zesto's on Chamblee Tucker Road," she told me as I opened the car door. "Not a fancy place," she added, "but the onion rings are good." She flashed a toothy smile. I tapped her shoulder and said, "I will miss you," and hugged my friend.

I can't believe that I am a stay-at-home mom again, I thought as I walked toward my front door. *I must reframe my thinking to stop feeling shame about quitting my job.*

I sneaked into the living room to surprise my girls, but they were hiding behind the red couch and hollered, "Mommy!" when they saw me. I kneeled down to put my arms around them. I had tears in my eyes, yet I smiled.

I didn't notice Joseph standing by the curtains until he said, "Babe, we are going out tonight. Remember the movie *Jaws*? It's about the great white shark on the beach."

I responded, "It's scary, but I want to go." I loved that Joseph planned something to take my mind off my troubles . . . until I remembered that we couldn't take the girls. But Joseph had thought of that, too.

"I took care of the babysitter; Rose is coming over to stay with them so we can go out, just the two of us." Then Joseph turned to the girls and announced, "Girls, I bought Hot Pockets with melted cheese," but you would have thought he told them he'd bought them each a pony; they ran over the toys and blocks on the floor while yelling with excitement.

"You thought of everything," I murmured, embracing my husband.

28
A Homemaker Once Again

I MISSED BRINGING HOME a paycheck with my name on it since I quit my job. Working at Anna Café gave me an identity beyond being the cleanup lady at home, and work provided a sense of pride. And I learned that I enjoyed talking to random people and hearing their thoughts and ideas. Those conversations made me realize that I have a rich life with my family.

I was once again a stay-at-home mom, but I now had a new appreciation for the time I spent with my daughters. I still enjoyed getting up in the morning to comb and braid the girls' hair. Then, after they brushed their teeth, I served Fatima and Rabia their Lucky Charms cereal for breakfast in their pink Disney bowls before the school bus arrived. As they ate, I watched Aisha tear into her waffle while Joseph waited for his sunny-side-up eggs with wheat toast, and Coco sat by his bowl waiting for puppy bites.

In the afternoons, I enjoyed sitting on the grass in the backyard while Aisha rode around on her yellow and blue Big Wheel. I had plenty of time to think while I drank my sweet tea and the sun shined on me.

One day, I had an idea to start a sewing club. I thought about my mother on the plantation sewing quilts with her neighbors because it was necessary to keep warm covers for her family at night. After I moved to Aberdeen, my mother taught me to use the Singer sewing machine with its metal foot pedal. She bought me a blue floral sewing basket with needles, a thimble, scissors, and measuring tape. I put them all to good use by making things like curtains for the girls' room when we first moved into our house. I also made a shirt for myself, purses for the girls, and a bandanna for Coco.

A sewing club seemed like a good way to motivate myself to make quilts and also spend time with some friends. After I talked to Lila, my friend from the mosque, and Rose, they were excited to join my group. I decided I would cut pieces from Joseph's old shirts and purchase pieces of cloth from Goodwill to get started. *I'll teach my friends our family traditions*, I thought, and I couldn't wait to get started.

Quilting

In my childhood home in Aberdeen, my momma had a quilt that served as an important possession, and she loved to tell us stories about each quilt she made. She often draped a quilt across the couch or gently folded it at the foot of the bed. So, I decided to dedicate my quilt to my grandmother, Mary Jane Pruitt. When I was growing up, she lived in a shack on a plantation about eight miles away, near Prairie, Mississippi. Grandma was skinny but had swollen legs because of health issues; she'd had a stroke, which left her with muscle weakness and stiffness. I remember her stiff, bony hands when she hugged me.

My club met twice a month in my dining room while my older girls were at school. Aisha played in the corner of the room with her pretend kitchen set. Each meeting when I served sweet tea and coconut cupcakes or brownies, Aisha used her imagination and whipped up cookies and cakes with her brightly colored dishes and spoons and a small white stove.

I asked my friends to bring their own sewing baskets. For our first project, a small baby quilt for Aisha, I decided on a pattern with light and dark squares, and we worked on it together to learn since we were all beginners. I used the cut-up squares for the patchwork to sew together with a needle. After finishing the baby quilt, I made a new neck bandanna for Coco, and Rose made a purse with a strap. Although Leila often pricked her finger with the needle, she still sewed two potholders. Later, my neighbors Viola and Dixie joined us. We kept meeting until I moved away.

*

As a stay-at-mom home (again) in 1979, I sometimes felt like I was fading into the woodwork. I felt irrelevant and unimportant without an income. Even though I enjoyed preparing my family dinners and nurturing my daughters, I thought about the stereotype of women who stayed at home as having less value than women in the workplace. I was a housewife, and that wasn't considered a "real" job.

Even so, I enjoyed stepping back into my old routine with my daughters and taking care of my husband. I kept our home neat and clean, but Joseph wanted our home to be organized and disciplined, like in the military. He liked certain things placed on shelves and expected everything to be orderly when he got home. And so, I talked with him and let him know that I was in charge, and he could offer suggestions. I was the first to acknowledge that sometimes I was messy, with open mail on our nightstand, my typewriter on the kitchen table, and my teacup on the floor by the bed. But I also had three daughters to care for, and living like we were in the army wasn't my idea of how to raise a happy family. I was doing my best to make our home cozy with bright sunlight and a green peace lily in the living room.

Still, after a few weeks at home, I again considered returning to work, but I knew I would face limited opportunities because of my race and gender. Despite the civil rights movement, I saw little real change as an African American woman. I believe that my thick Afro, dark skin, and tone of voice offended many people. I was often uncomfortable working with white people because of my experiences growing up in Aberdeen. I was also realistic about my lack of work experience and a college degree, and I knew I'd probably be limited to a job as a service clerk, cashier, or factory worker.

I planned to be more productive with my daughters. After I went to the PTA meeting one Monday and learned our Black school received less funding than white schools, I decided to volunteer for the bake sale at Ben Hill School. I learned that the school's library needed more books by and about African Americans. Donating my time would allow me to work for a cause that I was passionate about. When I told my daughters, they were so excited. And I thought about baking my moist, three-layer lemon cake made with freshly squeezed lemon and fresh butter and eggs from my mom's recipe book. (I did end up making this cake, and it sold for twenty-five dollars, which was a pleasant surprise. Mostly, I was just happy that I could help the school.)

I loved being with my children, and I really appreciated the time I got to spend with them after the months of working outside of our home. From my earliest days as a mother, I watched my children grow and took note of their milestones. I enjoyed telling them stories about my childhood. One of their favorites was my story about being a naughty child. Momma kept her good Sunday dishes in a white and glass cabinet in the dining room, and I liked putting my food on the silver-rimmed plates and drinking out of the tall silver glassware. Usually, only the church members used those dishes. I often sneaked into the cabinet when Momma was at work, but one day, I broke two round plates that had belonged to Mary Jane Pruitt, my grandmother

A Homemaker Once Again

who had lived on the plantation; the plates fell while I was trying to return them to the tall cabinet. I didn't mean to break anything; I was just a curious child. As punishment, my mother cut a long switch from the oak tree and whipped my legs. I stuck my lips out at her at the time, but I realized later that spanking was her way of disciplining me. Fatima wondered if I was angry about my whipping. I replied, "I was angry for a few days, but I knew that she cared about me."

I needed to cut our food budget because I was no longer working, so I started using coupons that I cut out of newspaper ads. I remembered how my momma found ways to keep our family from hunger, so I did the same thing she did: I planted a garden to grow tomatoes, greens, and squash.

Many afternoons while I prepared dinner for my family, I turned on the radio to the Braves game on TBS, channel 17, and listened to broadcaster Skip Caray build excitement for every pitch. I became a Braves fan when I moved to Atlanta, and sometimes I watched the games on my black-and-white TV in the kitchen. Even though the team was not winning, I was inspired when I watched Hank Aaron, who later became known as the Home Run King. The team name—the Braves—is controversial today, but at that time, I didn't consider that it might be disrespectful to Native Americans, and I enjoyed wearing my team's hat and shirts. I didn't have much self-worth nor value other minorities. I had a lot of fear from my upbringing in Mississippi, so I just thought what are now considered racist behaviors and ideas to be normal.

I continued preparing my dinner for Joseph; he loved my hearty meatloaf. I added spicy pepper, onion, and tomato sauce. I also prepared fresh mashed potatoes, cabbage with okra, and a side of our homegrown tomatoes. I usually made some sweet tea, and sometimes a batch of old-fashioned cornbread, which reminded me of my daddy in Aberdeen. Anyway, I was grateful that I could prepare a good meal for my family, and I loved every minute of cooking.

When my baby girl, Aisha, turned five years old, I learned there was no kindergarten for her in our segregated area, so I decided to homeschool her. I displayed drawings of animals on the door and colorful posters of numbers to count on the walls as though her bedroom was a small classroom. I taught her phonics, shapes, and how to write her name, and even on our limited income, I did what I could to teach her to dress well and have good manners. I also got books from the library. The Ben Hill library did not have any children's books by Black authors, so I got books she enjoyed because of the silly names, pictures, and rhyming structures like *The Cat in the Hat* by Dr. Seuss and *Stuart Little* by E. B. White.

I sat at the kitchen table when it was time for schoolwork, but Aisha did not want to sit down, so it took a while to get her attention. I remembered that when I went to a one-room schoolhouse in the woods, I did not read well. But I loved my teacher, Miss Jenkins, because she inspired me to learn. I wanted Aisha to take pride in learning and have a positive experience in school. I bought a handwriting tablet and #2 yellow pencils and invited her friend, Olivia, to share story time with us. We sat in yellow and blue beanbag chairs for story time, and it was fun.

When they got home from school every weekday, Fatima and Rabia had a list of chores to do. The list included not only washing the dishes, but also hanging clothes outside to dry on a clothesline, wiping the counters with Lysol, and mopping the bathroom. When I heard Fatima complaining, she had to do extra homework; one time, that was writing a four-page essay about her family. After their chores were done, I went outdoors with my daughters and watched them jump rope like I did in Aberdeen. I watched the twirling of the two ropes while they sang the rhyme "Miss Mary Mack." Fatima was quick with her feet; Rabia's feet got caught in the ropes, but she couldn't stop talking about it because she had so much fun, and sometimes, their friends joined them. They stayed outside until the streetlights came on.

At least twice a month, I allowed the girls to have a sleepover on Saturday nights with their friends Alexia and Amelia, who were their classmates. Although Joseph always grumbled because he said they stayed up all night giggling, he helped buy snacks like Pizza Spins, Bagel Bites, Twix cookie bars, Star Wars cookies, and Blow Pops. I oversaw the popcorn and Hawaiian Punch drinks, and sometimes, I prepared potato skins dressed in cheddar cheese and green onions. Fatima gathered the extra pillows and blankets. Rabia decided on a Disney movie like *Biscuit Eater*, a family drama about friendship and dreams, and they all played the game Simon Says. Even Aisha was excited about the sleepovers.

Monopoly

About a year earlier, I bought the game Monopoly at Kmart. It took a while to learn the game, but I practiced with Joseph. He was a wise player and always figured out a strategy to win. After that, Fatima and Rabia wanted to play Monopoly, and Rabia soon asked her dad to teach them. Joseph said he would be happy to show them. The following Friday, Joseph came home early. Then he asked Fatima to grab the board game from the bookshelf, and Rabia trailed her.

I took Aisha to the living room with me so they could focus on playing the game. Aisha had her Raggedy Ann doll, and Coco gnawed his treats nearby. I opened *TV Guide* to see which of the latest shows like *The Twilight Zone*, *The Bionic Woman*, and *The Jeffersons* was on that night. I turned on our twenty-five-inch screen, black-and-white TV to CBS, one of the six available stations, and I decided on *Mission Impossible*, a spy story. I looked forward to seeing Greg Morris, a young Black man, playing an essential role as an electronics expert. Aisha lay on a cushion beside me in her Mickey Mouse pajamas, and we snacked on cheese puffs.

Joseph and the girls started the game with a bowl of Doritos on the side table. Joseph explained the rules and how to play the game to our excited daughters. First, each player gets $1,500 from the bank. Second, each player picks a token; Rabia grabbed the iron, Fatima picked the boot, and Joseph choose the top hat. Next, he shuffled the deck of property cards and placed them on the board; each property group is a different color. If a player lands on a property that someone owns, they must pay the owner "rent." The player can also land on a space that sends them directly to jail, and each time they pass the start, they collect two hundred dollars.

Joseph explained that the strategy is to accumulate properties in the same color group and enough money to put houses and hotels on them so when your opponent lands on them, they must pay you a lot of rent. If you are unable to pay your bill, you go bankrupt.

Of course, the winner has accumulated wealth. For a few months, Joseph kept winning. But Rabia and Fatima liked being competitive with their dad, so they learned the strategy and eventually worked together to take their dad's money and property. One night, I heard two voices hollering, "We finally beat you, Daddy!" I went into the room to see Joseph shaking his head, saying, "You were just lucky!" and Rabia telling him, "I think you should take us to Pizza Hut." Their dad happily agreed.

29
Joseph's Security Job

AFTER OUR MOVE to Atlanta, Joseph was the best husband because he still bought me flowers and our bills were paid on time. Although Joseph worked long hours, he always found time to play chess with our daughters. He loved being a dad and spoiling our daughters with teddy bears and books.

Worries about money always seemed to be in the background, though. A year earlier, Joseph was looking for another job because he wasn't making enough money. He checked with his friend Tony, who knew Joseph had worked for the Pinkerton security agency in New York. Tony told him about the Jessup Security Agency on Decatur Street. My husband called first and then decided to go there in person.

Joseph reached the brick building, opened the glass door, and a bell jingled to announce his arrival. As he entered the small, dimly lit office, he observed the Confederate flag hanging on one of the gray walls and a trash bin overflowing with coffee cups. He was the only person in the room at first, but finally, a middle-aged woman came from the back room to the desk and greeted him in a squeaky voice.

"Good morning, can I help you?"

If Grits Could Talk

"I am here about the security job," Joseph said.

"Just a minute," the desk clerk said, then turned and hollered, "Teddy!"

A moment later, a tall man with gray hair and wearing cowboy boots entered the room and introduced himself as the manager.

"Hey, what is your name?" he asked Joseph.

"Joseph Halliburton, and I am here about the security job," my husband responded.

After shaking Joseph's hand, the manager led him to the back office and pointed to a metal chair. Teddy continued talking while Joseph sat down, and then he handed Joseph a clipboard with the application attached.

The room where they sat wasn't air-conditioned, and Joseph smelled a pungent odor, like a garbage can that had spoiled food in it. When Joseph completed the application, Teddy pulled a Pall Mall cigarette out of its green box and lit up. Teddy leaned back in his chair, read through the application, and finally said, "I read your application. I see you worked at Martin Security for one year; you were a soldier in Vietnam. Do you smoke marijuana?"

"No."

"The job includes inspecting and patrolling the building and monitoring surveillance equipment. The pay is $2.65 an hour, and you work weekends. Can you start on Wednesday?" After Joseph responded yes, Teddy told him, "Good. I'll order a uniform for you."

Teddy told Joseph he would meet the other members of the crew, Leroy, JT, Tim, and Jerome, when he started. "You'll meet Rodney, the assistant manager, when you come for your uniform. Let's go; I'll show you your locker."

When Teddy stood up to take them to another part of the office, Joseph looked at a metal sign on the wall that read, GUN RIGHTS FOR SOUTHERNS. When Joseph stood up, a gray Doberman pinscher about two feet tall began sniffing at his pant leg. Teddy smiled.

"Buster is gentle, just like a baby; he protects this place and is a good dog." When Joseph was growing up, his family owned a bulldog, so he wasn't afraid of dogs. He studied Buster for a few minutes and decided the dog was sociable when he wagged his tail.

In the afternoon, Joseph came home with a smile on his face. "I am looking forward to working as a security guard and bringing home more money so I can buy our new car," he said. "I know our car can barely get out of the driveway."

"Honey, I hope you won't be cheated," I said with concern, "because our credit is not good."

Joseph set his jaw and looked determined. "Babe, I am going to buy us a new car." And that was the last word about that.

Joseph liked wearing his uniform, working patrol, and getting to know the other guys on the crew. He also learned CPR. Joseph worked with Rodney, the assistant manager, on the weekends. Rodney was the person who had trained Joseph in security procedures at stores and warehouses; for instance, how to check locks and doors, how to handle unauthorized vehicles on the premises, and what to do if someone was loitering around the property or making noise near the building and "looked suspicious."

Joseph believed Rodney felt threatened by his size and skin color, especially since he had a beard. He also thought Rodney saw Black men as stupid and lacking moral values and integrity; he thought of them as criminals.

The other men had been working at Jessup for a while, and they were good friends. JT, who was about twenty-five years old, was bald and looked like a boxer. Leroy was from Barbados and had been in the country for two years but was still waiting for his immigration papers. Freddy, a single dad who was white, was a short guy with stringy hair. Joseph was soon their friend as well. He encouraged them to take care of their families and support each other.

Things weren't great at the job. Joseph told me that Rodney had threatened to call immigration to report Leroy for stealing uniforms, and when Freddy was sick with asthma, Rodney told him he had to come to work or be fired, even though he had a doctor's note. The guys made it clear that neither the manager nor his assistant were to be trusted and that Rodney was sneaky and always complaining that the workers were lazy.

After Joseph had been on the job for a year, he expected to get a raise, but he did not. He had been hired at poverty-level wages, which were often shortened. Also, he and his friends were not paid for their overtime either. One day, he and the other guys were eating their lunch in a small room with a hole in the ceiling, a bucket on the floor to catch the leaking water, and a new Coke machine. Joseph and JT listened to the Braves game on Leroy's boom box. Afterward, Joseph went to his locker for his badge, and the door of his locker stood open; so did the door to Leroy's and TJ's lockers, but Freddy's was untouched.

"Guys, come here!" Joseph yelled. When Leroy saw his own locker open, he banged on the table and then started pacing the floor. JT chain-smoked cigarettes in frustration. Joseph was on edge as he thought about losing his job, and he balled his fists in anger because he knew he was being exploited.

Joseph immediately went to Rodney's office to confront him. While pointing his finger in Rodney's face, Joseph loudly and angrily accused the assistant manager of tearing the lock off his locker and his friends' lockers and opening them without their permission.

Rodney announced the keys were missing from the warehouse. "Have you read the company handbook? I have the right to check your lockers," he added. His manner toward my husband was arrogant and rude.

Joseph got in his face and said, "You don't own me."

"You better watch your mouth if you want to keep this job," Rodney snarled.

After work, Joseph talked to Terry, the owner, who apologized and said the company didn't discriminate. That evening, when Joseph finished patrolling a nearby clothing store and was ready to go home, he noticed two of his tires were slashed. He stiffened and thought, *I'll never let these ignorant people hurt me.*

Joseph went back to the other men and told them what had happened. He was upset and didn't know how he would get home, so he called his friend Tony for help. (Tony was the person who told him about the job in the first place.) Several hours later, Tony finally arrived. "Man, I am sorry about your tires, but you got to be careful," he warned Joseph. "I can help you get new tires, though."

While they drove, Tony told Joseph to tone down his behavior. "As Black men, we have to blend in on the job and not show our anger to stay safe," he reminded my husband. "Even though you are not respected, you must adapt in order to earn an income to take care of your family. Brother, I had to swallow my pride to keep my job and my mean boss made me feel ashamed. I appreciate you wanting respect, but you got to think about your wife and children."

On the drive home, Joseph worried about how he was going to break the news to me about the slashed tires and other troubles on the job since we were struggling financially.

Not only did Joseph now have two slashed tires to fix, but he wasn't getting paid for the overtime he earned either. Working conditions were sketchy, too; Joseph was sent to monitor a warehouse of dangerous chemicals and had blurry vision for several days afterward. When he complained to Rodney, he was ignored. That's when he decided to call a meeting with his friends and told them he planned to start a union. Leroy scratched his head and said, "Man, that could get us fired." Even though the boss had cursed out JT in front of everyone for being late, JT said, "That is dangerous talk." Joseph recognized their concern; he had been around Black men from the South who had a deep fear of going to jail or losing their jobs. But Joseph answered simply, "We got to take action."

Joseph came home that night and sat in our driveway for hours. Finally, I went outside to see what was wrong.

"Babe, I told them that I wanted to start a union."

"You did what?" I became alarmed because someone could be arrested for doing that. Finally, he got out of the old Impala and mumbled that these people were messing with his family.

On Tuesday morning, Joseph went back to work. Terry, the manager, met him at the door holding Buster, the Doberman pinscher, close on a short leash. Looking scared, Terry announced, "You're fired," and handed Joseph his belongings in a cardboard box.

Joseph was owed a week's pay plus fifteen hours of overtime, so his response was, "What about my paycheck?"

"We don't owe you any money," was Terry's icy reply.

Fighting Workplace Discrimination

Joseph decided to call the Equal Employment Opportunity Commission (EEOC) about filing a complaint against the company for violating the law by firing him and refusing to pay him when they thought he would start a union. He told the clerk that he wasn't afraid of retaliation from the company. "I knew this company was unfair when I saw the Confederate flag in the office," he said.

The clerk asked him to come in to file a complaint in person.

Joseph was doubtful any action would be taken on his case, but he decided to try anyway. The day he went in for his two o'clock appointment, he wore white shirt and slacks.

The EEOC office was on the sixth floor of a tall office building on Peachtree Street. Joseph was greeted by Irene, his counselor, who had a puffy ponytail and wore a blue blazer. She told him she had just graduated from University of Georgia with an MBA, and this was her first job.

"I talked to you on the phone," Irene told him. "Let's head to my office." Once there, Joseph sat in a leather chair across from Irene's shiny desk. Irene opened the folder on my husband's case. "You are courageous to file a claim. I see your complaint against the Jessup Security Agency is for discrimination, and there should not be discrimination based on race or color," she told him. "Can you tell me more about what happened while working at Jessup Security?"

Joseph told her how his boss had smashed open his locker, and that he had worked at a warehouse with the smell of chemicals.

"I will help you file your claim," Irene replied. She reviewed his written complaint again. "You included missing pay, missing overtime, and the slashing of your tires. Did you feel that you were in danger, Mr. Halliburton?"

"Yes, and the next day, I was fired!" Joseph told her.

Irene suggested he seek legal advice. "The EEOC can provide a list of local attorneys to represent you and give you advice. First, the agency will file a formal complaint with your employer for discrimination. If the EEOC finds the company guilty, you may be awarded damages, including back wages and overtime. I will be giving you a call about your claim in a few weeks."

Joseph left the office thinking the counselor seemed confident, and he was more optimistic about getting fair treatment than he had been before walking into that office.

After two months, the Jessup Security Agency admitted wrongful discrimination, and an agreement was reached. Joseph was awarded a financial settlement, but he was disgusted and angry that the small settlement supposedly compensated him for his pain and suffering. Even though my husband received $3,000, he felt it was not enough for the malicious actions of the company. He asked the EEOC about a hearing, but he felt the situation was too complex for him to continue waiting in the hope that he'd be awarded more; the lack of income hurt us, and he had to think about his family.

Joseph remembered that his dad had faced the same type of meanness and hate on the job, and he believed not much had changed in the workplace for Black men. He was out of work for four stressful weeks. He learned the lesson that he needed to start his own company and be in charge.

30
All Is Not Well

AFTER JOSEPH'S TERMINATION, he was concerned about the bills not being paid. He had assumed the job was stable, so he felt betrayed and disappointed, especially because the family depended on his paychecks.

He began his job search immediately, and for the next two weeks, he scoured want ads, made phone calls, and checked with friends. He was looking for a security job or a warehouse position, hopefully at Sears, Roebuck and Co. or Aaron's Warehouse. He also filled out applications in Decatur and Lawrenceville. Unfortunately, he had been rejected at two places because his employer gave him a bad reference.

On Friday evening, I was cooking chicken from Kroger for dinner. I decided to make curry chicken with ginger and minced garlic. I recalled that Joseph's mom's, Carrie, made this recipe in New York; the aroma of these spices filled the kitchen. *I'll surprise him*, I thought.

I browned my meat and added it to a curry sauce. Next, I boiled jasmine rice and cut my carrots and potatoes.

While I was cooking, Aisha began pulling out my pots and pans, beating on them with two long wooden spoons and giggling. I was a little annoyed, but she was happy. When the green phone on the wall rang, I couldn't hear well after I said hello, so I followed up with, "Joseph, is that you?"

"Yes, hi Babe," my husband mumbled in a low voice.

I asked if he was all right, and his response was, "Well, I am okay."

His tone worried me; he usually said kind things or asked about our daughters in an upbeat way. I didn't know what to say, but I decided to wait till he was home to ask. "Dinner is almost ready," I said instead.

"I'll be home soon."

About thirty minutes later, I heard a grinding noise from the engine of my husband's car as he pulled into our driveway. I took off my apron and ran to greet him in the driveway with Aisha trailing behind me. As Aisha got closer to the door, she hollered, "Daddy is home!"

Joseph wore his wool cap and his wrinkled green sports coat. I knew Joseph normally cared about how he looked and hated wearing wrinkled clothing. To me, between the wrinkled jacket, his labored movements, and his body language, he just looked so defeated. He exited the maroon Impala, picked up Aisha, and cradled her tightly. Fatima and Rabia, who were riding bicycles outside, rushed over to meet their dad. And Coco began barking, so Joseph reached down to rub his head.

Fatima asked, "Daddy can we play chess tonight?" When her dad told her, "Maybe tomorrow," she pressed with "And Rabia says you did not play chess with us last night."

"Hey, girl," I interrupted. "I want to talk to Daddy for a while." I leaned down and whispered, "Girls, I want you to wash your hands and set up the silverware on the table for dinner. Fatima, you are the leader tonight."

"Why can't I be in charge?" Rabia whined.

"No, Rabia. Tonight, you'll listen to your big sister."

I stood beside my husband's car and looked at the yellow mums blooming in our yard. I felt hopeful, and I just knew things would get better. In the meantime, my husband reached into the car and grabbed his sports magazine with Muhammad Ali on the cover.

While Joseph closed the car door, I said, "Your friend, Tony, came looking for you this afternoon." He darted his eyes at the magazine like he was not interested. We walked in the driveway path to the steps, which he climbed ahead of me. He opened the screen door with its loose handle and stepped into our living room, which had toys scattered on the linoleum floor. I moved past my husband to sit on the red couch, and he sat beside me.

"How was your day, Joseph?" I asked gently.

With tight lips, he replied, "Okay," followed by five minutes of silence. I felt he did not want to share his feelings. As we sat there in silence, the thick rotary phone on the coffee table rang, and I answered it.

"Hi, Rose," I said quietly. "Can I call you back?"

After hanging up, I turned my attention back to my still-silent husband. "Joseph, did you have any interviews this afternoon?"

"I did not get a job. Is that what you are asking?" he demanded. I ignored his loud, angry response and, instead, told him I'd made a special dinner of curry chicken. "I am not hungry," he snapped.

"It's seven, do you want to watch the *CBS Evening News* with Walter Cronkite?" I asked. I didn't know what was wrong or how to get him to talk to me.

"No, I am going to listen to my jazz music."

Before I could respond, Fatima yelled from the kitchen, "Mom, the table is ready."

"I'll be there shortly." I turned my attention back to Joseph, who wore a gloomy expression. As I thought about it, I realized he hadn't smiled much since losing his job, and he'd been staying up late every night. I asked him to join us for dinner, but he just shook his head no, saying he didn't have any appetite.

After dinner, kitchen cleanup, and getting things ready for the morning, I tucked my daughters into bed and said goodnight to them at 8:30 p.m. Once the girls were asleep, I went to check on Joseph in our bedroom. The sound of Oscar Peterson's "Things Ain't What They Used to Be" playing was soothing to my ears. I knew Joseph liked that song; I bought that album for him at a music store on 125th Street in Harlem.

Slowly, I opened the bedroom door, and I smelled incense. I recognized what that meant because he'd done it when we lived in New York to lift his mood. Maybe he felt restless and tense; the smell was unusual now.

Joseph was lying on the right side of the bed in his white T-shirt and underwear, and the lime green sheets had been pushed onto the floor by the side of the bed. I asked quietly, "Joseph, are you all right?" No response. I stood in the doorway and called again, but he still did not answer, which really concerned me. His eyes were open, and I could barely see his face. As I stood there, my throat tightened, and my knees became weak.

From the light coming through the silver shade on the bedside lamp, I saw the shiny .45-caliber automatic pistol. I balled up my hands and began to tremble.

Anxious, worried, and afraid, I stepped into the room and sat down on the left side of the bed. My shoulders slumped and I held my head in my hands. I tried not to panic; I needed to stay calm for my children.

I had seen the gun in the glove compartment of the car when we first moved to Atlanta, but this was the first time saw it in the house and in our bedroom. I thought about my husband being a Vietnam veteran. I had seen him in distress and sad in New York, but he never acted this way. Joseph would talk to me. Now, he wouldn't share his feelings.

I just sat there, thinking about how overwhelmed he'd been when he got fired. Joseph needed to snap out of this, and I was worried. After about fifteen minutes, I left the bedroom and rushed to my daughters' room, where I held Aisha's pink teddy bear. Shortly, I prayed over my daughters, asking God to look after my family. I couldn't shake the question that kept coming to my mind: did Joseph plan to hurt himself?

Next, I took a pillow and the striped blanket from the closet, and I slept on the red couch in the living room. I cried myself to sleep while holding onto the blanket my sister had given me. Finally, I checked on Joseph around 3:00 a.m. He looked asleep; once I was sure he was, I tiptoed into the room to pick up the heavy, brown-handled revolver, and I wondered if it was loaded. Once I was out of the room with it, I did not know what to do with it, so I took the gun to the backyard in the dark and hid it with my garden tools.

Back in the house and with a tight stomach, I paced the floor until daylight. Promptly at 6:00 a.m., Joseph opened the bedroom door and walked into the living room wearing a flannel shirt and slacks.

"Hi, Estell," he greeted me, but his voice sounded flat, and he didn't smile. My heart pounded, but I stayed calm. Joseph stood near the walnut coffee table and, looking a bit confused, asked, "Where is my gun?"

"I'm not telling you. I hid it."

"Why?"

"Because I was afraid."

Joseph said, "Babe, I felt a lot of anger last night, but I will never hurt anyone in our family."

"Why do you have a gun in our bedroom?" I already knew part of the answer: he believed that he needed the gun for protection, and he worried about the police ever since he had witnessed them kill his childhood friend. I added, "Could you get rid of it?" When Joseph said no, I told him it made me uncomfortable having it in our home. "For now," I told him, "it will stay hidden."

"Honey, I am sorry for my behavior; please forgive me." My husband gave me a slight smile. "Can you make me some coffee?" I shook my head no. I always made my husband's coffee, and it seemed to relax him, but that morning, I was in no mood to do so.

Joseph made his own coffee and abandoned the rest of his morning routine—there was no breakfast, no speaking with the children, no goodbye to me. After he got his own coffee, he mumbled defiantly, "I am getting a job today," and then proceeded to walk out the front door to his car. He seemed not to be thinking about us at all. I believed he was hurting inside because I knew he did love us.

As soon as I heard his car leave the driveway, I rushed to call my family in Mississippi.

"Hi, Mommy!"

"Sis, you sound tired. Are you all right?"

"Yes, Mommy. I was just thinking about you and Daddy."

Momma sounded concerned. "Sis, I am headed to work in my garden to plant turnip greens and cucumbers."

"I miss eating your home cooking," I remarked.

"Are the girls all right?"

"Yes, just fine," I said, realizing she was worried by my call.

"Tell Richard hello."

"Bye, Momma, I love you." After I hung up the phone, I felt better. I even smiled after talking to my momma. I thought, *I'll wake up my daughters and cook breakfast, maybe waffles with strawberries.*

Can We Talk?

I barely spoke to my husband for the next week. We hadn't exactly argued, but it certainly felt like we had, and I was hurt and angry. The only thing we discussed was caring for our daughters. During that time, I saw a bouquet of red roses and a box of candy wrapped in a silver box on the dining table with a note that read, "I am sorry." I threw the roses and the candy in the garbage. When Joseph called on the phone, I wouldn't answer. I just ignored him since I was not ready to listen to him. I still loved him, but I was hurt by his actions of shutting me out, and I really wanted to slap him a few times. I calmed down after a while.

On Friday evening, I sat in the kitchen with my daughters. On the menu: Sloppy Joes with chopped meat and red sauce, lightly seasoned with spices. Aisha drank out of her pink Disney cup. I opened the window, and the bright sunlight shone through my yellow curtains. I knew my daughters were concerned about me and their dad. When the girls and I sat down to eat, I said the blessing as we held hands; I held Aisha's tiny ones. "We are thankful, dear God, for the many blessings and our food."

Rabia lifted her bowed head and asked loudly, "Mom. Where is Daddy's plate? I miss him. He didn't eat with us last night."

"Rabia, your daddy and I disagreed, but we are working things out," I assured her.

Fatima chimed in, "Daddy looked unhappy. And he did not come to say good night."

"Daddy will never stop loving you, girl," I assured her. Fatima nodded her head and looked uncertain; her usual smile was missing.

Aisha climbed onto my lap and ate off my plate, and she managed to spill sauce on the pink tablecloth as well as her yellow sundress and white sandals. She giggled and drank sweet tea out of her pink Disney cup.

When I finished eating, I said, "Girls, clean up the kitchen, and I am going to bathe Aisha." I paused for a moment. Then I announced, "Your daddy is taking you to McDonald's near Greenbriar Mall tomorrow for a Happy Meal." Suddenly, I noticed big smiles, which made me feel good. Even though I was unhappy with Joseph, he still took care of the girls.

I was hurt and displeased with the tension in our home, but I continued my daily work. I thought about my mother and her strength in Aberdeen. During this time, I confided in Rose at our sewing class that I was arguing with Joseph. Rose asked, "Do you want to talk about it?" but I told her no, maybe later. But I did not discuss it with her. I don't share my personal business with anyone. I am a private person, and my husband felt the same way. Besides, how could I tell her my husband had a loaded gun on the side table by our bed?

After another week went by, Joseph came home one evening and said, "I want to talk to you."

I sat down on the red couch in the living room. "I may have a job offer," he told me. I didn't look at him.

"Babe, please listen; I want to talk to you about my attitude."

I lifted my head to look into his brown eyes; I knew how much I loved him. However, he made me feel anxious at times.

"I still think about the Vietnam War," Joseph said slowly. "I've had nightmares many nights about being in the jungle. I went to war to show my patriotism like my dad. Then I realized I was in a foreign land in the same uniform as the other men in my platoon, but I wasn't viewed as a true American. Even coming home, I felt like an outsider because it took months to get a job, and I was ignored. Looking for a job and trying to pay our bills after being fired was so hard, especially when I kept getting rejected."

As I listened, I laid my head on his shoulder, and my eyes welled with tears. Filled with love for him, even with his imperfections, I embraced him with a warm hug. I remembered when Joseph first joined the Black Panther party; I was so scared for him with police raiding their offices in Brooklyn.

I thought about us moving to the South with big dreams. Joseph embraced his cultural identity growing up in Harlem, New York. He came to the South for a better life for our family and bought a home. He endured blatant biases in the workplace. Joseph was unwilling to change or hide his identity.

For instance, when he worked at the Jessup Security Agency, Rodney, the assistant manager, broke into Joseph's locker when he thought the keys had been stolen. Tony never inquired about the missing keys; he just assumed that Joseph was a thief and unethical.

Further, the boss was insensitive and thought Joseph was unintelligent and did not know his rights. Joseph knew that even after the civil rights movement, some attitudes hadn't changed; there were still signs in the restaurants in downtown Atlanta that read WHITES ONLY. My husband continued speaking up and protesting, and he could be jailed for his social activism. I believed that America's promise of freedom and justice were beyond the reach for Black people.

After Joseph finished speaking, I told him I needed us to come together. He held my hand and promised to do better and would spend more time with our daughters. He said he regretted his behavior, and he looked sincere.

"I felt doubtful about paying our mortgage and buying clothes for our daughters, and I was embarrassed. Babe, I respect you, and I will do better."

I appreciated his apology and said, "I decided to mark two days a week the calendar to talk about our marriage and about you carrying a gun."

Joseph took a deep breath. "Where is my gun?"

"I am not telling you," I answered.

My husband looked disappointed. He shrugged his shoulders. but I knew he wanted to make peace and mend our relationship. Finally, Joseph walked over to the twenty-five-inch black-and-white TV and turned it on. After turning the dial, he found a movie on channel 6. "Babe, what about this movie? *Close Encounters of the Third Kind*? I know you like science fiction and adventure stories."

"Yes," I told my husband with a smile, "I'll grab the popcorn and some cherry ice cream."

31

A New Beginning for Joseph

ON A THURSDAY afternoon, while I listened to *WSB* radio to hear the weather report, I washed the dishes and rinsed them in the sink. But my mind wandered, and my thoughts returned to a common refrain: *I would like to get a job and help with the bills.* Suddenly, Joseph tapped me on the shoulder, and I turned around to a beaming smile.

"Hey, Babe, I got a job." He lifted me off the floor and hugged me.

"Joseph, you got hired!" I yelled. "I am so happy for you." I squeezed him while my mind raced forward. "Tonight, I am preparing a fresh peach pie; you know you love the flaky crust and the smell of cinnamon."

Joseph sat down at the table, and I followed him, asking for details. "You know I am curious about your new job."

"I put my application in at Mountain Warehouse Company, a home improvement retailer on La Vista Road; I received a phone call this morning that I got the job."

I pretended to scold him with, "You kept this from me!" and he laughed.

"I drove to the company to talk to the supervisor, Jacob, who said I could start work on Monday. Then I filled out a form for insurance and a tax form." When I asked my husband what he would be doing, he said with pride, "I am a clerk assisting customers, stocking shelves, and organizing merchandise." I clapped my hands together in delight as he continued, "In addition, I am driving a small truck to deliver and pick up appliances and equipment. My starting pay is $4.50 an hour, and I don't have to work on the weekends. Plus, I will pick up my uniform on Monday. It is khaki pants and a blue shirt."

I asked about the location of his new job, and he replied, "About twenty miles from our home, and I get off I-85 North in the city of Tucker, Georgia."

We chatted about how the drive might be with traffic, and then Joseph told me, "After filling out my application for the job, I was interviewed by Jacob, a short guy with a bald head and a cigar hanging off his lips. Babe, this guy asked me ridiculous questions."

"Tell me."

"After I took the two tests, he was surprised that I got above average on the logic test. He said, 'I see that you are a smart fellow. Where are you from?' When I told him 'New York,' he asked, 'Have you ever been to jail?' He seemed friendly and wore a Falcon's hat." Joseph paused before continuing, "Although I am still determining what to expect from this guy, I am ready to start work."

"Joseph, this is the right job for you. I can just feel it," I told him.

"I will be training for three weeks for certification to drive a truck and be registered by the company."

I could hear the pride in his voice, pride that had been missing for far too long.

"I can't wait to tell our daughters the good news," he said with a smile.

After we talked for another minute, Joseph said, "Babe, I am headed to Walmart to fix our lawn mower. Do you need more seeds for your garden?"

I couldn't believe how motivated Joseph sounded now that he had a job. "No, I am good," I told him, and then gave him another hug before he left for the store.

Once he was gone, I made myself a sandwich with Skippy peanut butter and sliced bananas on white bread with a glass of milk. I recalled eating this delicious sandwich in Aberdeen as a young girl with slices of Wonder Bread that came wrapped in red and white plastic. I decided to sit on the back porch in my purple chair to eat, and Coco lay beside my chair while I rubbed his fur.

After I finished my sandwich, I pulled out my red bound journal from my garden basket along with my silver pen. As I turned the pages, I saw a black-and-white photo of my brother Wardell and me and my gray puppy, Spooky. I was living on the Thompson plantation at the time, and Wardell looked after me when Momma went to town. I was always sneaking into the woods behind our house. I smiled at the memory. "I don't remember wearing shoes with my faded overalls," I muttered aloud, "with about six braids sticking up on my head." I still had dreams about living with my family in our small shack. Sadly, the photo was faded, and I could barely see the images and the date written on the back: 1952. *Oh, I've learned so much since then*, I thought.

I picked up my silver pen and began reflecting on the events of the past few weeks.

May 17

> I am thankful for my family. I am still trying to make sense of my marriage to Joseph after 15 years and I am discovering what truly matters to me. Certainly, I've been shaped by my values of growing up in Aberdeen. With my husband, I am learning more about him, and it gets kind of rough at times.

32

Joseph Gets His Groove Back

I HEARD A KNOCK at the door one Friday morning in June and peeked through the curtain; it was Charlie, the mailman. He handed me a loosely tied cardboard box with a return address from Aberdeen along with the newspaper. Then, I told Charlie to wait just a minute; I ran to the kitchen to grab two homemade oatmeal raisin cookies for him. He smiled and said, "Thanks, Ms. Estell."

I put the box on the table to surprise my daughters when they came in for lunch. Momma had told me she was sending sundresses for my daughters and some freshly made Kimmel's fudge. Then I opened the *Atlanta Journal-Constitution* and saw a picture of Andrew Young, one of the leaders of the civil rights movement, who marched with Dr. Martin Luther King Jr. In 1963, Dr. Young also mediated between white and Black communities during protests. I planned to teach my girls about his courage and leadership. *Since he lives in Atlanta*, I thought, *I hope they can meet him one day.*

The phone rang; it was Joseph, who wanted to let me know he would be late coming home that day.

"How are you feeling today?" he asked. That surprised me because when he called, he usually asked what was for dinner, but he didn't this time. When I told him I was good, he said, "I got a surprise for you."

I wonder what's happening with him, I thought. *Well, I know he sounds happy.* I didn't have time to think more about what the surprise might be because the doorbell rang; it was Jessie Lee from the diner. She was a sight for sore eyes as she stood on my front porch in her waitress uniform.

"I brought your Avon order, the White Rose perfume, in that cute narrow-neck bottle," Jessie Lee greeted. "I don't make much money at the café; this weekend job keeps food on the table." She handed me the silver bag with a couple of coupons inside.

"I'll pay you next time," I told her.

She shook her head and told me not to worry about it. "Are we still on for lunch at Paschal's Restaurant on Hunter Street next Saturday?"

I gave her a big smile. "Indeed, I can't wait to eat their sweet buttery pecan pie."

"See you soon, sweetie." Jessie Lee smiled and waved as she headed back to her car.

Next, I set up my ironing board with a smooth cotton cover. I grabbed Joseph's shirt and began pressing out the wrinkles. I decided to turn on the small black-and-white TV to watch my soap opera, *All My Children*, which came on at 1:00 p.m. My favorite character was Eric Kane, who was charming and a troublemaker. I must have paid too much attention to the show while I continued ironing because soon, I realized I had just burned Joseph's shirt; it now had a brown stain printed on the front pocket in the shape of the iron. I later learned the iron had a faulty cord and was defective, but at the time, I thought, *I got this iron from Kmart, and it's a piece of junk.* I decided I would just hide the shirt from Joseph.

I was still ironing when I heard what sounded like screaming. I ran to the front door with my apron on and saw a bright yellow station wagon in our driveway and my daughters were yelling and jumping up and down in excitement. Next to it stood my husband, looking cool in his sunglasses and a blue floral shirt, his shoulders back and his head held high. And circling him were our daughters, whose outside play stopped in their excitement of seeing their daddy step out of a new yellow station wagon. For a moment, I could barely catch my breath. I ran to see this car and bumped into Fatima's bicycle in the yard with my house shoes.

"Joseph, you bought us a new Ford station wagon!" I felt proud to see his success after losing his job and feeling stuck.

I hugged my husband tightly, hollering with my daughters, "We've got a new car!" Joseph wore a big grin like I hadn't seen in weeks. He swaggered around the car like he had regained his power. In the meantime, four-year-old Aisha held up her hands to be picked up by her dad. Rabia pulled on her daddy's shirt and kept asking, "Is this our car?" Fatima danced around the car and rubbed the wood side panel. Then, she looked confused and asked, "Daddy, where is our old car?"

"I gave the keys to the dealer when I bought our new car," he told her.

I looked at the Ford's shiny chrome grill and wondered how much this station wagon cost. I had some questions for my husband. But as I looked at Joseph's beaming smile, I knew he was setting us on a path to success.

After hearing all the commotion, our neighbors Tony and Rose came over. Tony said, "That yellow Ford station wagon you bought is top of the line, and it looks like it just came off the showroom floor."

"Joseph, you got a smooth ride, and I like those chrome hubcaps; looks fancy," Rose added, and then turned to me and whispered, "Girl, I am so happy for you. I can see you riding to get your nails done at Miss Betty's place." I stretched out my hands and wiggled my shoulder, of course.

After we all chatted in the driveway for about twenty minutes, Tony said, "Come on, Rose, let them enjoy their new car." Tony and

Joseph slapped their hands together in a high five. I was grateful that these two men had formed a brotherhood because they understood their struggle as Black men.

As soon as Tony and Rose were gone, Joseph shouted, "Are you ready for a ride?" The girls all squealed with delight, so Joseph pulled the handle in the back, opened the rear door, and flattened the seats. Our older daughters scrambled into the car with their dirty sneakers, and Joseph lifted Aisha into the back seat with her sisters.

Joseph opened the car door for me with a flourish as he said, "Step inside, Babe." With my shoulders thrown back, I pulled off my apron, stepped inside, and buckled my seat belt. I sat beside my husband on the soft brown leather bench seat; it smelled like new leather. Joseph turned on the air conditioner and took off his sunglasses. "Wow, cold air blowing in my face," I said with a smile, and he chuckled, then grabbed the wood steering wheel.

I reached over to turn the dial to the R&B radio. Soon, Stevie Wonder's "Superstition" filled the car, and I bobbed my head to the beat while my daughters sang along.

As the song ended, Fatima asked, "Daddy can we go to Burger King?"

Joseph reached over and turned off the radio. He looked into the rearview mirror to the back seat. "Listen up. Rabia, how many books did you read this week?"

"Daddy, I did not have time. I was working on my science project with glitter and dish soap."

"That's no excuse, " Joseph told her. "Fatima, did you get an A on your algebra test?"

"Well, I got a B last week," she admitted.

Joseph pulled off the road and stopped the car. He turned around to face the girls without saying a word.

Aisha volunteered, "Daddy, I read my book, *The Frog and the Toad*, and I know my shapes."

Joseph Gets His Groove Back

"Good job, Aisha," he said without much enthusiasm. "I am thinking about taking you girls back home. What did I tell you about training your minds to think and focus on your work?"

I said softly, "Joseph, we are celebrating tonight. Can you talk about this later?"

He sighed. "All right, Babe." He started the car again and pulled back into traffic.

About ten minutes later, Joseph turned into Burger King on Greenbriar Parkway, and by then, he seemed relaxed. The Braves game played on the radio, and he turned the tiny metal knob to a low volume, and then he shouted, "Let's eat in the car!"

The girls giggled in the back seat.

"Don't spill your drink on the seats," their dad warned. "Babe, do you want to take their orders?"

"Do you girls want your usual, the hamburger with cheese, fries, and a strawberry shake?" I asked them.

Fatima answered. "Yes, Mom. I know Rabia wants extra ketchup, and I want extra pickles."

Aisha held up her hand and asked, "Mom, can I order? Do they have a happy meal?" That sent Fatima and Rabia into a fit of giggles.

"No, this is not McDonald's," Rabia told her baby sister.

"I know what you want," I said to Aisha, "chicken nuggets, fries, and an ice cream cone."

Aisha smiled and said, "Thanks, Mom."

"Joseph, I'll order you a Whopper with onion rings, Mountain Dew, and a slice of chocolate cream pie."

I placed our orders at the drive-thru, then Joseph parked the car and went inside to get everything. He soon emerged from Burger King with two bags of food, and a drink carrier nestled between them. As Joseph approached the car, I could see his satisfied smile, and the girls let out cheers of joy. When he handed me the bags, I noticed a small piece of paper peeking out through his fingers, a neatly folded receipt in the amount $3.97; this dinner was a great deal. As we pulled out of the parking lot in our new yellow station wagon, the tantalizing smell of burgers filled the car.

We headed home, happily chatting and eating our celebration dinner. All the while, I kept thinking, *Tonight was special, and I am truly grateful for this delicious meal with my family.*

33

Fun in the Yellow Station Wagon

A LTHOUGH I WAS CONCERNED about my husband buying a new car, seeing the yellow station wagon parked in the driveway at our modest home made me smile. I couldn't wait to visit my parents in Aberdeen. As I sat on the side of the bed on Friday morning, I daydreamed about shopping at Rich's department store on Broad Street, walking down the aisles, picking up name-brand purses like Calvin Klein with their gold chains, and seeing the kind salesladies. *I am tired of wearing these faded jeans and sweatshirts and shopping at thrift stores on weekends,* I thought.

I recalled shopping with my daughters six months earlier so they would have new clothes for my husband's birthday. I wanted to get them each a new pair of patent-leather shoes with a T-strap and a dainty bow, and the shoe department was on the second floor. My youngest daughter, Aisha, was reluctant to ride the escalator, so I practically carried her up. Her big sisters giggled, saying, "Aisha is still a baby," which upset me. Sensing my attitude, Fatima knelt to comfort her sister at the top of the escalator. I was glad to see my daughters being kind to each other.

I heard the doorbell ring, followed by Joseph hollering, "I'll get it." That was my cue to return to my daily duties. Hearing Joseph speaking to the person at the door, I grabbed my pink house shoes and strolled into our kitchen.

When I entered the small white kitchen, I heard the announcer talking on the radio about the Hawks basketball team and saw Joseph listening intensely.

"Good morning," I said.

"Hey, Babe," he replied.

I grabbed a chocolate donut from the covered bowl and walked past him; he smelled like Old Spice.

Joseph asked if I had slept well, and I told him I had. Joseph was wearing his khaki shirt and pants for work. He stood in front of the electric stove, adding coffee grinds to the percolator basket for his coffee. While he did that, I began fixing his lunch of tuna fish and an apple.

Joseph smiled at me and announced, "I am coming home early this evening because we are going on a road trip."

"Oh, that sounds like fun in our new station wagon," I said happily.

Joseph added, "I was told at the mosque that the houses are cheap in Forsyth, Georgia, and we can buy a home there."

We had talked about this before with a couple of friends as we daydreamed about owning farm land and growing our own vegetables.

"No," I said firmly, "I am not going outside of Atlanta. Besides, this small place is probably one of those sundown towns and unsafe for Black people. As a girl growing up in Mississippi I listened to my dad's and uncles' stories about Black people being put in jail for driving through these places."

Joseph rubbed his chin. "Babe, I did not grow up in the South, and these stories are new to me."

"Joseph, I am not ready to integrate into this small town." At the time, Forsyth only had white residents.

Fun in the Yellow Station Wagon

My life changed in 1964. I was a country girl and a bit rough around the edges when I met tall and handsome Joseph R. Halliburton in New York City.

In this photo, he is 38 years old and charming. He is wearing his white T-shirt and has a thick Afro and beard. On the day I met him, Joseph was a private in the army and stationed in New York. By the way that he spoke, I knew this guy was articulate. On our first date, he told me about the Harlem Renaissance, and I could see how much pride he had in our culture. Six months later, I married this soldier.

As a father, he was always there for our daughters. He listened to them and spent hours playing chess with them. He encouraged them to read books about our history. Not only was Joseph the breadwinner and provider, but he was the leader of our family and set our moral values. And I can recall that he always brought me red roses and respected me as his wife. For sure, we had our ups and downs in our marriage, but I found my soulmate in my husband. We loved spending time watching old movies together. He believed in us leaning on each other and guarding against losing our identity and our heritage.

"All right, then," Joseph replied. "We'll stay in Atlanta and raise our family here. But I've got a road trip planned for you and the girls this evening."

"Please tell me where we are going!" I began dancing around and laughing.

Suddenly, he grabbed his lunch and kissed me on the cheek. "I'll be home at six-thirty, and I'll surprise you." He waved bye and left!

In the afternoon, I sat down with my daughters on the front porch as they ate popsicles. I told them to be ready at six that evening for our road trip.

Aisha asked, "Can I bring Coco?"

"No, baby girl," I told her. I sat her on my lap, and she leaned her head on my shoulder. I told her Coco would be fine in his bed with the new gray blanket. "Why don't you go inside and hug him?" I suggested, and she hurried into the house to see Coco.

As the sun was setting, Joseph pulled up in the yellow station wagon wearing his sunglasses. He had a Kroger's bag full of snacks for the girls that included Hostess Twinkies snack cakes and Hubba Bubba bubble gum. He always brought goodies after work, and he received lots of hugs.

He hopped out and opened the rear doors for our daughters. The girls were dressed in white pants and tunic shirts, and I had braided their hair. I wore my yellow maxi dress with gold sandals and hoop earrings.

In the car, with the cool air conditioner flowing, I put on my seat belt. As Joseph started the engine, Fatima asked where we were going.

"Our first stop is Auburn Avenue to see the home of civil rights leader Martin Luther King Jr.," Joseph announced, sounding like a tour guide. "Second, I am driving to Collier Heights, a middle-class Afro American neighborhood. Then, we'll go through Buckhead, where the rich white folk live."

I felt comfortable with the stereo sound of jazz music playing and lots of giggling from the girls. I looked over at my husband, who looked handsome even in his work clothes.

He caught me looking at him and smiled. "Babe, I am taking you out on Saturday to see the movie *Shaft*."

"I can't wait to see this action-packed movie with a Black man playing the lead role in Harlem," I told him excitedly.

After being on I-85 for a while in heavy traffic, Joseph started gliding past slower cars, shifting lanes, and overtaking slower vehicles.

"Joseph, slow down!" I shouted. "Why are you driving at eighty miles an hour?"

"Sorry, Babe, I lost track of my speed. I promise that I'll go the speed limit."

For the rest of the evening's drive, the only sound was Fatima and Aisha playing pat-a-cake, a hand-slapping game with rhymes. I smiled, remembering how I had played that game when I was growing up in Aberdeen. I settled down in my leather seat with a small cushion behind my back and felt comfortable. I was enjoying this road trip with my family in our yellow Ford station wagon.

34

An Afternoon of Quilting

I FINISHED DUSTING the living room furniture and placed a vase with vibrant yellow mums on the polished coffee table. I was excited about meeting with my quilting club in just thirty minutes. Hurrying to get ready, I chose a floral print dress with puffy sleeves and gold loop earrings. When the doorbell rang, I opened the door and I was greeted by a Black man dressed in a uniform and carrying a toolbox. He said politely, "I am looking for Joseph."

"My husband is not here."

"I am a contractor, and he wanted me to fix the back porch."

I assured him that I would let my husband know. As he departed, I wondered why Joseph had not mentioned this, but I decided he probably forgot.

I was putting away the broom in the kitchen when I heard knocking on the screen door. "Come in," I greeted, and in walked Daisy, who was wearing a bright yellow sun hat and carrying her green sewing basket.

"Hi, sister, I saw your husband driving that new Ford station wagon; you've moved up," she teased, and I chuckled. I gestured for her to sit on the red sofa and took the small bags of fruit she'd brought along to share. About five minutes later, Rose, Leila, and Viola arrived with their sewing baskets and a side of treats to celebrate our get-together. Daisy and I followed my friends into the living room. Then, she mentioned that Margaret, our new neighbor, was not coming that day. Rose clicked her teeth and said, "I am glad she is not coming; she brings that nasty potato salad with dill pickles and raisins," and Viola added, "How could she mess up that classic soul food dish?" We all giggled.

Shortly, I jingled the tiny bell that announced the start of our gathering. My friends took their seats at the dining table. First, I carefully laid out the wide homemade quilt in the middle of the table. Our quilt had a horizontal pattern with bright floral squares. I felt a sense of joy and saw warmth in my friends' eyes as they touched the sewn pieces. Rose's expression was filled with admiration, and she said, "Our quilt is a work of art, but it still needs a border and more padding."

"Just a moment," I said, and I grabbed my old Kodak camera and snapped their picture. We began finishing the quilt by sewing the padding, and we chatted the whole time. Then, Viola suggested she could finish the quilt on her grandma's Singer sewing machine instead of sewing it by hand.

"That's a great idea," I said because our hands were tired after an hour of sewing. "Who's ready for our delicious treats?" Leila and Daisy said to go ahead.

The rotary phone rang just as I was about to serve the food. I heard my husband's voice on the other end, and he said, "Hi, Honey. I'll be coming home late tonight. Bye, Honey."

I smiled as I hung up the phone. *Joseph is always so thoughtful.*

I turned to Rose and asked if she could help me serve the food. She began clearing the sewing baskets from the dining table and then spread a red-and-white polka dot plastic tablecloth on the table.

An Afternoon of Quilting

Wearing my pink apron, I placed my spicy chicken wings on the table with celery and a blue-cheese dip. Rose neatly arranged the corndogs, baked beans, and corn on the cob. As we unwrapped the other bags of food from Food Giant, there were sweet goodies of Twinkies with creamy filling, Skittles candies, Almond Cluster bars, and bottles of Dr. Pepper.

While everyone else was filling their plates, I noticed Daisy also wrapped food in a napkin and put it in her purse. I thought, *This woman is greedy, and she didn't even bring any food.* I pretended I did not see her sneak food into her purse. While we ate and chatted, I told them about my dream vacation: going to Tampa, Florida, and walking on the sand. "Can I join you?" Rose asked, and the fun continued with lots of laughter. After that, we ended our sewing luncheon with many hugs before my friends departed.

Finally, I had some time to relax. I sat on the comfortable love seat by the wooden coffee table, picked up my gold pen, and began writing in my red leather journal about my friends. I thought about my mother in Aberdeen, who spent many years sewing and patching old quilts to keep our family warm on cold nights when I was a young girl. While she worked, she shared stories about her mother, Mary Jane Pruitt. Like Momma, I enjoyed quilting with my friends and sharing childhood stories. While sewing the square pieces onto the quilt, I used bright yellow squares that reminded me of my mother's curtains in her living room. To honor my daddy, I sewed blue pieces to represent the shiny neckties he wore to church on Sundays.

I turned on the black-and-white TV and heard the familiar theme song of *Diff'rent Strokes*. It was one of the comedies about African Americans, with the talented Gary Coleman as the star. I settled down in the corner with a square gray pillow under my arm, and my furry companion, Coco, lay beside me with his thick fur. I felt content, and happy that my husband would be home soon.

Hands Up

I sat in the living room watching my black-and-white TV one evening, and at first, I assumed the sound that caught my attention was a fire truck passing by. Within a few minutes, I walked over to the window and pulled back the curtain.

What I saw alarmed me. A police car with sirens and flashing lights followed my husband in his yellow station wagon and was pulling into our driveway. A tall white officer emerged from a dark vehicle and approached Joseph, who handed the officer his driver's license through the window. I felt my stomach tighten. As I stood watching from the safety of our home, I gripped the dark green curtain; my eyes widened with dread, and I began praying that my husband wouldn't go to jail.

Within minutes, Joseph stepped out of the car with his hands up. I held my breath as the officer patted him down and continued talking to my husband. Meanwhile, a second officer inspected the yellow station wagon's license plate with a flashlight. I had troubled thoughts as I watched. *Was my husband being targeted because he was a member of the Black Panthers, a militant organization?* I wanted to run outside and plead for him because he was a loving father to our daughters. After what seemed like an eternity (but was only a few minutes), the two officers returned to their car in the dark of night and drove away. I did not hesitate; barefooted, I ran down the steps and onto the driveway.

I embraced my husband tightly, relieved he wasn't arrested. He seemed tense, his body rigid and his face so tight he looked like he had sucked on a lemon. Tears ran down my face, and my legs felt weak.

We walked silently back to the house together and entered the living room; Joseph threw his keys on the coffee table. In a low voice, I asked, "Honey, what happened?" I thought he would lash out, but he was silent. Instead, he walked swiftly to our bedroom and slammed the door so hard the walls shook.

An Afternoon of Quilting

I knew better than to disturb Joseph when he was upset like that, so I stirred around in the living room for a while, sat in my big armchair, and wrote in my journal. There, I could pour out my thoughts and feelings. *Today, I am feeling so upset and ready to bust with anger,* I wrote. *However, I am grateful that my husband is sleeping safely, and it was a good day bonding with my friends.* No matter how bad things were, I always tried to stay positive and be grateful for the blessings in my life.

The following morning, I woke up early, brushed my teeth, and dressed in my lime-green jogging suit. My daughters had spent the night with my friend Jessie Lee, who lived across town. At 7:30 a.m., the doorbell rang. "My goodness, my girls are here," I exclaimed. I opened the door to smiling faces.

"Hi, Jessie Lee," I greeted my friend.

"Good morning, Estell. I took the girls to McDonald's for breakfast."

Aisha mumbled, "Mom, I ate my pancakes with syrup and sausages," and Fatima and Rabia joined in to share about their breakfasts. I listened to their excited explanations and then smiled at Jessie Lee.

"Thank you, and I'll call you soon," I told her. I put my arms around my children. I walked with them to their room while Aisha skipped ahead with her Raggedy Ann doll. Fatima asked, "Where is Daddy?" and I told her, "I believe that your dad is getting dressed for work."

I headed to the kitchen to make coffee for my husband, but Joseph had already made his Folgers coffee and was wearing his cap and uniform for work.

"Hi, Honey. Did you sleep well last night?" I asked sweetly.

He hesitated. "I barely got any sleep."

I didn't want to upset my husband, but I had to ask. "So, why were the police following you?"

With a bit of anger in his voice, Joseph said, "The police were looking for someone driving a stolen yellow station wagon. And when they stopped me, the officer asked if I had been drinking. I said no. I was agitated. That was the third time the police stopped me since we moved to Atlanta."

I studied his face for a moment. "I am glad you got out of the car with your hands up."

"I learned that in Harlem when I was a teenager," Joseph told me. He looked so serious. "Babe, I was so enraged and scared that I could barely lift my body from the seat. I waited for them to arrest me, but the officer said I was the wrong Black man."

I put my hand on my husband's shoulder and said, "God was protecting you last night because I need you to pay these bills." My husband grinned.

"Honey," I continued, "I just remembered this contractor stopped by looking for you. I forgot to tell you."

Joseph replied, "Our back porch has cracks in the wall. I will call him this afternoon." He picked up his car keys and kissed me on the cheek. "I'll grab lunch at Morrison's Cafeteria and talk to my daughters tonight."

35

The Inspection

ON SATURDAY MORNING, Joseph put on his sunglasses and went outside after breakfast to wash the yellow station wagon. He wore jeans and a white T-shirt and carried a bucket with a sponge, a stiff brush, and a spray bottle. Before he started cleaning, he turned on the boom box, put in a cassette tape, and listened to George Benson, a jazz guitarist with the smooth sound of his guitar. I smiled when I saw my husband nodding his head and falling into a groove.

Although he was busy scrubbing down the back window, he began checking his Timex watch because he was waiting for the maintenance man, who was supposed to arrive at 9:00 a.m. to work on the back porch.

I followed my husband outdoors. Wearing my straw hat, I carried a watering can to care for my purple pansies. I felt happy with the sunlight beaming on my plants. Aisha, snacking on a Twizzlers red licorice stick, soon joined me to play with her pink ball.

In the meantime, Joseph's friend Tony, our next-door neighbor, waved at Joseph while walking his dog. Just then, a green truck bearing the bright red logo for Hunter Street Home Services pulled into our drive behind the yellow station wagon. A young Black man wearing a green uniform stepped out holding his toolbox.

Joseph paused his washing and walked over to greet the maintenance man with a warm smile.

"Good morning," I heard him say. "I am Joseph."

"Hey, man, I am Bobby; glad to meet you."

Then my husband said, "Let's walk around to the back of the house."

Bobby, a tall man with a red handkerchief peeking out of his side pants pocket, followed Joseph around the building. I heard him compliment my husband on the lush green grass and the bushy stalks of red tomatoes he saw growing. Joseph nodded his head and said simply, "My wife loves her garden."

As they reached the backyard, Joseph stepped up onto the porch. He pointed out the bubbling white paint on the wood. At the same time, Bobby pressed his finger against the wood and said he felt tiny holes. He pointed out how the wood looked dry and damaged, which was a likely sign of termites. Joseph just stared at Bobby in disbelief.

After completing his inspection, Bobby handed Joseph his business card and said with confidence, "I'm sure you can get rid of them," and suggested a professional exterminator. He told Joseph there was no charge for him to inspect the porch.

The men walked back to the front yard with Coco, our energetic poodle who had followed them on their inspection, trotting alongside beside them. Seeking to show his kindness for the complimentary inspection, Joseph asked, "Can I get you a glass of tea?" Bobby declined, saying he was running behind schedule.

Before heading to his truck, Bobby tapped my husband on the shoulder and said, "Call me if you have any questions."

"Thanks, man," Joseph replied.

I was weeding the plants in the front yard when the men returned from the back and was anxious to hear what Bobby had told Joseph.

The Inspection

Frankly, I had become concerned when Joseph first noticed the damaged wood about a month earlier. I recalled that when Uncle Curly had termites while I was growing up in Aberdeen, he used termite baits. Although Joseph was unfamiliar with termites, I suspected that we had them now.

After Bobby drove away, Joseph called me over, urging me to sit on the steps with him.

"Do we have termites?" was my first question. I rubbed my forehead as I imagined these flying bugs eating our house.

Joseph grabbed my hand and promised we would find a way to get rid of them. Trying to lighten the mood, he suggested taking me out to dinner that evening.

"What about Mary Mac Tea Room in Buckhead?" he asked, reminding me of my love for Southern fried green tomatoes.

Worried about our limited income, I hesitated and then replied, "Honey, we can't afford that place. Let's go to Chili's on Tilly Mill Road instead." Then I remembered we needed a babysitter.

Joseph had a solution. "Fatima and Rabia can do it. They are eleven and nine years old. Of course our daughters can watch their baby sister."

"You know that Aisha is spoiled and gets attitude sometimes with her big sisters," I reminded him.

"I'll talk to them," Joseph reassured me. He glanced at his watch and told me it was time to grab his lunch box and head to work. Leaning in, he whispered, "Babe, I'll see you tonight," and he planted a kiss on my cheek.

As Joseph backed out of the driveway in the yellow station wagon, I couldn't shake the feeling that he wasn't being entirely truthful with me. *Still, I am going to remain optimistic. Besides, I am going out to dinner with my husband and without the girls—like we were on a real date.*

36
Flying Bugs Are Eating Our Home

THE NEXT DAY, which was a Saturday, I woke early for my morning walk. While I sat on the side of the bed watching the sun peep through the window, I recalled the fantastic evening with my husband the night before.

I decided to take a walk with my daughters, so I hollered for the girls to get ready and join me. I strolled into the bathroom to brush my teeth and dress in my lime-green jogging clothes, and I noticed a scribbled note attached to the mirror.

> Hi Babe, I had to leave early for work. So, the exterminator will be here at 6 p.m.

I had a sinking feeling in my stomach after reading those words. I knew I would be counting the hours until my husband returned home.

Just then, Aisha peeked in the door wearing her Star Trek pajamas and asked, "Mommy, can I wear my sunglasses for our walk?"

"Sure, baby girl."

I grabbed my straw hat and water bottle and headed to the front steps. The girls were waiting with our puppy, Coco. They wore colorful T-shirts, jeans, and white sneakers. Fatima held the leash for Coco, who was patiently waiting for us and wearing a bright yellow collar.

We began walking on the broken sidewalk, my girls following me past the green shrubbery in front of the house next door and continuing farther down the street. Daisy was sweeping off the porch and waved at us. Once I felt the warm breeze on my face, I began sweating and sipping on my water bottle. After four long blocks, Rabia and Aisha ran up beside me and said, "Mom, we are tired. Can we rest?"

"Girls, I didn't realize that I was walking so fast. Anyway, let's turn around and head home." I had been thinking about our home and the termites that might be in our bedroom, and it scared me. The more I focused on the idea, the faster I walked, and my poor girls had to run to keep up with me.

We turned around and were home in no time. I told the girls I would sit on the steps in the sunshine, but after a restless fifteen minutes of thinking about the upcoming exterminator visit, I was too anxious to do nothing. For the rest of the afternoon, I did housework like scrubbing out the bathtub, mopping the floors, and washing clothes. I thought doing housework would help me focus on something that would keep me busy until I learned the truth about the termites.

After I finished cleaning up, I made green tea with ginger in my Atlanta Braves mug and sat at the kitchen table, focusing on the chair that Aisha had scratched when she was two years old. I reminisced about how Joseph and I had picked out the perfect house with the burgundy door, and how much I loved our home. To distract myself, I looked through *Ebony* magazine, but I was in such a daze that I couldn't read the stories; I just looked at the pictures.

At five-thirty, Joseph came into the kitchen with his lunch box.

"Hi, Babe," he greeted me. "I called, and you didn't answer the phone. Are you all right?"

I took a deep breath before saying, "Well, I meant to tell you that I saw termites dropping at our back door."

"You did not tell me last night."

"I could not bear to speak about termites."

He looked at me, tightening his lips. "I'll shower quickly before the pest control man arrives."

While Joseph showered and changed, I sat in the living room; the sound of the rotating fan helped me stay calm. I wore my faded jeans and my husband's shirt, and I was barefoot. I didn't feel like putting on my regular clothes because I was scared about the future of our home.

As soon as Joseph returned to the living room, a horn beeped outside. Joseph opened the screen door as a red pickup truck advertising Billy's Bug Control pulled into the driveway.

I peered out the window, wondering if we could trust this guy to get rid of the termites.

As I stood at the front door, an older white man got out of the truck wearing a gray uniform and cowboy boots. He walked to the back of the truck to grab tools and a white container that looked like pesticide spray.

Joseph strolled over to greet him. "Hey, I am Joseph, and you must be Billy; I talked to you on the phone."

"I came here to help you get rid of these termites," Billy said. "Can you show me your back porch?" Billy wiped his face with a red handkerchief. He talked rather slowly because he had snuff in his lower lip. When I was growing up in Aberdeen many years ago, I remembered sitting on the porch watching old folks dip snuff.

Billy said that he'd brought a potent pesticide to spray the termites. He explained that some folks called termites "swarmers" because they build colonies inside the wood. "Did you see them in your house?" he asked.

Joseph replied, "My wife noticed them at the back door." Looking concerned, Joseph pointed to the peeling paint and the dry-rotted wood.

Billy pulled out a spiked tool to check the solid beam. He shook his head and clicked his tongue before saying, "There are hollow spaces; you got those little rascals in the wood."

Next, Billy got on his knees with the flashlight in his hand to look under the house. He grabbed a long stick to dig small holes and check the dirt for mud tubes, which are pencil-width tunnels the termites make on the side of the house. Billy told my husband, "I need you to stand back while I'm spraying because these chemicals are strong. It might take about thirty minutes." Billy put on a mask and gloves and began poking holes and digging around the side of the house to spray the mud tunnels with pesticide.

While we waited for the time to pass, Joseph first sat on the outdoor bench and fidgeted with his glasses. Feeling anxious, he put his hand into his pocket to feel the small brown stone his mother gave him that served as a token of comfort. As he sat for a while, sweat rolled down his forehead.

Finally, Billy removed his mask and revealed the damage to our home.

"The termites are burrowed deep into the wood of your home and building nests in the framing beams."

"How can we get rid of them?" Joseph asked, his eyes fixed on Billy.

"You could rebuild this back porch. Or I could continue spraying for the next five years, which could be expensive. But there is no guarantee that you can get rid of them."

Joseph just stared at the exterminator as his heart sank. He listened in disbelief as Billy explained how termites would totally destroy our home within five years.

He wondered how this white man could be right, but when he thought about the obviously rotted wood, he knew the evidence didn't lie. Then, in a loud voice that I could hear from where I waited, Joseph fired off questions about how we could save our home. I could tell from his tone that he still had hope.

"That would take a miracle, because the pale, wet worms of the larvae stage can spread quickly in your home," Billy explained.

"Listen, Joseph," Billy continued, "I see that you are upset about your home. You can pay me later; I can find my way out."

Billy gathered the pesticide containers and his tools and walked to his truck. I watched from the front door as the man drove away, and then Joseph made his way to the living room. He had a serious look on his face, and his shoulders slumped down; his shirt was drenched in sweat.

"What did he say about flying bugs?" Joseph said loudly, then paused momentarily before continuing. "Termites are destroying our home."

The words hit me like a deep pain in my heart. Joseph continued delivering the bad news. "The pest control guy says they are inside the wood of our house."

"What can be done?" I asked.

"We might never get rid of them."

I felt my teeth gritting in anger and frustration and tears welling in my eyes. I was paralyzed with fear and felt as though I could not move. Joseph put his arm around my shoulders and led me to the red couch, where he sat down next to me.

Joseph's gaze seemed fixed on the wall. He began rubbing his beard and shifting in his seat. "Why did I not notice the wood was rotting?" he mumbled. "It's all my fault that we are losing our home. I am responsible for our home."

All I could hear was the rhythmic tick-tick-tick sound of the clock on the wall.

I moved closer to my husband, and I told him, "We are going to work this out."

He stared into space for a while longer. Suddenly, he hit the coffee table with his fist in a burst of anger and frustration. The sound echoed through the tense air like a thunderclap. "Babe, I've got to get out of here," he said as he grabbed his car keys.

"Where are you going?" I called, but he just continued toward the front door. Concerned that he was so angry and hurt, I chased after him, but he was already headed to the car. *I am sure my husband feels powerless and overlooked because of his identity. Still, he works long hours to keep our family together.* Soon I heard the roar of the car's engine and the tires squealing. As I stood in the open door and watched the taillights disappear in the distance, I worried about Joseph, who had poured his heart into our home.

"Oh, God, what has happened to our house?"

As tears streamed down my face and my nose ran, I flopped down in the armchair. I was glad our girls were spending the night with my friend Jessie Lee again. Eventually, I stopped crying and began praying for a miracle to save our home and my family. I thought about my dad, who was always had faith in God and our family on Matubba Street in Aberdeen. Finally, I fell asleep.

I woke up around 4:00 a.m., and the green knitted throw covered my body. That throw let me know that Joseph was back and had settled down. I thought again about the silent invader of our sanctuary, and I vowed that we would never give up.

37

Family Meeting: Let's Tell Our Daughters About Our Home

ONLY TWO DAYS EARLIER, we'd learned we had termites in our home. I tossed and turned all night, and after waking up feeling anxious, I was still sleepy. I turned off the alarm clock and turned the dial to WCLK, an Atlanta jazz station. To my delight, "What a Wonderful World" by Louis Armstrong was playing, and I lay in bed listening to his velvety voice. The lyrics of the soulful melody lightened my mood. By the time the song ended, the sunshine was drifting through the canary-yellow curtains bathing my green-leaved houseplants nearby and making me feel more hopeful.

I slipped into my worn and comfortable house shoes, and as I strolled to the bathroom, I could smell the aroma of coffee percolating.

I brushed my teeth, washed my face, and gently rubbed in my Fashion Fair moisturizer. I smiled at my reflection, feeling positive about my looks. For years, the makeup made for dark skin made me look pale, and beauty brands ignored Black women. I was happy to have found a brand made specifically for us.

If Grits Could Talk

I walked into our small kitchen and greeted my husband, leaned down to rub Coco, our poodle, who was crunching on his treat, and then I sat down at the square table.

Joseph took a deep breath and began, "Babe, I am sorry about how I acted on Saturday night; I was overwhelmed just talking about the termites in our home."

I gave him a warm, a polite smile. "I understand, and I want us to share our feelings about our home."

He nodded. By then, he had prepared a cup of Lipton tea with lemon, which he placed in front of me along with a cheese croissant on a round plate. Then he placed a red rose in a mason jar before me. His sincerity touched me. He sat down, joining me with his tall cup of Folgers coffee.

After we sat for a few minutes in silence, I asked, "Honey, how can we tell the girls about the termites? I don't like telling them flying bugs are taking over our home."

Joseph thought for a moment. "I'll call a family meeting to talk to them. Sure, I will tell my daughters." He glanced at the clock on the wall. "I have to leave for work soon, but I should be home around six. We can tell our girls then and take them out to Dairy Queen for a Blizzard afterward."

"Joseph, we must seek a solution. I plan to call my dad in Aberdeen and get his advice. Then I will talk to my friend Rose and tell the rest of my friends. I am considering getting another inspector to come out." I hugged him and said, "Let's think it over for a while before we decide how to handle these termites."

At 6:00 p.m., my daughters were playing in the backyard, and I hollered for them to come inside. I had decided to have our family meeting in the dining room with the wooden China cabinet that had a glass panel for my silver tea set from New York. I put a white tablecloth and with tiny red flowers on the table with snacks. I laid out several small bowls with white nacho chips, a side of spicy salsa, and cheese puffs for Aisha, plus a glass pitcher of sweet tea.

Family Meeting: Let's Tell Our Daughters About Our Home

As my daughters entered the dining room, I smiled at how they had changed. Fatima was tall with skinny legs, a soft voice, and a thick head of hair like her dad. She enjoyed her Etch A Sketch tablet and freestyle drawing. Rabia, with her cute smile, liked having her clothes pressed and her hair braided with pink and yellow beads. She asked open-ended questions and tested my patience, but I felt proud that she was so inquisitive.

Aisha, who was now five years old, could write her name in cursive; she wore a ponytail tied with a pink ribbon. She loved putting together a puzzle with her friends next door. I had to admit that the family spoiled Baby Girl, and she sometimes acted naughty.

Watching my daughters enter the room, I felt immense pride. I genuinely loved my daughters, which would never change, but they could try my patience at times. I loved playing with my daughters in their bedroom and seeing them giggle and laugh out loud. Sometimes I wished my mother could have sat down and played with me when I was growing up in Aberdeen. Momma worked as a domestic and barely got paid any money. Other times, she brought home old, crusty bread instead of her paycheck. She didn't have time to play with me because she worked from dusk to dawn. I wish I'd had those tender moments with her.

While we waited for Joseph to arrive home from work, chairs scraped the floor as my daughters settled down in their seats, still playing with each other. I turned on our air conditioner; I heard a humming sound, which meant it was not working. I wiped beads of sweat off my brow.

The engine roared in the driveway shortly afterward, and I knew my husband was home. Soon, Joseph entered the dining room and tapped me on the shoulder, a simple gesture of warmth.

"Hello, family," Joseph greeted us. He sat down at the head of the dining table and seeming relaxed; he rang the tiny bell to signal the start of the meeting. Suddenly, the crunching sound of the chips stopped, and we focused on him.

At times, Joseph acted like we were all in the army, making rules for our family like those he followed in the military. He could be somewhat overbearing at times.

For instance, he insisted the girls must learn African American history. He would often tell me how to prepare meals in the kitchen. He sometimes got on my nerves, but he showed a strong love for our family. He remembered his grandma, Helen Hunter, who lived in Harlem and said that family is our strength and will help us live a good life. Joseph believed the family shared a sense of belonging and spiritual values.

When the girls heard the tinkling of the bell and knew the meeting had started, Rabia asked curiously, "Why do we need a meeting on Monday? I am going to miss *Little House on the Prairie*."

"Just settle down," her father scolded her. "I discovered that we have termites, tiny dark brown insects that chew through wood, and the pest control man agreed."

Fatima said, "I saw this flying bug on the windowsill of our room. I just assumed it was a regular bug and swatted it. Will they bite us?"

"No, they like to live inside the wood and leave behind a trail of germs," Joseph told her. "I first noticed these pests on the back porch. And the paint on the wood was bubbling and peeling. I learned from the exterminator that they are destroying our house." Joseph paused and seemed overwhelmed.

Fatima continued, "Was that the reason the guy was here in the red truck, and why you did not tell us?"

"I needed to share the news with your mother," Joseph mumbled.

Rabia asked, "Dad, can we get rid of them?" When her dad said he wasn't sure, Rabia stood up and said, "This makes me angry." Her voice wavered. "And you are telling me those bugs might be in my room?"

Fatima, her eyes filled with tears, chimed in. "Daddy, how could you allow this to happen?"

Joseph grappled with his emotions and began rubbing the side of his face. "Please calm down," he implored them.

Family Meeting: Let's Tell Our Daughters About Our Home

In the meantime, Aisha hopped down from her chair and ran over to her dad for comfort. He picked her up to sit in his lap and embraced her. She said in her tender voice, "Daddy, I am afraid of those tiny termites."

Joseph looked nervous; sweat dripped off his forehead. "Your mom and I promise to combine our efforts to lead us forward."

At that moment, my emotions spilled over from witnessing my daughters' anger and sadness about the looming threat of the termites. I felt my knees knocking together; I felt tears welling up. I said I wanted us to gather for a family hug.

I wiped away my tears as we stood shoulder to shoulder; I felt the warmth of our love. In our closeness, I was reminded of our ability to bounce back.

"I am glad we came together tonight and shared our feelings," my husband said with sincerity.

Then Aisha told her daddy, "I am hungry." We all began to laugh. I felt happy that our family meeting brought us together.

Afterward, we hopped into the yellow station wagon and headed to Dairy Queen for thick and creamy Oreo Cookie Blizzards for the girls. I had a Royal Rocky Road Trip Blizzard with Joseph to commemorate this memorable evening.

38

Sharing Our Unhappy News

ON THE WEDNESDAY following our family meeting, I fixed lunch for the girls before they went outside to jump rope with their friends. Fatima and Rabia had bologna sandwiches with sweet pickles, and Aisha had a peanut-and-jelly sandwich cut into squares; I made myself a pimento cheese sandwich with fried green tomatoes. As soon as they were finished eating, the girls bounded outside followed by Coco, who had a ball in his mouth. As I stood by the back door and watched them play, I noticed my roses finally had two blooms, one pink and one red.

I decided to journal a bit, so I grabbed the bound red journal and my gold pen from the bookshelf. In the first section, I read what I had previously written about my children—how I enjoyed washing my daughters' thick hair, massaging their scalps like my momma did for me in Aberdeen, and braiding it, too. In the second section, I wrote about dropping out of college. It had been fourteen years since I attended Tuskegee University, and I still had recurring dreams of returning there. *Being a housewife is a valuable experience*, I wrote, *but I feel stuck without a college degree. Indeed, I want to learn more skills to help my family.* I closed my journal and laid my pen in the pencil holder.

I paused for a while, knowing I needed to call my best friend, Rose. I was still trying to decide whether to share the news about the termites in our home.

I dialed the green rotary phone on the coffee table and greeted her when she answered. After we exchanged a few pleasantries, I asked, "Can I come over for a while?"

"Sure," Rose said cheerily. "I have a doctor's appointment for my son at Grady's clinic at three, but we'll still have thirty minutes to catch up on things."

I grabbed my sandals and put on my lime-green straw hat and headed out the door for the short walk. About seven minutes later, I knocked on Rose's front door, where her puppy waited patiently to be let inside. Rose opened the screen door, and the puppy and a few flies followed me into the house.

Rose was medium height like me, with brown skin and a mole on the left side of her nose. That day, she wore shorts that showed her dry, ashy knees. *Her skinny legs could use some Jergen's lotion on them*, I thought. Rose gave me a quick hug, and I smelled the Avon perfume I had bought for her birthday last year.

"Come in and sit in the rocking chair with the cushion in the back," Rose invited.

"Oh, girl, I've got news about our house."

Rose leaned in, a look of expectation on her face. I took a deep breath and then said, "My husband and I learned that we have termites in our home."

Rose just stared at me. Finally, she asked, "How did you find out?"

"Joseph saw tiny holes in the wood on our back porch and hollow places in spaces in the wall. So he called pest control and learned that the termites were inside our home."

Rose pulled up her chair beside me and held my hand. "This news deeply saddens me. What can I do to help?"

Sharing Our Unhappy News

My best friend's kind words touched me. "I don't know," I told her, "but I am glad I can count on you."

"How do the girls feel about the termites in your home?"

"My daughters were upset and asked a lot of questions. Yet, after our talk with them, they seemed to understand."

Rose shared what little she knew about termites. "In Waycross, Georgia," she told me, "my sister, Mamie, used these two home remedies: a cup of white vinegar and lemon juice in a spray bottle to spray. Then she sprinkled Borax power in the corners of her rooms to stop those wood-loving pests." She looked sad and shook her head. "None of those things worked; my big sister had to move. Hopefully, you can get rid of them."

Rose surprised me next when she said, "Estell, I want to plan a party for you and Joseph to show our support."

"No, I don't want a party. I don't feel comfortable with all those people around me. And I feel like people are watching me. But thank you." I stood up and grabbed my hat. "I know what it takes to drive in traffic downtown, so I'm heading home, but I'll be over tomorrow to spend the day with you and help you in your garden with your tomato plants."

Later that afternoon around 5:00 p.m., I was in the kitchen starting our dinner. The sun was shining through the pink curtains over the sink. The girls were spending the night with friends from school, so I decided to heat up my husband a TV dinner: Hungry Man Salisbury Steak with gravy, potatoes, peas, and chocolate pudding. I also warmed up fish sticks and added yellow mustard and tater tots. So that's what I decided to make for my dinner. While I got things ready, I turned the radio to the Braves game on *WSB-TV*.

Joseph peeked into the kitchen and hollered that the licensed inspector had just driven up to check for termites. I instantly felt nervous, so I began drying the dishes I had washed. After twenty minutes, I changed the radio to a rhythm-and-blues station and listened to Gloria Gaynor singing "I Will Survive." I began weaving my head to the beat; this disco song with its fast tempo put me in a different mood.

As the song ended, Joseph came into the kitchen wearing a solemn look on his face. I turned off the radio.

"Let's sit in the living room," he said gently, and I knew from his expression that the news wasn't good. I followed my husband into the living room, and we sat down beside each other on the red couch.

"The inspector said the termites have eaten wood under our house; they are in the firewood in the backyard. Babe, there is no way to save our home." Joseph's eyes glistened with tears.

"Oh, no!" I shouted and then covered my mouth with my hand while I shook my head from side to side. My husband reached over and held me tightly in his arms. I burst into sobs. I felt so hopeless and sad.

Joseph mumbled, "I should have seen those termites; we are losing our home!" The phone rang, but we couldn't move to answer it. We felt paralyzed as the reality of the situation sunk in. I kept saying, "What about our daughters?"

Joseph squeezed my hand with my wedding band. His jaw was tight, and he kept blinking back tears and squeezing my hand, sometimes so hard that my ring dug into my skin. We sat there together for a long time until the silver clock on the wall chimed, letting us know it was 9:00 p.m. I will never forget that moment.

I stopped crying, brushing away the tears with my hands. I told my husband, "I am scared, but we are a good family. I know we will stand together with courage, just like my family in Aberdeen!"

39

Silver Linings

ONLY TWO DAYS earlier, I had learned we were losing our home. I spent those days just walking around, thinking about my home and trying to make sense of things. That Friday morning was warm, and I had not slept much, tossing and turning all night and worrying about my home.

I went to the bathroom to brush my teeth. In front of the mirror, I thought about how much I enjoyed standing in the same space with the tacky yellow shower curtain and Aisha's scribbled writing on the wall. In the background, I heard Joseph mowing the yard. When I was finished, I walked to the girls' room and knocked on the door.

"Girls, get up and brush your teeth for breakfast," I called. I thought about telling them about the inspection, that we were losing our home. But I decided I'd let Joseph talk to them.

About thirty minutes later, as I finished preparing breakfast, I listened to Coco barking and my daughters running in the living room. When I asked then to calm down, Rabia said it was Fatima and Aisha chasing the puppy.

"Okay, wash your hands, breakfast!" I set out the spread on our dining table with a red checkered tablecloth: bacon, scrambled eggs, grits, and biscuits. The biscuits came out a little hard and dry as usual, but my daughters loved them.

"Fatima, can you set up the plates on the table with silverware?" I asked.

"Rabia, will you tell your dad that breakfast is ready?" She hopped out of her chair and ran to the back door to call her dad.

After washing his hands, Joseph came into the dining room. He sat down at the head of the table. He asked us to hold hands while he said, "Dear God, thank you for my family and my wife preparing a good breakfast, Amen."

"Mommy, can you fix my plate?" Aisha pleaded. I grabbed the pink Mickey Mouse plate and put two pieces of bacon and a biscuit on it with a big spoon of grits. "Mom, I don't want grits," she said, shaking her head.

"You ate them in Aberdeen," Fatima said with a smirk on her face.

Rabia, who liked sharing her opinion, chimed in. "Aisha, you are big enough to fix your own plate."

I wasn't in the mood for this and said, "Girls, I taught you to be polite to your sister." That ended Fatima and Rabia's commentary.

While we ate, Joseph explained to our girls about the second inspection of our home. "And the termites are rapidly destroying our home," he finished.

Looking confused, Rabia said, "You mean we are moving?"

"Mom and I are discussing that together" was her dad's response.

Fatima wiped the crumbs from her face. "I want to stay on this block with my friends."

Aisha looked at Joseph earnestly and asked, "Daddy, why can't we spray them with Raid?"

"It will not get rid of the termites."

"What about our puppy, Coco?" Our youngest daughter looked worried.

"Coco is part of our family," I assured her. "I know you like rubbing his fur while you read your books. And I can't wait to see him sitting by my bed and wagging his tail wherever we live." Joseph glanced at his silver Timex watch and stood up to grab his lunch box. "Babe, I need to leave for work," he announced and then leaned down to whisper softly in my ear, "I love you."

Fatima asked, "Daddy, can you come home and play Scrabble with us tonight?" and Joseph agreed to come home early.

As he backed the car out of the driveway, the phone rang in the living room, and Rabia answered.

"Mom, sister Lila wants to talk with you."

I met Lila when I moved to Atlanta and went to worship at the mosque in the West End neighborhood.

"Hello, Lila. I am doing fine." I listened for a moment. "Yes, you can come over this afternoon. See you soon." I hung up the phone and immediately turned back to my daughters.

"Girls, clean off the table and wash the dishes. And Fatima, scrub out the pots and pans." I believed my daughters learned discipline from doing chores in addition to their homework, just as I did when I was growing up. It was also a way for them to earn their allowances.

After the girls were off to school, I worked in the garden for a while. Keeping my hands busy helped me stay calm. I gently pulled off dead leaves and stems from my azaleas and sunflowers. The smell of the flowers in the warm sun brought a smile to my face. Soon, it would be time for Lila to arrive as we had planned.

I wanted to look good, so I changed out of my jeans and shirt because I had dirt on me from working in the garden, where Fatima and Rabia were playing. I decided to wear a light blue maxi dress with my handsewn headband. I vacuumed the living room and put the potted peace lily by the sofa. At four that afternoon, the doorbell rang.

I opened the screen door, and my friend Lila greeted me with "As-salamu alaikum, peace, and blessing upon you." She was short and skinny with skin the color of a brown paper bag, and she wore a lime-green dress with a tightly wrapped headscarf that looked stylish. I received a warm hug, and then I pointed to the red couch and invited her to put her basket on the coffee table.

As soon as we sat down, Lila told me, "Sister, I know I talked on the phone about the termites, but I had to come over to be with you. I am so happy to be in your home."

We chatted about drinking green tea with ginger and eating croissants in her home, and then I said, "Lila, I remember us going shopping at Walmart for a stroller for Aisha's birthday. It was raining and our clothes got soaking wet, but it was fun."

Lila said, "I bought something for you." She handed me the basket, which was covered with plastic wrapping and a yellow ribbon. First, I laid my eyes on a bean pie that smelled good. I remembered my husband buying me this delicious pie in New York. And there were more presents: a tall jar of dates covered with a burlap cloth, an Islamic journal with gold lettering, and a wrapped bar of African Black soap, which was a special gift. African Black soap is unlike drugstore and supermarket soaps because it is made from ethically sourced ingredients from around the world. This soap is unscented and can be used as a moisturizer for your face and a shampoo for your hair. After admiring all the gifts, I hugged her shoulders. "You brought me hope and love," I told her.

"I am glad we understand each other through faith and friendship," Lila said. "By the way, are Joseph and the girls doing all right?"

"Yes, I am keeping them in line," I assured her, and she grinned. Soon, she opened her green purse and pulled out her car keys.

"Estell, I am leaving to pick up my son from the afterschool Sunshine play school. Anyway, I'll call you tomorrow. Thank you, my friend. We will be friends forever." She squeezed my hand tightly. As Lila walked to her car, I smiled and waved bye.

After Lila's visit, I spent a few minutes looking at photo albums on the bookshelf in my dining room and straightening up the books Rabia had checked out from the Ben Hill School library.

The yellow rotary phone rang in the kitchen, so I went in there, picked up the heavy receiver, and said hello. My friend Rose was on the line.

"Hello, Estell. Can you come over and see my new curtains?"

I told her I'd be over soon, so I grabbed my lime-green sun hat and walked the seven minutes to her house.

I knocked on the frame of the screen door and heard Rose call out, "Come on in."

I stepped into the darkened room, and suddenly, the lights came on. "Surprise!" came shouts from behind the couch and from the bedroom. I stood there by the door, shocked, and looked at the faces of my friends. Rose came over and grabbed my hand. She told me to come sit down in the leather armchair. The living room was filled with balloons and streamers that read HOUSE PARTY in bold letters of red and white.

As I looked around, I noticed a vase filled with red roses on a round table near the fireplace. In the center was a big, white cake with peaches and cherries and some writing on the top. I observed bowls of food on the table: mac and cheese, chicken wings, pizza, fresh salad, and chocolate brownies topped with nuts. On the side table were bottles of Mountain Dew, Pepsi, and Root Beer.

Rose brought me a plate of chicken wings and potato salad with a bottle of hot sauce. I chatted with my friends Daisy, Margaret, and Jessie Lee about enjoying the party. After a while, Lucinda, the babysitter who had mistreated my baby, Aisha, came over to shake my hand. I pretended that I didn't see her and continued my conversation with my friends.

Rose's husband, Tony, had a turntable record player and acted as the DJ for the party. He spun Otis Redding's rhythm-and-blues hit tune, "(Sittin' On) The Dock of the Bay." It was the right song to liven my spirit. I began to enjoy the party, and I forgot about why I was celebrating; termites did not enter my mind. I was glad that Rose had organized this party for me and my family.

As time passed the living room filled with people, and musky perfume permeated the air. Rose's cousin was there, and she was puffing on a cigarette. I had not seen many women smoking. I wanted to ask her to put out that cigarette, but instead, I sat closer to the rotating fan.

After a while, Rose stopped the party.

"Listen up, everyone. We are here tonight because of my best friend, Estell. She and her husband need our support for their home. While taking care of her children, my friend organized the Quilting Club. Our members are here to honor her tonight." Rose handed me the large quilt we had all made together, wrapped with a pink bow. "I'll let Estell speak."

I stood up, my leg wobbly. "Umm," I stuttered, "I enjoyed sewing those cut pieces of fabric with my friends and telling stories that reminded me of my mother sewing quilts in Aberdeen. Thank you, sisters."

As soon as I finished my short speech, Joseph walked in with our girls. Aisha shouted, "Hey, Mommy!" I hugged Rose for looking out for my family.

I felt so proud that we were together. Baby Girl Aisha gave me a hug and ran to pop the balloons, and then she began hiding under the dining table. My daughters acted shy sometimes, but they were lively at the party. They mingled with Rose's children, Candy and Randy, who were twins and liked to make funny faces. My friend Rose loved dressing her children alike, even down to the same brown lace-up shoes. Wearing big smiles, the girls grabbed crispy fried chicken wings and slices of thick and greasy pizza. Fatima liked her food spicy with Louisiana Hot Sauce, and Rabia had this thing about ketchup on her pizza and her eggs. Later, they all sat on the floor and played with a jigsaw puzzle and made a lot of noise.

Joseph came to the party in his leather jacket. When I first saw him walk in, I thought that he hadn't changed much since I married him. He leaned down to hug me. Next, he sauntered over to chat with his friend Tony, who was the DJ. Joseph did not have many friends because he was always skeptical of new people. Yet he and Tony always hung out together in the yellow station wagon and watched wrestling together on Friday nights. Tony knew that my husband cared about jazz, so he picked old jazz tunes like Miles Davis's "So What." Joseph tapped his finger in time to the music and moved his shoulders like he was in the groove.

While Joseph was with Tony, I opened the wrapped gifts some of my friends brought and a pink envelope with one hundred dollars in it. I decided to pick up my gifts later, but I grabbed the envelope with the money.

Then, I gathered around the table with my daughters. I was proud to see an icing message on the top of the cake that read BEST WISHES, ESTELL. I sliced through the thick white frosting for two hefty slices of cake, one for the girls and one to share with Joseph.

Before the end of the party, Margaret asked me to sing karaoke with her. "What about the Beatles song, 'I Want to Hold Your Hand'?" she asked me.

I shook my head no. "I don't want my friends laughing at me." They were singing karaoke in the hallway. Eventually, I changed my mind and decided to sing. I chose "The First Time Ever I Saw Your Face," which was a big Roberta Flack hit. I liked this song because the tune had the rhythm of jazz and gospel. It reminded me of when I met my husband. My voice was shaky, but I did it.

After an hour, we walked home in the dark with the girls skipping and running ahead. Joseph carried the quilt and held my hand. As we strolled, I told my husband, "I didn't realize I had so many friends who cared about us. We are a good family!"

40

Leaving Our House with the Burgundy Door

LIFE WAS CHANGING for our family, but I needed to learn that change makes us stronger and wiser.

The sun was shining bright in June of 1979, and I had a pitcher of fresh lemonade on the metal table in the backyard for the girls. Aisha was barefoot and playing in the sandbox with her shovel and bucket. Fatima and Rabia played on the outdoor swing set and climbed the monkey bars.

My mind drifted to the good times momentarily, making me smile. When I moved here, the backyard had patches of grass and weeds. Over the summer, I began planting tomato seeds and watering them weekly. To my surprise, they sprouted, and after a few months, I had my first red tomatoes and picked one and ate it.

Other times, I joined my daughters and my husband at the picnic table. We sat down to eat ripe and juicy watermelons from the garden, and the juice exploded in our mouths, causing many giggles. I recalled swatting mosquitoes that were feasting on my ankles.

I'd been in shock since we discovered the termite infestation the previous month, and I was sad about moving and unsure what to expect. Yet I was mentally transitioning in my mind, knowing we had to leave our home. This space belonged to us, but the termites ate their way through our house. I had waited a while before I talked to my husband about moving, but I was ready to get it done. He had seemed worried and told me he wanted to stay in our house for several months.

Later that afternoon, I stood in the living room, swatting at the flies coming through the windows that were propped open with a stick to allow the cooler air inside. I observed my husband pulling into the driveway in the yellow Ford station wagon and watched as he exited the car in his khaki work clothes. Joseph carried a beige shopping bag from Kmart; I knew he probably had bought our daughters toys, Twinkies, and Ding Dongs. I wished he would stop spoiling our children.

Joseph opened the screen door and greeted me.

"Hi, Honey." I kissed him on the cheek. "We could talk about moving before dinner."

"Can this wait for tomorrow?"

"No, I am putting together our budget."

Joseph sighed. "I worked twelve hours today, and my feet are aching from walking around up and down the stairs in the warehouse with packages."

"Sit on the brown leather chair and remove your boots. And I'll bring a tall glass of sweet tea."

When I returned to the living room, I sat on the stool beside my husband.

"Joseph, you remembered Shirly, the real estate agent who helped us find our house."

"You mean that lady from Jamaica who had that fancy car?"

"Yes, I talked to her on the phone. I explained to her about the termites, and she told me that after we moved and hired a professional pest control company, she would help find a buyer."

"That's good news; we need the money," Joseph replied. "I am not ready to move, but I looked in the *Atlanta World* newspaper and talked to my friends."

I took a deep breath. "Honey, I want to live on the south side of Atlanta and am interested in Collier Heights and Summerhill. Our girls can attend schools with children who look like them and feel comfortable. Segregation continues to mean less money for teachers and insufficient books. As I see it, a lot has stayed the same since I grew up in the South in the 1960s. I went to Shivers High School in Aberdeen. The White schoolchildren used the books first, and we got them with scratch marks and torn pages."

"Babe, I had some of the same issues in Harlem in high school," Joseph said. "Still, I want to live in a diverse neighborhood. Last week, I had lunch with my supervisor, Earl, who lives in Woodstock; he says it's a nice place with good schools."

"Honey," I said, "that sounds like a small town outside of Atlanta with no Black people."

"Estell, I want to live in a zip code where my daughters will receive the best education. I want to live in an area with a lower crime rate and grocery stores within walking distance. Like other families, I want to live the American dream with a lovely home. Estell, I don't wish my girls to attend an all-white school, because they would feel alienated by stares from the students and teachers." Joseph wore a serious expression. "I want our children to attend schools on the Northside like Sandy Spring, Brookhaven, and Norcross."

I was concerned about my daughters going to an integrated school because many of the white teachers were unfamiliar with our culture and our roots. I was also alarmed by unintentional bias and lack of sensitivity, like mispronouncing ethnic names and frowning at braided hair, which is a cherished tradition for Black girls. Besides, I wanted them to be in a nurturing environment to get a good education.

The doorbell rang, and I opened the door. "Hi, Tony," I said to his friend. "I like your Falcons shirt, and you must be a big Falcon fan."

"I am ready for them to be in the playoffs. We'll see." Tony turned his attention to my husband. "Hi, Joseph, do you want to go to the Falcons game on Sunday?"

I excused myself, and I then decided that now, before dinner, was the time to tell the girls we were moving. I had worried about telling them for two days. I took a deep breath before walking into their room, where I stepped on crayons, art drawings, and toys. The sun shone through the bright pink curtains and onto the floral wallpaper.

"Hey girls, can you stop playing for a minute? I need to tell you something important."

The three girls sat on the pillows on the floor in a circle, their eyes fixed on me.

"I had a conversation with your dad, and we are moving soon." I held back my tears, but looking at their fallen faces made me sad.

Rabia leaned in. "I want to stay in school; I like my teacher, Miss Roberts. In the afternoon, my teacher sings with us while we stand in a circle."

Fatima drew her lips tight. "I enjoy climbing the trees and catching butterflies. When are we moving, Mom?"

"I'll let you know soon." I tried to look strong for my girls, so I pushed out a smile.

I sat by Aisha, who lay her head on my shoulder. "Mom, I am scared." I held her close with her long braids next to my chin.

"Fatima and Rabia, do you remember moving to Atlanta from New York? It was hard, but you excelled in your classes at Ben Hill Elementary school." I looked each girl in the eyes. "Hey. I want to see some smiles. Let's hold hands and say this together: 'We are a family, and we stand together!'"

Finally, I saw lots of smiles. "Girls, I have an idea." I stood up, and the girls all jumped up too. "I decided to clean out my closet, and I need your help."

Fatima stood next to me and lay her head on my shoulder. "Mom, can we do this another day?"

As I said no, Aisha ran into my bedroom and began rolling on the bed. "Baby girl, get down off the bed with your shoes on," I scolded.

I pulled open the door to the closet I shared with my husband, and purses and hats fell onto the floor with my shoes. Rabia asked if I had collected all this stuff, and I told her, "Yes, I saved these things because I want to hold onto old memories. Finally, I've decided to get rid of them." I got two plastic bags, one for donations to Goodwill and the other for trash. Meanwhile, Aisha sat down and began putting my leather high heels on her tiny feet, then plopped my pink straw hat onto her head.

"Mom, look at me!"

My baby was missing two front teeth. "You're cute, Aisha, with my straw hat over your eyes."

Rabia opened the gray purse with a buckle my momma bought in Aberdeen at Lasky's years ago. "Can I have this purse, Mom?"

It was a keepsake. "Yes," I told her, "you can have it."

At the same time, Fatima put on her dad's faded Vietnam cap. "My dad was a soldier in Vietnam," she said with a smile. I chimed in, telling them how proud I was of their daddy.

"Mom, why did you save all these things?" Rabia asked.

"When I was growing up, Momma did not throw away anything. She hid things under the bed and in the attic," I explained. "But I need to let go of these things."

While we chatted, the phone rang in the bedroom, and Fatima answered it.

"Mom, it's Granddaddy," she said excitedly. "Hi, Granddaddy, I miss you! Here is Mom."

"Girls, you can go outside to play," I told them as I took the phone from Fatima. "Hi, Daddy, I am so happy you called. I am more confident about moving because you encouraged me by writing me letters and telling me that you are proud of how I am raising my own family."

"Are you coming to Aberdeen?" Daddy asked.

I told him I hoped to visit the next month. "Tell Momma I will call tonight."

"I am sending a money order with twenty-five dollars for the children."

"Thank you, Daddy."

"Love you, Sis." Daddy's words touched my heart, and I couldn't wait for our trip to Aberdeen.

About two hours later, Joseph's friends from his job knocked on the door. I had met them some months ago.

"Hi, good morning, ma'am," they greeted me.

"Hi, JT and Leroy."

They told me they had talked to Joseph on the phone and came to help him clean out the shed. Joseph was in the backyard; I pointed to the left side of the house. I was touched; those guys worked with my husband, and he stood up for their rights on the job. Now they were best friends.

On Sunday night, I sat in the living room with my family; we began watching the movie *Superman* with Christopher Reeve. The girls liked Superman's blue "uniform" and his red boots.

I laid back on the couch with Joseph beside me and held my baby girl, Aisha, who wore her pajamas. Next to the coffee table, the girls sat on the yellow bean bags; Fatima and Rabia kept laughing and nibbling on popcorn. Joseph held my hand and whispered "Love you" into my ear. I smiled and kept eating my popcorn.

After the movie ended, we were thinking about watching the science-fiction fantasy *Star Wars: Episode IV – A New Hope* when there was a knock at the door. *Who is stopping by at eight o'clock at night?* I wondered.

I opened the door to see Rose and Tony standing there wearing big smiles. Rose held takeout boxes from Piccadilly Cafeteria. Tony held two small brown bags and sodas.

"Something smells good," I said.

Rose looked excited. "Estell, I bought this for your family." She opened the box filled with spicy chicken wings and blue cheese dipping sauce, celery sticks, and a bottle of hot sauce. I couldn't wait to grab my plate when I saw those wings. In the second bag were fries and chocolate brownies. Aisha found a gummy bear in the bag for her. Joseph and I thanked them and invited them to stay for a while.

I sat down with Rose. "You feel like kin folks to me," I told her, "And I remember how you cared for my girls when Aisha was born at Grady Hospital."

Her eyes began tearing up, and I reached over to hug her. I said, "Remember coming to our house for a cup of sugar at dawn?" We both giggled, and when Joseph joined our conversation, reminding us that we would see each other the next day, we both laughed out loud. Rose stood up, tapped her husband on the shoulder, and told him, "Let's go."

"Bye, best friends, and thank you for the food!" I called as they headed home.

On Monday morning, I stood by the bedroom window looking out at an overcast sky that looked like rain. I wore my lime-green housecoat and had braids in my hair. I headed toward the dining room and inhaled the smell of lavender as I walked in. I sat down at my old Singer sewing machine, that made the clanking sounds. I stitched flowery sundresses for my daughters in the summertime. I enjoyed threading the needle like I did with my mom. As I sat there, I mused a bit.

> I am thirty-four years old, and I've gained wisdom from a different life perspective. I gained some weight in my thighs, and I see strands of gray hair when I look in the

mirror. I am getting older, with my own family. Anyway, when I left New York, we had a plan. However, this move seems different because it isn't our choice.

As a mother, I went back to work to earn a living, and I felt guilty not spending time with my daughters. I cherish my role as a stay-at-home mother, but I had to leave my children with a babysitter and rely on my husband for support. Still, I felt good working and contributing to our family as a waitress. It hurt my self-esteem when I was rejected at several jobs because of my brown skin. I take pride in being a Black woman, and I am still working to be heard and seen. Despite the challenges, I still want a career to help my family.

I love being a girl mom, and I always enjoy talking to my daughters; I am raising them to be strong women who are kind to others, hold their heads up, and embrace their identity.

Joseph came from Harlem, and I am a country girl from Mississippi. Yet our differences helped us learn from each other. Joseph and I are on the same path with our marriage, and we are soul mates. Even though my husband can be hardheaded and stubborn, we find ways to make our marriage work. When I look at my wedding ring, I realize we are connected forever.

When Joseph got fired from his job at Jessup Security, it was a struggle for him to keep the lights on and to keep a roof over our heads. After three weeks with no job, he felt angry, fearful, and unvalued. But my husband will do whatever it takes to protect our family and handle responsibility. Since he is from Harlem, it is hard for him to get used to the ways of the South. However, he has learned to adapt, and he knows our family comes first.

I stood up and headed to the kitchen to make myself a cup of green tea. As I made my way through the house, I thought about the work ahead of us with the move.

> We are losing our home because termites are eating the wood of our house. Sadly, we have no choice . . . but we still have each other. The main thing is that we love our children and each other. We are resilient. We are a good family. Losing our home is not something we expected, but we will make the best of it. Losing our home has cast a shadow over our lives, but our family will continue its strong bond.
>
> I learned many lessons from my family on Matubba Street in Aberdeen, especially concerning their family values and their resilience. Although they are gone, I am carrying their beliefs and their courage.
>
> I am not sure what to expect, but my family is beginning a new chapter. Sure, I am a bit uncertain, but I am open to new possibilities. Where will I live in Atlanta with my husband, Joseph, and our daughters? I am somewhat scared, but I know that we can conquer any challenges that come our way!

Acknowledgments

Writing this book was a journey filled with joy, including discovering the many rich and dynamic untold stories about landmarks like Hunter Street and Auburn Avenue in Atlanta in the 1970s. As I finish my book, I find it imperative that I express my gratitude to those who played a key role in bringing my book to life.

First, I would like to mention the extraordinary individuals who helped me bring this book into fruition, and I am grateful to leave a tangible story for the next generation. Once this book started moving from a concept in my head to a manuscript, many friends and family members sent letters, cards, emails, and flowers that fueled my determination to voice my narrative. I appreciate the notes, scriptures, and messages from my friends, neighbors in Aberdeen, Mississippi.

I must extend my appreciation to my editor, Candace Johnson. Although we've never met face-to-face, I find that she is kind and friendly. We worked together on *Leaving Aberdeen* and her commitment to help me with my creative process for the sequel, *If Grits Could Talk*, was demanding. Her guidance and wealth of information were essential in shaping my manuscript. I sincerely recommend Candace as an editor for her consistency and trustworthiness.

Researching my stories

I did my literary research at the Auburn Avenue Research Library, which became a pivotal resource for my stories about Atlanta and the South. I want to express my gratitude to a dedicated individual, Frederick Cox, who played a significant role in unearthing valuable information and the landmarks in Afro American culture.

Educator and mentor

A special acknowledge to an amazing teacher and mentor, Dr. Natasha Johnson. Her passion for education, engaging presentations in the classroom, and personal interest in my work during our class at Georgia State University-Perimeter College was motivational. Even after I graduated in 2021, Dr. Johnson's words of encouragement and uplifting emails became a beacon of hope during my writing. I am grateful for her kindness and encouraging words.

To my daughters Fatima, Rabia, and Aisha

I never knew when I held the three of you in my arms at the beginning of your lives that our relationship could blossom into a source of strength. We are a circle that continues to push forward and withstand anything together as a family. Our mornings having breakfast at the Flying Biscuit with eggs and grits make for heartfelt conversations. You encourage me to share my wisdom and pursue the importance of documenting our stories to preserve our historical moments and our legacy. Even though your dad is no longer here, he would be proud of us sticking together. Indeed, I want to thank my daughters for inspiring me to share my creativity and bring awareness to our untold stories.

About the Author

Writer, author, lecturer, and businesswoman **Estell Sims Halliburton** grew up in a small town in rural Mississippi. Her love for her family has always been her foundation—the tight-knit sharecropping family she grew up with in Aberdeen, Mississippi, and the family she created with her husband, Joseph. Her debut book, *Leaving Aberdeen: Memoir of a Southern Girl*, delves into her formative years and is set against the backdrop of systemic racism, oppression, and the social upheaval of the 1960s.

In 1964, Estell attended Tuskegee University for one year, where she awakened to the joys of learning. After moving to New York City, she met Joseph R. Halliburton, a handsome Army soldier on his way to Vietnam. Following a whirlwind romance, the couple married, and Estell worked in accounting and as a fashion model while her husband fought overseas.

Her dream of having a family of her own came true, and the birth of the first two three daughters highlighted for her the importance of motherhood and advocating for her views. She discovered her voice and carved her place in the world as a Black woman, the wife of a Black Panther, and a young mother who dreamed of a better life for her daughters.

After her daughters were grown and her beloved husband passed away, she returned to college, where she discovered her love for storytelling. Majoring in education, Estell graduated from Georgia State University Perimeter College in 2021.

That same year, she started her own company, Halliburton Publishing, to help other writers tell their stories. She is continuing her research to learn more of her family's history and to share this knowledge with others who want to preserve their own family stories. Estell's love for her family has always been her foundation, and it has carried her through many challenges times.

Today, Estell lives in Atlanta, Georgia. She is a mother of three daughters, a grandmother of six grandchildren, and a great-grandmother of two. She gets up every morning before dawn to drink her green tea and complete her morning exercise before she begins her writing schedule. Some days will find her shopping at Permitter Mall for a new purse. One of her granddaughters lives with her, and they watch old movies together. Learn more about Estell and her ongoing plans for writing about her family by connecting with her through LinkedIn, Facebook, and Instagram.

Thanks for reading *If Grits Could Talk, A Southern Girl's Return Home.*

Please visit me for more updates in this series:

LinkedIn: https://www.linkedin.com/in/estellhalliburton/
Facebook: https://www.facebook.com/estell.sims/
Instagram: https://www.instagram.com/estell.s/
Tiktok: https://www.tiktok.com/@brownsugar1945
Email: authorestell@gmail.com

Printed in the USA
CPSIA information can be obtained
at www.ICGtesting.com
LVHW011601030624
782149LV00009B/320